Old Somenos School, 1953

Joy's school photo below: I am the chubby little girl on the extreme right in the first row wearing a white blouse.

COWICHAN KID

Hijinks at Stratfords Crossing, Duncan, B.C.

in the

Fifties

By Joy Sheldon

Canadian Cataloguing in Publication Data

Sheldon, Joy 1947-

    Cowichan Kid: Hijinks at Stratfords Crossing, Duncan, B.C.,

    In the Fifties

Includes song and poetry references and glossary

17 illustrations and photos

ISBN 979-8-689354422

  1. Biography-women-920.72 I. Title. 2. History-Canada-(1945-99)

971.053

Humor-adult

Independently Published by Amazon Books and JS Books

Available at most local bookstores

Printed in the U.S.A.

The cover showing mountain in background is a photo of Mt. Prevost, Duncan, B.C.

COWICHAN KID CHAPTER HEADINGS

THE DEMISE OF STRATFORDS CROSSING   GLOSSARY
1950'S SKIPPING SONGS   SPECIAL NOTE: Eaton's at Xmas

List of Photos and Illustrations: (17)

Frontispiece Stratfords Crossing c. 2020 p.10 The Old Homestead (drawing) p.12 Mother in Winnipeg c. 1926 or so p.20 Flapper in Bath (drawing) p.29 My Pioneer Family c.1900 p.35 My Dad up North p.43 Katzenjammer Kids (cartoon) p.48 wringer washer p.77 sign on my shed c.1990's p.120 Punkinhead doll p.129 Milton's Letter p.154 Old Somenos School p.171 The Mikado p.202 Duncan Elementary School p.205 Mt. Prevost and Mountain View Cemetery p.208 Class of '65 Reunion folder (cover drawing) p.214 Graduation Diploma, 1965 p. 232 Old Stratfords Crossing House site p.234

List of Song and Poetry References:

Ch I Just Try to Picture Me p.11 Old Homestead (drawing) p.12 I Ride An Old Paint p.13 Trees (poem) p.14 Two Little Kittens (poem) p.15

CH II There are Fairies p.19 Roll 'Em Girls p.20 La Marseille; Georgie p. 21 Happy Wanderer p.22 Horatius at the Bridge; Rabbi Ben Ezra p.23 Alice Blue Gown p.25 When Father Papered...p.27 Pax Canadiana; My Boy Billy p.30 Rock of Ages p.31 Ivanhoe; Skye Boat Song p.36 School Days p.39 Bringing in the Sheaves p.40 Old Rugged Cross; Waltz Me...p.41 Little Brown Jug; Big Rock Candy Mountain p 45 'Somewhere'; O, Dem Golden p.46

CH III The Inquisitive Kid p.51 Where Be Ye Going?/ Go Down Moses p. 65 Quickly, Quickly/This Time of Year/ The Forest p.66

CH IV RECIPES- Brown Beans and Hog Jowls p.81 Quick Spaghetti; Anything Cobbler; Mom's Pudding Sauce p.82/83 Goldmine in the Sky p.109 Santa (Original poem) p.130

CH IX Clap Your Hands p.165 Horatius at the Bridge (long poem) p. 169; Roll 'em Girls p.170 The Pirate Don Durk of Dowdee (poem);The Old Dog Barks p.174 Daisy Bell p.181 The Rubaiyat p.183 (poem) Pease Porridge (nursery rhyme) p.189 alary rhymes p.193 Let's Go Fly A Kite p.196

CH X Come On, Let's Cheer... p.209 Cowichan High We Salute You (School Song) p.215 Entre Les Etoile p.225 Shakespeare quote p.230 Pax Canadiana full text p. 237 1950's Skipping Songs and Rhymes p.240/41

PROLOGUE

Statement: S.C. April/94 and May/2003

I am no historian. The following stories are merely the reminiscences of a young child and should not be taken as fact. To the best of my recollection, I attended Old Somenos School in 1952-53 and New Somenos from 1953-58. As much as possible, I have changed the names of most of the players, but have kept the place names intact.

When we became adults, my younger brother would often lament that we had a lousy childhood. I never thought so. In retrospect, I think we were incredibly blessed to have the many benefits of a 'country' upbringing. We had the hearty, nutritious foods that only a truck garden and good home cooking could give. We had the fresh air and freedom that is rarely experienced by kids today. We could go barefoot from June to September. We were free to roam the fields, fish the streams, and hike the mountains.

And we were lovingly and expertly schooled by elderly parents. They were heavy on wisdom if sometimes light on patience, (especially where my brother was concerned!) My cultured, Latin scholar mother, instilled in us a love of language and a love of people and animals. My pragmatic farmer father- a love of knowledge and insatiable curiosity about the meaning of life. The little three-room schoolhouse down the road provided me a more than fitting foundation for fulfilling my later dreams.

It was this humble country upbringing that shaped what we later became. In my case, I think it gave me an early naivety which later countermanded the hard facts of life I learned in the city. It gave me an abhorrence for all things evil or artificial or phony. It instilled in me a strong sense of justice, a desire to stick up for the 'underdog'. And a sense of triumph and hope which even numerous years of Big City living and Big City people could not destroy.

The Seventies and Eighties were a time of relaxed morals. 'Free Love' and all that. But nothing is ever free, not even love. It all comes with a price-the A.I.D.S. epidemic, unwanted pregnancies, broken marriages.

However, the Fifties and Sixties were, for me, almost idyllic by comparison. I had not yet learned the consequences of the Hippie or Women's Liberation movements. I had not experienced the evils of the Big City. My country upbringing, in fact, morphed the person that I am today. In other words, it didn't hurt me a bit to be raised a- Cowichan Kid...

'Ah, the gift of poverty. We didn't feel poor. But we just didn't have any money.'   -David Foster

'They are not dead who are immortalized in print.' (me)

7

DEDICATION

TO ALL THE GOOD OL' COWICHAN KIDS

WHOEVER AND WHEREVER

THEY MAY BE!

Note: All names have been changed with the exception of most place names.

STRATFORDS CROSSING

In the Fifties, on Vancouver Island, halfway between Duncan and Ladysmith, there used to be a turnoff out to Westholme. That turnoff has since been blocked off by the highways department. We called it The Cloverleaf. Both the Old Highway and the New intersected there with four sections of road radiating out in a 'floral' pattern. It also caused the dreaded Death Corner which you will read more about later.

If you traveled back along Somenos* Road a mile or so, you came to our place. If you continued on past Old Man Whyte's apple orchard and past a small shale pit, you came to a railway crossing. In those days it was marked with two large white boards painted with the words RAILWAY CROSSING. The words crossed over one another, with 'Railway' painted on one board and the word 'Crossing' on the other making it seem to read 'Rail Crossing Way'. I think the sign is still there today, but pretty faded.

To the right, as you headed South, was a 'crossing house' painted brick red and about the size of a small cabin. It was made of rough-hewn boards and comprised a massive door which was usually open. There the locals would occasionally come to wait for the train. All the locals knew it as Stratfords Crossing. The Cowichan archives report it as being only one hundred square feet in size. I remember it as bigger. However, all things are magnified in the eyes of a small child. It supposedly had a self-appointed agent without salary named Charles Edward Pearmine. I don't remember ever meeting him, so, perhaps he was before my time.

I don't know for sure how it got the name of 'Stratfords' (strat, Latin 'street', and ford, a river crossing). However, the tracks crossed low bottom land, so there may have been a river there at one time, or the existing creek was much deeper. In the following stories, I will tell you a little more about this, now defunct, landmark. I will also tell you about the intriguing, sometimes downright weird, people who lived around it....

Note: Words marked with an * are in glossary at end.
          Acknowledgements are also at end.

Stratfords Crossing on Somenos Road c. March 2020

CHAPTER 1

THE OLD HOMESTEAD

Song: "Where roses round the door
 Made me love Mother more
 And friends I used to know....."
  -song: 'Just Try to Picture Me.....' Jerome and Donaldson 1915

The weathered bread loaf mailbox stood sentinel beside the makeshift metal gate. The gate led to the front door of the old, rough-shingled house. It was stained in friendly, faded shades of two-tone green. A riot of hot pink tea roses hung heavy on the fence as you passed through. No one ever knocked on the front door, of course. If they had, I doubt that anyone would have opened it. As a child, I never remembered us using that door. We always took the sidewalk around to the porch on the right. The only people I ever remember knocking on it were unsuspecting Jehovah Witnesses. Someone would always yell at them and tell them to come to the side door off the front porch. Boy, were they ever in for a shock when they encountered my father! But I'll leave those details for later in this tale.

I think my brother and I were both in High school when, for some reason, my dad decided to open that door. He couldn't. I guess, over the years of non-use, it had swelled shut. Dad planed it down until it would open and then it probably sat a few more years before being opened again.

Story goes, Dad had purchased the entire property-about an acre- from his best friend, Ray. In those days, an acre comprised a piddly amount for a farm. But because my ol' prairie dad was an accomplished truck farmer, it was amazing what that little farm produced.

We were poor by today's standards, but my dad knew how to glean every bit of value from every foot of land. 'Waste not, want not', was definitely a mantra at our house. Unfortunately, that philosophy included 'clean your plate' and 'the starving kids in China would love to have what you are wasting!' (Our stock answer: 'Well send it to the starving kids, then!') Could be a large part of the reason why my figure as a child and young adult, was definitely rotund.

It seems that when my father purchased the house in 1952 (for the princely sum of $1000.00), it was little more than a three-room shack. By the time my stepmother appeared on the scene in 1964 or 65, it comprised three bedrooms with two added porches, a basement, and several out-buildings. All this created by my father between the ages of sixty to seventy-three! Simultaneously, he had raised two small children and tended an invalid wife. Then, he and my stepmother, (twenty years his junior!), added two more bedrooms in the attic which she rented out to male boarders. Dad was over eighty when they completed the final renovation project!

There was a huge homemade garage near the road which for many years doubled as the school bus stop. An enormous, heavily-hewn woodshed stood to the right of the house with a pump house for our deep well just behind it. Along the right-hand side of the property was a short roadway which sloped almost to the creek. It bisected about a quarter acre of marvelous truck garden before passing an egg candling shed (which later became my brother's hideout). There were also two large chicken houses for the twelve hundred leghorns Dad at one time raised.

There are no existing photos of the Stratfords Crossing homestead, so my granddaughter drew one:

Drawn by Brandi Sheldon, Age 13

(In this drawing, the huge maple has been removed with only the Bing Cherry tree remaining to the right of the house.)

Below the chicken houses the wooded expanse sloped rather steeply down to the creek. Our property line ended at or just before the creek. But in those days property lines were often blurred. Kids just roamed free wherever they wanted with little concern for 'trespassing'. Behind it stood a huge meadow which stretched to the foot of Little Sicker Mountain. That, I believe was part of the large pasture owned by the Smythe family. Beyond that, the mountain. But- before I get on with my story about the land, I'd like to tell you a little bit about the man my father purchased it from:

Montana Cowboy

I Ride an' Ol' Paint   (Johnny Cash Western Song)

'I ride an ol' paint,
I lead an ol' Dan,
I'm goin' to Montan' for
To throw the hooley ann...'*
            pub. 1927 coll. Carl Sandburg, American Songbag

Ray was an interesting ol' codger. Tall and lanky, weathered like a prune in a dust bowl, he spoke little, but told much. (My ex-husband possesses that knack; I don't.) Said he hailed from Montana years ago-cowpoke country. His accent was unidentifiable to a little kid from Cowichan, but his Western drawl was intriguing. I think he was a few years older than my dad which put him early seventies when we kids first met him. Unlike my balding father, he possessed a thick headful of long, almost white, hair. Always wore jeans, vests, and the cowboy kerchief. Unfortunately, he no longer wore his ten-gallon hat. Darn! As little kids we'd be enthralled with his tales of the 'cowboy days' absolutely none of which I can remember in their entirety. I have a vague reminiscence of a story involving a burr under a saddle and a set-down in a cactus bush, but the details escape me.

Suffice it to say, my brother and I thought ol' Ray was a great guy. We looked forward happily to news that he and his plump wife were coming to visit. We would get even more excited when we were told that we were going to town in Dad's old puddle jumper to visit the Hayes. They had a modest house on Dingwall Street.

However, for us, the most interesting fact about Ray was his ability to do rope tricks. He'd often show up unannounced, and call us kids out to the front lawn. I do know that watching Ray do rope tricks was nothing like watching it on T.V. today-especially, if you happened to be on the receiving end of the Big Loop Treatment-good for runaway cattle and mouthy kids.

Upon hearing his Western baritone boom from the front yard, my brother and I would tear out to the lawn. Often a huge loop of rope would settle around one of us as we were racing along the sidewalk. No matter how much you pulled or struggled you could not escape its boa-like coils. The only escape was to beg for mercy. This you learned to do quickly before being ignominiously deposited on your face in the soft grass. Incredibly, Ray could free the rope without ever touching it. A light tug and a practiced flick and you were free.

Ray would then coil big loops in his enormous, weathered hands and, if more begging ensued, the tricks would begin. He would usually start with a small loop then dance it out onto the lawn. It grew as it danced. When the loop became about as big as one of us, he would snap it in all different shapes - circles, figure eights, snake-like lengths all hopped along the ground before us. Then requests to 'rope things' would be honored. The big cherry tree, a distant fence post, the wooden dog house, all fell prey to Ray's ingenuity.

Unfortunately, we didn't own a horse and Ray said he had long since given his up. We were confident that, even at his advanced age, he could have shown us some trick riding and roping from the back of a galloping steed. (Or, at least, to hear him tell it, he could.)

We had known both Ray and his chubby wife Ethel for about ten years. Unfortunately, she was diabetic and when I was still only a teen, she died. A year or two later, my Dad took us to visit Ray in a small trailer park just on the outskirts of Victoria. I don't know why the old cowboy had moved there, but my brother and I were mildly shocked when we walked in. Ray, now nearing ninety, was sitting on the couch holding hands and almost necking with an extremely elderly, and heavily wrinkled, old lady. He later told us she was ninety-three to his eighty-eight. They were madly in love. (he didn't tell us that part, but we soon figured it out) They planned to marry soon. Dad quipped on the way home that 'they better hurry up' or time would run out. We kids thought the whole idea was gross!

The Demise of the Big Maple

I think that I shall never see
A poem lovely as a tree.
A tree that looks at God all day
And lifts its leafy arms to pray .....
Trees, Joyce Kilmer, 1914

The narrow cement sidewalk formed an L-shaped curve in front of the house and over to the brown porch door. To the right stood a lovely Bing cherry, its canopy of white blossoms providing a cheery welcome in Spring. In Summer, it produced the fattest, juiciest fruit you have ever tasted and provided a goodly portion of our annual home preserves. Yet the immense Maple tree, which hung over the house, dwarfed the cherry. I am not good at judging feet, but our old farmhouse must have been over twenty. The enormous maple was easily twice as high. Its huge branches provided shade for the entire home on hot Summer days. Standing under it was like being in a dappled, welcoming forest. The variant shades of green filtered down as if one were under an enormous stained-glass window in church. I could take an entire chapter to describe the wonder of that immense and spreading monolith. Suffice it to say, I loved that tree.

Sadly, when I was about eight, Dad decided the huge maple had to go. I guess it posed too much of a risk on stormy days. It was a real production in those days for a lone, elderly farmer to fell such a big tree. But-Dad did it. First he had to limb the big son-of-a-gun. That process took about three days. Then he cut off most of the largest branches. They had to be hauled down to the 'Back 40' in the old stoneboat* (see glossary) with the help of one of the neighbour's horses. By then, we must have had four or five huge piles of branches and stumps stretching from the back of the chicken houses to the creek. Years later, the huge decaying piles were still there.

Our fat old cat, Minnie, loved to have her kittens in the middle of the piles where they were safely hidden from any danger. I can remember spending hours buried, often up to my chest, in the disorganized debris. In Spring or Fall, Mom would yell: 'Scour out back and see if you can find where Minnie has hidden her kittens this time, dear'. Minnie's batches would average about eight or ten each time and, of course, there was no way we could keep them all. We would give away as many as we could, usually pick one to keep, and then Dad would drown the rest down at the creek.

In keeping with Dad's annual sojourn to the creek, my mother had taught us a poem: (my apologies to the poet who, to this day, remains unknown):

The Two Little Kittens

There were two little kittens, a black and a grey
And Grandma said with a frown:
"It will never do to keep them both, the black one we'd better drown.
Don't cry my dear (to tiny Bess)-One kitten's enough to keep
Now run to nurse, for it's growing late, and time you were fast asleep."
The morrow dawned and, rosy and red,
Came little Bess from her nap:
Nurse said, "Run to Mama's room and look in Grandma's lap."
"Come here, my Dear," said Grandma, from the rocking chair
Where she sat.
"God has sent you two little sisters, now what do you think of that?"
Bess gazed at the babes a moment with two heads, yellow and brown,
Then to Grandma soberly said, "Which one are we going to drown?"
(anon? or did my mother write this?)

I remember thinking that poem incredibly sad, even horrible, when, as a young child, I first heard it. I guess my mother felt it would 'soften the blow' when we found our kittens disappearing and soon figured out what Dad was doing with them.

However, those huge piles of small logs and branches fueled evening bonfires for months to come. We happily toasted marshmallows and weenies on the end of a stick. No such thing as a smoke by-law in those days! Everybody burned either wood or oil. I remember we had a 'brown box' oil stove in the living room when we first moved to Stratfords. A more sightly or stinkier heating device has never been invented. Not only that, it was expensive.

Dad ripped it out of there and replaced it with his (homemade?) and somewhat makeshift wood furnace. I'll tell you all about that project later on. Finally, the big day arrived. Dad was going to fell the massive tree. I honestly don't remember whether Dad used his big chain saw or had to get a neighbour on the end of the old bucksaw. The reason I knew that Dad had a bucksaw is because I can remember many's the time I stood on the other end of it! Eventually, my arms would feel like two lead weights from the exertion.

A bucksaw was a long, heavy strip of metal about six inches to a foot in width. It had a large wooden handle at each end. The ability to use a bucksaw was a practiced art. First of all, you had to hold it correctly. Two hands were necessary-one at the top of the heavy wood handle, the other at the bottom. Then a tentative cut was made. The cumbersome instrument had to remain correctly balanced in the cut or it would bind. Then, using two hands, you would move the saw in concert with your partner in a steady push-pull, push-pull, back and forth action. If you got 'out of sync' with your partner, the saw would bend ominously and soon after bind. Being a kid with a good sense of rhythm, I became quite a good 'bucksawyer' at an early age.

I may have been a plump kid and an academic, but I definitely did a large share of the work around the farm. I was a year-and-a-half older than my brother, so I had to help Dad a lot for those extra years before my brother became strong enough to act as a hired hand.

But-back to my story of the big tree. My father had it all limbed and ready to go down. I think every neighbour and neighbourhood kid for miles around was there to see it. Dad made them stand outside the fence for safety. He had predicted exactly where it would fall. And, 'by gum' as the old man would say, there it did. My brother and I cried when it fell. I don't know what Dad ever did about the huge stump. Probably just ground it down to ground level and left it there. The bucking, splitting and hauling to the large, recently-constructed wood shed at the side of the house took several weeks of concentrated effort. That big old tree provided heat in our homemade furnace for more than a year.

The Demise of the Stinky Oil Stove

Before we got our, much treasured, Westinghouse T.V. we had the oil stove. An uglier, smellier, noisier old stinker never disgraced a living room. There it stood, smack in the middle and not-quite-up-against the wall. Gunmetal grey with blackened oil stains and a few rust marks. None of us ever thought to clean it. However, we only had to suffer its malodorous presence for a few years before Dad got the bright idea of replacing that oil stove with one he built himself! Since the demise of the big maple, he had tons of wood to burn. So-it made sense (to him) to dig out a basement under the house and install a different metal contraption of his own making. I think he made it out of some kind of an old boiler. What it had originally boiled, I have no idea.

Then, he had to cut an approximately one foot-square hole in each floor.

That was so that the heat could come up from the basement conduits which he had also constructed himself. They were covered with wooden grates of some sort. He probably made those, himself, too. The house was definitely more evenly heated. The old oiler had mainly only heated the living room and the rest of the house remained quite frigid on Winter days. Unfortunately, the smell of the recently-cured wood was only marginally better than the oil had been.

However, that old boiler furnace stood us in good stead for many years and was still operative long after my brother and I left the home. My Dad rarely, if ever, paid for any wood. He became a Wood Scrounger Extraordinaire. More evidence of his pioneer ancestry- his ability to be self-sufficient!

When I was in Grade Seven, our eagerly-awaited cabinet model Westinghouse T.V. arrived. (second-hand, of course). It took the place of the unsightly stove, becoming the central feature of the living room.

Woodsheds and Pump Houses

As I said, we had a large 'woodhouse' to store all that wood from the old maple and other large trees Dad felled at the back of our property. It was a rather pleasant-smelling wooden structure, completely enclosed but with an oversized door. It was unpainted. I used to like going in there and smelling the fresh-hewn wood. It never had any of the nasty connotations several of my school friends imparted to their woodsheds. For Dad never took us 'out behind the woodshed for a strapping' as many of them suffered. In fact, I can only once ever remember my Dad ever hitting us. And that was after we were both well into our teens. And we deserved it. We both knew we did. Details later.

As far as I know, Dad never laid a hand on my brother, although, God knows, he had good reason to. Gary was about the most careless, accident-prone, interfering, 'get-insky' kid ever on the face of the planet- to quote my long-suffering parents. Read Chapter III.

Therefore, the wood shed was used strictly for housing wood. Next to it stood a small, and rather tall, if compact building we called simply 'the pumphouse'. It held our well pump. If it held anything else besides that, I don't recall. Luckily, we did not have an 'outhouse'. But we had only one bathroom and the old four-legged tub was in pretty bad shape. We also had the luxury of an INDOOR toilet. We kids plugged it up from time to time, but Dad became quite proficient at the use of the plumber's 'snake'.

I used to like it when I was small and Dad would be working in the pump house with the door open. The regular thump, thump, thump of the pump, pump, pump, I found quite soothing. In the more than twelve years I lived at Stratfords, I only remember one Summer when our well went dry. We simply took buckets to the creek and carried fresh water up to the house! My Dad would never have been able to get his head around the idea of actually PAYING for bottled water!

He also had at least two other outbuildings at the back of the property. One, a very large chicken house and a smaller, but heavily-built egg candling shed. Several years after we arrived on The Island (and when Dad was almost

17

in his dotage,) he decided he was sick of selling Raleigh's products. This I think he did to augment his small Old Age Pension (or it was just before he was old enough to get one). 'Road selling' required a lot of travel. With mother being an invalid and sick in bed much of the time, Dad needed to be home. Yet he needed to have some way of earning an income.

When I was about eight or nine, he decided to become a chicken farmer. He built a large, heavily-constructed 'chicken house.' You could hardly call it a coop as it eventually housed more than twelve hundred Leghorns! I'll tell you more about the joys of chicken farming and the function of those rather ingenious chicken farm accoutrements in the section on our outdoor work (of which there was always plenty).

CHAPTER II   OUR FAMILY Ma and Pa

Once upon a time there was my brilliant, beautiful, eccentric mother, to
whom I will give the name of Millicent:

I'm a fairy!! Mother. Stark naked. Holding up a large bath towel behind
her as wings. Singing exuberantly:

"There are fairies at the bottom of our garden,
It's not so very, very far away......"

I'm a butterfly!"
Naked again. This time flapping the towel at her sides.

"The butter flies and bees make a merry little breeze,
While the rabbits stand about and hold the light".
There are Fairies....R.A. Fyleman (1877-1957)

Usually just after she got out of the bathtub. Brilliant. Beautiful. Creative.
Fun-loving. Crazy? Perhaps. We were only little kids back in the Fifties when
Mom used to do her fairy and butterfly routines. She'd been a serious nudist at
one point, so we were told. Didn't see anything wrong with flaunting her
chubby, naked body in front of her small children. (Or so we surmised.) At the
time, we thought it was funny. We didn't see it as conflicting with her many
moral platitudes: 'Keep your knees together and your skirts down at all times,
dear.' And Dad never discussed it. If he had, he would have merely said: "Oh,
that's just Milly, being Milly."

At the time, we thought her behavior was normal. I didn't see anything
wrong with it till years later. But I never told any of my friends (or anyone for
that matter) about my Mom's strange doings. I don't know what my little
brother thought about it. Never discussed it with him, either. He was
hyperactive as a child. Mother used to hit him with the fly swatter. She'd get
terribly upset and even cry with remorse afterwards. He'd just laugh it off!

At fifty, Mother was considered elderly. My bro was about nine. Mom was
chubby, but tiny. Stood about five-feet-nothing and that was with shoes on. She
was about as wide as she was tall. A foot shorter than my six-footer father.
Long, black straight hair halfway down her back with very little grey. I used to
brush it for her most mornings and sometimes pin it up on top of her head in
braids. Her grandmother had been a full-blood Alberta Cree.

'Roll 'em girls, roll 'em. Go ahead and roll 'em.
Roll 'em down and show your pretty knees.'
Billy Murray, 1925

Mom was a great singer. Voice low and sultry. Mother sang lounge-singer style. A la Mama Cass, in the days long before Mama Cass. The story goes she had spent two years in Europe when very young. Took off at age sixteen from her palatial home in Winnipeg with a girlfriend. Unusual thing for two young girls to do in the Twenties, they said. Was it just adventure? She said she had graduated high school, an exclusive all-girls' finishing school in Winnipeg, a year early. She wanted to go to nursing school but, at only sixteen, they wouldn't let her in. Said that, she had to be at least eighteen. I guess she had to fill in the two years somehow.

Above is a photo of Mom from that era.

Her father was dead; supposedly 'assassinated' in the Winnipeg General Strike of 1919. Her boilermaker father was supposed to be one of two casualties. However, I have researched in several venues and cannot find any mention of a Frederick Webster* being killed in that strike. He may have owned the business or been just a worker, I'm not sure.

But, back to Mom. It was said that her mother couldn't control her. Perhaps my grandmother was a bit ditsy herself. Seemingly, she was busy spending the family fortune ($30,000) she had inherited. Gave a big chunk of it to the Catholic church, so we heard. She ended up running an old boarding house in Vancouver years later. In conjunction with her rather strange oldest daughter, my aunt Edith. Before Edith married (late).

'Allons enfant, de la patrie
Le jour de gloire est arrive!'
La Marseillaise (French anthem) Rouget de Lisle, 1792

Paris, France. 1924, 25. Mom had a ball from the sound of it. She sang in cabarets, played the tambourine, even danced on the tables as she told it. She taught me many Roaring Twenties songs which I still remember. Some of my friends today are amazed at the words I can sing:

'Georgie used to come to court his little Mary Ann.
I used to think that he was my young man.
Till mother caught his eye and they were married on the sly.
Now I have to call him Faaaaatheeer!!'
Now I Have to Call Him…….Collins and Godfrey 1920's

I can picture her now in the short, fluffy bright skirts with layers of crinolines. Dancing the Can-Can. She was a good ballroom dancer, too. Mother was a buxom girl. They liked that in the Twenties. My father claimed Mom had been deported from Europe for 'lack of funds'.

'Bone-lazy' according to her acid-tongued Cousin Jane. She said that, as a teenager, Mother wouldn't get off the couch to wash dishes. Jane said she slept a lot. Depression? Perhaps, or maybe Jane was just jealous. I met Jane years later and she was pretty ugly. Looked a bit like the Wicked Witch of the West from The Wizard of Oz-tall, skinny, and always wore black.

'Passez-moi du lait, s'il vous plait.'(French) 'Kla-how-ya,Tilikum (Cowichan).' 'Aufiderzein.' (German) 'Kimurihashinjoo.' (Gallic, I don't know the spelling).

Mom was multi-lingual. She spoke twelve languages fairly fluently and parts of others. That even included Alberta Cree, her grandmother's native tongue. She even spoke a little 'Cow-it-chun'. Learned it from Old Mrs. Johnny, her dear friend. She had been a famous carder, spinner and knitter of Cowichan Indian sweaters. She was a very large lady and couldn't walk. When she'd show up in her old American car to visit my mother, her big sons used to carry her in. Even though she couldn't seem to walk on her own, we really enjoyed her visits. We used to see her on the reserve, too. She taught me how to card wool and gave us a black Labrador pup, named Boots. Whenever another one of our dogs got killed on the Highway, we'd go to old Mrs. Johnny and get another one. We had about five in all.

Mother loved animals and small children. In fact, she loved everybody. She was outgoing. Dad was an ol' codger and more reserved. People? He could take 'em or leave 'em. His family was all that mattered to him. He was a hard worker. Had to be-in his sixties with two small children and an invalid wife. To this day, I don't know how he did it! We had a good 'country' childhood; healthy and rich in experiences most kids today will never have.

> *'O, I love to go a-wandering*
> *Along the mountain track.*
> *And, as I go, I love to sing,*
> *My knapsack on my back.'*
> (Probably Mother's all-time favorite; we sure heard it enough times!)
> The Happy Wanderer -by Schaumberger Mauchensanger

Mom had to have people around her. She craved excitement. I remember her taking me to Vancouver when I was a small child. (This was when she was still well enough to travel on her own.) She saved a hundred dollar bill out of her disability pension, rolled it up in her stocking garter, and off we went. To visit her sister in Vancouver. It was my first time on the B.C. Ferry.

Another time I accompanied her when she flew in a small plane to Vancouver for a brain operation. We were both terrified; held hands. Her nails made big gouge marks in my palm. I was about ten or eleven. Dad had to stay home with Gary, I guess. The operation was supposed to stop the tremors from her Parkinson's. Didn't. She underwent that torment twice. Once for each side of her brain. 'cryosurgery' they called it then. I think her Parkinson's was caused or exacerbated by the old Forties and Fifties psyche meds. Dad called Mother's problems her 'spells'. Perhaps it was medication side effects. She sweated a lot and often complained of dizziness. She would have to lean on one of us or up against a wall or fall right over. Probably menopause symptoms, too.

'Tse-tse fly', Dad said. She was supposedly bitten during the Encephalitis epidemic in Winnipeg when she was only ten or eleven. She had been in a coma for six weeks and the only human to survive. Or maybe she was the only human who came down with it. I should research. She said that all the horses died. The brain swelling was supposed to have manifested itself as Parkinson's years later. But would that necessarily have affected her brain's dopamine levels? I think it was more likely a side effect of all the handfuls of pills she took.

'Alpha, Beta, Gamma, Delta, Epsilon.....'
The Greek Alphabet. She taught it to me by the age of five. In the Fifties, she used to take us to visit the wealthy Greek lady whose family owned the oyster company in Ladysmith. Mom would converse with her in her own language. I always picked up smatterings which I have now forgotten. But I remembered quite a lot of the French she taught me and and picked up the accent. Stood me in good stead at college. I even taught French a bit.

'E pluribus unum.' (Out of many-one)   *'Tempus fugit.'*   (Time flies.)

She was also a Latin scholar. Must have learned it from the nuns at the convent school. She was raised a devout Catholic and later flirted with Anglicanism. Her cousin was Archbishop of New Westminster Diocese. 'Hoity-toity'. He was a nice man; I met him once. Big, fancy house in, I assume, a posh area of Vancouver. I believe they had servants.

> *'Hail Mary, full of grace, the Lord is with thee*
> *Blessed art thou amongst women and*
> *Blessed is the fruit of thy womb, Jesus.'*

She taught me to recite the catechism and to say the Rosary. However, she converted to Mormonism just before she died. 'Why?' I don't know. That was Mom!

> *'Lars Porsena of Clusium,*
> *By the Nine Gods he swore*
> *That the great House of Tarquin*
> *Should suffer wrong no more.'*

Horatius at the Bridge   -Thomas Babington, Lord Macaulay (1800-59)

Lord Macaulay. She was also a good student of English Literature. For many years I kept her old, beautifully illustrated school textbook, circa 1922? Dark blue cloth cover. It had marvelous color plates of Lord Tarquin and other characters from 'Lays of Ancient Rome.' I can still recite the sixty verses she taught me. We always quipped that 'no-the book was not about the sex life of the ancient Romans.' 'Lays' meant long poems, in those days.

It was, sadly, destroyed a few years after I left home. I was 'moving house' and had cartons of books stacked in the back of my stepbrother's old truck. One box blew open and a few things were strewn along the highway. By the time, we realized, it was too late to go back and save anything. By a process of elimination, I surmised that the wonderful old school book was one of the casualties. I would love to locate another copy of it. I have looked in many old bookstores on the Island (both 'old' and 'new'), but no dice. It might be worth a fortune by now, if any copies of it still exist.

Lord Byron, Milton, the romantic poets. The Brownings:

Oscar Wilde was her favorite. 'The Ballad of Reading Gaol'. She didn't care that he was gay. Discrimination or racism was not in Mother's repertoire. Had he been her contemporary, he would have been a personal friend. Mother hobnobbed everywhere. With everyone. Equally comfortable with street cleaners or professors of Latin.

She had many pen pals; one was a Danish lady in Vancouver. Mother spoke with her in her own language, of course. The lady mailed me over small boxes of homemade handkerchiefs. They were made of coloured silk with lovely oil-painted flowers. I sold them for spending money. Mother encouraged our entrepreneurship even then. Another pen pal: the Queen of Tonga. I believe I still have a letter of hers from the Fifties addressed to my mother. Why, Tonga? I have no idea. But I know that Mom wrote to her on more than one occasion. An autographed picture of Hopalong Cassidy. 1958? Addressed to my brother, but I suspect my mother wrote the letter for him.

When I was just a toddler, there was also a tragic letter from her brother, my brilliant uncle. From a prison in Saskatchewan. I still have it, faded and dog-eared. But written in a beautiful hand. Almost calligraphic. You could tell that mom and both her siblings had been well-schooled and were, obviously, bright. Yes, my brilliant Uncle Milton whom I never met. I have no idea why he was in prison or what he was charged with. The letter was dark, depressive. Told of his perpetual sadness at his wasted life. I had to look up some of the words in the dictionary. 'Inimitable' and 'missive'. (see CH IV 'Our Relatives').

My mother was an invalid and I had learned to help her with the housework from about the age of four or five. We kids never did know exactly what was wrong with my mother. She was viewed in many quarters as an 'eccentric' with a 'flamboyant' personality. She took handfuls of pills. For exactly what, we did not know. Years later, I guessed. When we were older and we started asking questions about her shuffled gait, her palsy and her obviously curving spine, we were told simply that she had 'Parkinson's Disease'. I don't remember ever asking either my Dad or her any detailed questions about her condition. Mom was just 'Mom' and we accepted her condition(s) as part of who she was.

I remember baking my first pie when I was five. I still have the rather bizarre imprint of an old sad iron on the inside of my right arm. Mom said I had tried to help her with the ironing when I was only two. It matches the imprint of a dog's teeth on the outside of my left wrist. That, the result of an overly friendly gesture towards a strange mutt as a toddler. The bite happened in Vancouver before we moved out to the Island. We weren't constantly guarded in the old days as kids are today. But I later learned that my mother had been incompetent to parent. She perhaps didn't watch me as carefully as she should have.

In those pre-cartoon days, children did a lot more work from a remarkably young age. Both in the house and outside. I remember hauling laundry down to the basement every Saturday when still in Primary school. The basket was too big and heavy to lift so I, rather ingeniously, skidded it down the stairs. A kid was expected to 'pull your weight or you don't eat'. Of course, Dad never carried out the 'starvation' threat (I sometimes wish he had!). I guess parents thought the 'pull your weight' idea would make the kids more cooperative with chores.

But we seemed to fit in considerable time for leisure as well. I remember that, as a young child, one of my favourite pastimes was foraging through my mother's bedroom closet. Its colourful hanging garments held wonders at first mystifying and later, comforting.

Her bedroom was a shrine and a treasure trove. My brother and I spent many pleasant hours going through her things both before and after she died. She never minded. Her closet was a walk through history. When I was small, her coats seemed to hang high above me. I used to like to go there and hide., protected, under her furs and long dresses. I felt safe. It was my favorite inside play-place.

'In my sweet little Alice-blue gown,
When I first wandered down into town
I was both proud and shy as I felt every eye
And in every shop window, I'd primp, passing by...'
Alice Blue Gown   -McCarthy and Tierney, 1920

Long dresses, short dresses. Fancy nylon peignoirs, covered with ribbons. I never saw my mother wear a pair of slacks. Except in pictures of her fishing with Dad in Northern Manitoba when they first met. A long, black fur coat. 'Shortie' coats. Her gaily papered closet held colorful print house dresses for everyday. Lacy blouses all grouped together. A checkered black and white two-piece outfit. And, high above, her hat box shelf. Tiny black or navy-blue creations with feathers and little dotted nets that barely covered the forehead. I modeled them for my brother.

And the special wall hook that held her greatest treasure-her gorgeous, bright orange China robe. I never knew how she got it. I assume she brought it over from Europe, or perhaps it was given to her by a Chinese friend. She also used to take us to visit in Duncan's Chinatown before it was moved out to Whippletree Junction. I have only a vague memory of dark, diminutive buildings containing unusual people and exotic delights. Somewhat akin to the buildings at the old Tyee mine site Dad once took us to see.

Mother only wore the robe for special occasions. Or playtime. She'd put it on and turn her back to us. This time, when she became the butterfly, she'd open her arms to reveal a gorgeous dragon all outlined in China silk. Scores of tassles hanging down. It was a thing of beauty and a work of art. W. S.(Wicked Stepmother) probably used it for a floor rag after I left for College!

I guess it was reading a prominent movie star's recent bio-the section about her mother- that made me decide to write MY mother's story. The lady, it seems, killed herself with a razor when her daughter was only twelve. She had obtained it illicitly while on a home visit from a psyche hospital. The young girl had been told that her mother died of a heart attack. Years later she learned the real truth and it was extremely shocking to her.

In spite of their mental problems, I know both mothers loved us. What they didn't realize is, it wasn't really fair of them to take their own lives. Not when they had children. Single, they could do what they wanted. I agree with Dr. Laura on that one.

My mother starved herself to death at the age of fifty-six. They had put her in a care home in Victoria. She hated it. Told us she was going to do it, and did. The details too horrific to go into. She was shriveled up like a monkey, lying in the fetal position the last time my little brother saw her. 'Dehydration', they said. Freaked my brother out. I think the sight scarred him for life.

The fact that society may have thought of Mom as 'different', or 'eccentric', or 'emotionally delicate' didn't matter a damn to us kids. She was a lady-in the days when women knew how to be ladies. They knew how to be kind and gracious. 'Is there anything I can do for you, Mr. Elliott?' (Mother, speaking to the town drunk.) Or the movie star's mother inviting the exhausted model at Elizabeth Arden's to have tea with her instead of continuing to work. Just what my mother would have done.

Another example: Mother's visit to the local hermit, Nestor* Nelson:
Nobody ever visited Mr. Nelson. That's probably exactly why my mother went! Felt sorry for him. In fact, all the neighbours were afraid of him. All but my indomitable mother, that is. I had been told that he ate small children for breakfast. He was a huge, well-muscled man, even now in his sixties. A former boxer. Rumor had it that he'd left the big city after unintentionally killing a guy in a barroom brawl.

Ma somehow found out that he had a good gramophone and a huge record collection crammed into his little shack. About a mile down the road from us. Classical, actually. Every month or so she'd take me by the hand and march me down to 'invite ourselves for tea with Mr. N.' (The first visit she had to practically drag me until I got used to the idea.) He didn't have a phone so there was no way she could contact him beforehand to make an appointment.

One afternoon, we kids got the shock of our lives. I tell you that story later in this tale when I relate the saga of 'Nester Nelson'.

I recently reread the tragic story of 'Sybil'* In the film, her mother was portrayed as a monster. An unfortunate, tortured, mentally ill monster, but nevertheless a monster. There is now some controversy about the truth of that story. The mother was shown as a paranoid schizophrenic. My mother was nothing like her. In fact, just the opposite. Never laid a finger on me, except in a gesture of love. Always smothering us with hugs and kisses. Constantly told us how much she loved us and how much we meant to her. We were her 'miracle children'. Born at an age and under circumstances in which she never expected to have children.

And that's probably why she stuffed us with 'sweeties', and sugary, home-baked desserts. Because he ran around constantly, my brother didn't get fat as

I did. Back in the Forties, it was considered the fashion to have chubby-cheeked children. Perhaps a legacy from the Dirty Thirties when many children were starving. My Dad told me it was 'the mark of a man' if he could show that he provided well for his family. Plump children and a plump wife! Unfortunately, my mother took that a little too far. I was a little TOO plump. So was she. I have had to diet all my life, but my health has been pretty good, otherwise.

So-my mother was loving, brilliant, and feisty. Entertaining. We were never bored when Mom was around. Before she became profoundly ill, that is. As much as she was able, she, with my father, provided a well-run and stable home for us. She also took us on exciting 'adventures' both without and within the home. Her bedroom, as I have already mentioned, was a treasure trove.

She had the most marvelous dresser-Delfin blue. It had a three-way sculpted mirror and matching velvet-covered bench. She always kept it covered with one of her handmade ecru-coloured cloths she had crocheted herself. I still have three of them. But the beautiful, tasselled bedspreads were destroyed by W.S. (Wicked Stepmother) when she put them in the washing machine.

Over fifty years later, I can still remember the exact order in which Mother kept her feminine items neatly displayed on her dresser top. Mom made the hired girls put everything back in proper order, too. First-the silver-backed hairbrush and comb set my Dad had bought her. Next, her little floral face powder box. The pink music box that played 'Tales from the Vienna Woods'. It made a scratchy sound when there were earbobs hopping around in it. Usually she kept the bulk of her large earring collection in the perky, cylindrical-shaped Cowichan basket Mrs. Johnny had made her. Lastly, a lovely black satin make-up case.

> 'When Father papered the parlour, you couldn't see him for paste.
> Dabbin' it here, dabbin' it there, paste and paper were everywhere!
> Ma was stuck to the ceiling; the kids were stuck to the floor-
> You never saw such a bloomin' family so stuck up before!'
> When Father Papered the Parlour -Weston and Barnes, 1910

Dad had papered MY 'parlor' with a lovely greenish floral wall paper I can still remember vividly. It matched the paper in my mother's room. I also had my own dresser in my room. It, too, was what Mom called Delfin blue. (I have never been able to find a meaning for that colour unless it simply means 'woman from Delphi.' (in Greece?) Perhaps relating to the colour of the Mediterranean?)

Maybe Dad had painted it to match Mom's or maybe he just needed to use up the leftover paint. It was filled to the brim with my extensive comic book collection. Mother helped me keep them in order. Classics Illustrated, all numbered. Many Superman. Some Green Lantern and Wonder Woman.

Maybe others; I forget them all, but I know I had some #1's. I liked reorganizing them after my brother or friends had been in them. As I liked keeping mother's dresser organized. Gave me a sense of security and permanence. Maybe why I became an 'organizer' in my profession years later?

Eventually, I left home. When I returned on my first weekend visit, both the dresser and the comics were gone. W.S. again! She probably divided the collection amongst her needy nephews; or sold it. All done without asking my permission. Would be worth a fortune today. Then there were the bedspreads. It took Mom two years each to crochet them. I didn't dare ask W.S. what had happened to them. She always played dumb. Or 'Ask your father.'

Of course, he didn't know because he wasn't the one who had done away with my stuff. Or my mother's. She got rid of all my mother's clothes, jewellery, and makeup without my knowledge. My stamp and Mother's coin collections. My little blue sailor doll. My furry lamb, carefully preserved by Mom from my babyhood. Eventually, I traded W.S. for some of mother's crocheting and kitchen items. Took four items to 'buy' back one of Mom's crocheted tablecloths. Years later, I found my baby boots, flattened, in with some old papers in W.S.' small house in town. Stole them back. Heh! Heh! But I had to beg for the beautiful old wooden and glass tray that Father had made Mom for their 25th Wedding anniversary in 1955. I've still got it. Double Heh! Heh!

My father moved W.S. into our house within a month or two of Mom's death. I was just starting Grade Twelve. None of us got enough time to grieve. I don't think my brother ever grieved. My Dad and I did some. I guess my Dad, now age seventy-three and with a bad heart condition, was feeling desperate. Big, ugly, loud-mouthed European woman. Ignorant, no schooling. Dad said he remet her at Mom's funeral. Had been a friend of my mother's, according to Dad. I doubt it. Acquaintance, maybe. Took right over. Terrible food. She slapped me, hard, across the face. My mother never would have. I left and went to live with a strange lady in town until College started. Very traumatic. 'The sins of the fathers.' My (already troubled) brother went to live in our unheated egg house. We had a sort of a chicken ranch at the time. Although brilliant, my bro never did finish school.

Years later, I found my Grade Seven autograph book. And my high school diary. I don't remember where. I've kept them. I reread them once a year; on Mom's birthday. November 7. My best friend's birthday, too. My mother's album of old pics. It was a thing of beauty, although fairly small compared to today's. Rich burgundy cover held together with tassel cording. Faded tintypes, some hand-colored. A Twenties sketch by an artist friend of hers- a curly-haired flapper in a bubble bath:

The 20's sketch by unknown artist-Winnipeg? C.1929

'Come if you dare, to our Northmen's lair,
  The tramp of your armies shall not shake us.
Shout, if you will, we are freemen still,
  Words cannot break us!'
                    Pax Canadiana   -Millicent A. Webster, 1923

(for complete text of song see Appendix at end)

Mother may have written it. We heard she had won prizes in school for her writing and singing. War song, perhaps. Courting my father in the frozen North. Flin-Flon, Manitoba, circa 1930. (And knowing my Mom, she probably courted HIM, not the other way around.) Supposedly, first couple ever to be married there. I still have their beautifully lettered and illustrated marriage certificate booklet. Cherubims and roses on yellowed parchment tied with white braided ribbon and signed in a fancy hand (calligraphy style). A far cry from the sterile, typed single sheet the government gives us now. Signed by a minister and witnesses I've never heard of. Their official wedding photo. Outdoors. Heavy long Winter coats and white starched collars. Pics of them fishing thru ice on frozen lakes. The first house he ever built her up North somewhere.

Mutt and Jeff. My tall, relatively slim father. And my short, chubby 'squaw' mother. Wearing old pants and wool caps. Obviously in love. Dad was 38, she 21. Dad, 6'2" in his fishing boots. Mom, barely 5' 0, but wider than Dad. The Viking and the Squaw. Like me and Kurt (now my ex-husband). Her people were Alberta Cree. Kurt's, on his father's side, are Cowichan Coast Salish, Saltspring Band. But he looks like his mother's side. Viking. Kurt is 6'3". I'm 5'3". Coincidence?

Mother always had long, straight, shimmering black hair nearly to her waist, even in her 50's. I used to braid it for her every morning before school. That is, until she went into the care home that final time. And never came out. They had cut off all her beautiful hair. Easier for the care nurses, I expect.

I continued to haunt her bedroom after she died. As long as I could before W.S. took it over, that is. I think I always knew why Mom did it. And I was lied to, too. Like the movie star was. They told me she died because of her Parkinson's. I know different. She told me so herself. When I was about fourteen, two years before she died. Said she was going to starve herself to death. And she did, too. An ironic death for someone who liked to eat the way she did. Especially sugary foods and desserts. 'Finger Foods', she called them.....

'Can she bake a cherry pie, Billy Boy, Billy Boy?
Can she bake a cherry pie, charming Billy?'
             -My Boy Billy, trad folk song; coll. R. Williams,

She had learned fancy baking in France, I assume. Eclairs, coconut marshmallows, vanilla fudge, meringues-fancy foods the women can't make today. And she made the best deep-fried apple fritters and Johnnycake you could ever taste! They said she wouldn't even take water for weeks before she died. Shriveled up in a fetal position and turned black, according to my brother. From dehydration? They shouldn't have let him see that; he was only twelve or so. It was hard enough for me to face what we had to face. He was too young. He didn't really understand that, for her, it was a blessed release. After years of suffering.

She had also had a goitre operation about age fifty. After they cut her throat, she couldn't sing any more. That and eating had been her only pleasures left. She lost the will to live. I didn't blame her, or, for years, thought I didn't. I know that, in a way, she was content. She was finally going to her God.

"Rock of Ages, cleft for me; let me hide myself in thee."
-Rev. A. Toplady, 1763

But I know she missed us kids terribly and regretted leaving us. She told us so many times those last few years, even though she was rarely home. One benefit of her illness WAS that she told us sincerely and often how much she loved us. And missed us.

Born by Caesarean section to an ailing mother of forty, I was considered a bit of a miracle. Her age was unusual for the late Forties, not so much now. My father was considered positively ancient- 57! And almost sixty when they had my brother. He was often mistaken for our grandfather. My brother once told me that Dad told him Mom had had a miscarriage when they were first married. And then no babies after that for seventeen years. Perhaps they had used birth control. And then perhaps the doctors (?) thought she was too old and sick to get pregnant. But, she fooled them!

My Dad told a cute story of why I had been born on Dec. 31. He related that Mom was under the care of a prominent obstetrician in Vancouver. Her caesarian section operation had been scheduled for January 2. On the morning of December 31, Dad received a call from the specialist:

'Hello, Mr. McLeod. I'm going to be attending a couple of parties over New Years and making rather merry. I'm not sure I'll be in any shape to perform your wife's operation on the Second. Could you bring her in this afternoon?'

And that, supposedly, is how I came to be born on the 31st instead of the 2nd at 4 pm. Precisely. Or, as I like to quip: 'if I had been born one day later, I'd be a year younger!'

Aunt V. says she went to visit Mom one day when they were still living in

Vancouver. Mom wasn't home, but she found her down at the nearby beach. Turning somersaults in the sand at almost forty. Because she had just found out she was pregnant with me. I think we were treasured all the more by our parents because of their ages. They doted on us while they could. I was fat as butter by the age of two from Mom treating me with 'sweeties'. And loading up my bottles with Karo Corn Syrup. I was spoiled rotten till my brother came along.

But then, the hospitals. Always the hospitals. Since Day One. The costs broke my father financially. And finally, the care homes. Vile places that stunk. The stench of death. To this day whenever I smell a certain flower scent, it reminds me of the many visits to my mother at King's Daughter's Hospital in Duncan. We visited her there in the late Fifties before Cowichan District Hospital was built. There was a patch of blue something-or-other in the hospital courtyard where mother was brought out in a wheelchair to talk to us. Children were not allowed to visit in hospitals in those days. Every time I smell that flower scent, I get a nasty blast of memory. Of those sad visits to my unhappy, ailing mother.

I smelled a stench of death on her for several years. But I never really thought she'd leave us. Never believed she'd really die. Intellectually, I knew that the process was happening, but couldn't quite conceive of the finality of it. I don't think my brother could either. He and I had been warned. 'Your mother is dying.' But it came as a horrible shock nevertheless. I guess little kids always hold out hope. That someday we'd get up in the morning and there she'd be, back in her hospital bed in our front room. With the lifting bar she had become too weak to use. My brother, who was just getting into weight lifting, had even bought her a set of hand grips. To help her build up her strength. He couldn't quite understand that her condition had become hopeless. Couldn't take the grim finality of it.

'But I know you're better off where you are now, Mom.' And we can wait. We'll be joining you one day. 'On the Other Side,' as good ol' Kurt would say. ('Over the Rainbow Bridge' as his mother called it.) And I know just how and where you'll be. In the nearest fancy lounge. Wearing your prettiest Forties dress with the sequined shoulders. Your hair will be all done up in a fancy do or you'll be wearing one of your little pill box hats over pinned-up braids. With the dotted netting; probably the one with the jaunty feather. And you'll be raising a glass of the best champagne. Pink, probably. And toasting God. After spending a busy day telling him how to run Heaven. And correcting his mistakes; just like you did with father.

Maybe Dad'll be sitting beside you in his old tweed suit and jaunty Fedora smoking his annual cigar. He'll be raising a glass of that straight Scotch he only allowed himself every New Year's. And winking at God. And returning her toast with a sweeping gesture. With an exaggerated sigh and a 'there she goes again' expression on his face. My Mom.....

(My mother's death was, for me, the one traumatic event in an otherwise fairly happy childhood.)

Gorge Road Hospital. Rehab Unit. January, 1978:

Noises in the hallway. Voices. Muffled at first, then getting louder. I try to raise my head, but the body cast makes it almost impossible. I can just see a bit through the slatted bars of my bed rails. What the H.....! Here comes my nurse. But what's happened to her uniform? She looks like a ship under full sail. Sailing down the hallway and into my room. With something hanging on behind her and causing her skirt to bulge out.

An old-sounding voice booms out. "Where's my little girl?" Where's my beautiful little girl?" (I was thirty at the time).

'Omigod, it's the Old Man! What's he doing here?' Almost eighty-six and nearly blind. That's why he's hanging onto the nurse's skirt. I never expected to see him. I am overjoyed and utterly shocked.

The nurse pulls up a chair and he sits down at the foot of my bed. I can barely see him. But, I'm so glad he's here. He's only the second person who's come to visit me since my Hellish ordeal began.

"What the Hell, Dad? What are you doing here? Where is Hattie?"

"She didn't want to come in. She's waiting out in the car with Boris." (That figures, I thought). Leaves the blind old man to struggle in on his own.

"But, how did you get all the way down to my ward?" (Remembering the many lengthy corridors the ambulance guys had carried me down from the front entrance.)

"Oh, I just grabbed onto the skirt of the nearest nurse and asked her if she could lead me down to the Rehab wing."

Sounds like my Dad. We had a great, if short, visit. I don't remember too much of what we talked about except he would have asked me how I had weathered the scoliosis* operation. I told him it had been pretty horrible, but the morphine injections had worked pretty well (a lie) and I would soon be allowed to walk for short periods. I told him the surgeon said I would be in the body cast (from just below my neck to below my hips) for six months at least.

I asked him about his eyesight (as I noticed that he no longer wore any glasses). He replied that he could now only see shadows. There was no point in wearing glasses since they no longer helped.

At one point he told me he was hungry. I told him there was a tray there with some food on it. Even though he could barely see, he scarfed the remains of my lunch. Good ol' Dad. No matter what disaster befell, he didn't believe in going hungry!

Eventually, the nurse came back and told him it was time to go. I was heartbroken, but joyous all at the same time. He was the one person I had not expected to see. Imagine him, travelling over thirty miles to get here at his age. Then, almost stone blind, stumbling down the dark, unfamiliar, hallways to make sure that his little chick was all right. And to give me some much-needed moral support. To let me know that I was not facing this alone. I had felt so abandoned.

We said our good-byes and he leaned over the bed to give me a big kiss. That was to be the last time I would see him up and about and able to somewhat get around on his own. It had been several months since I had seen him. I noticed how much shorter and how frail he was. His poor eyes were grey and lifeless. But-he wasn't. As he grabbed onto the butt of the big nurse, he gave me a wink. And off he toddled. Back into the intimidating darkness. His indomitable pioneer spirit never daunted......

My grandfather, grandmother and five of their six children. Circa 1900. My father, age eight, is second from the left standing next to his father.

Pioneer Dad

'Gee Haw! Up, Betsy! On, Buck!'

(Dad. Early 1900's Yelling at his ox team. Urging them on as he plowed his father's quarter section in Rossendale, Manitoba.)

Dad was an old dude and a good one. He came from strong Scottish stock (in the days when people still cared about such things). Ayreshire, they said, like Robbie Burns. Lowlanders. Hated by the Highlanders because his family sided with the British at the Battle of Culloden in 1746. Oh well. Dad never did have much use for the bagpipes, anyway. Said that all that unGodly squealin' and squawkin' was never meant for Christian ears. Guess they were meant to lead a phalanx of huge Highland laddies over the moors. Enough to loosen the stiffest of British upper lips! Never meant for listening music, said Dad. Ironically, my cousin, Gay, in Edmonton, Alberta, is a piping instructor. She plays in the Canmore Highland Games wearing full Scots regalia! I guess nobody ever told her we were lowland farmers! My mother, of course, was English. Oops!

My father was born on the Canadian Prairies in 1892, the second oldest of six. Story goes his grandmother, back in the Old Country, had had twenty children and his dad was the youngest of fourteen. Interesting story that. My dad's grandfather had emigrated from Scotland in the 1850's. His people had been glove-makers and I often liked to fantasize about some rich young knight of the realm entering my multi-great grandfather's castle keep. Therein he would order from my old ancestor, of course an expert tradesman, the best of jewel-encrusted gauntlets for his impending joust. Or a fine pair of soft leathers for his lady.

'Ivanhoe, Ivanhoe-All the knights come out to ride with Ivanhoe.
At his call we spring to help him, right or wrong
The song we sing is freedom's joyous song.......'
        'Ivanhoe'   -Edwin Astley, 1922-98

My great-grandfather and his young wife, Nancy, came over on one of the many emigrant ships which fled the potato famines of Ireland and the wicked tenant lairds of Scotland. He came from the area of Dumfries, Scotland, in Ayreshire, the Scottish Lowlands.

'Speed bonnie boat like a bird on the wing
Onward! the sailors cry.
Carry the lad that's born to be King
Over the sea to Skye.......'
                -Skye Boat Song, Boulton and Macleod, Songs of the North, London 1884 (My grandmother was a McLeod from Isle of Skye-hmm?)

As far as we know his existing handful of children survived the journey. He had several more after he arrived in the New World-fourteen in all. My grandfather was the youngest. As history tells it, by the 1850's over 1000 ships had sailed from Europe, bringing immigrants to the Northern U.S. and what is now Eastern Canada. Many died of cholera, and other dreadful diseases. My family was lucky that they made it over, largely intact. However, once the locals discovered that these Scots were United Empire Loyalists (that is, loyal to the English crown), they were chased up into Canada.

All survived and another handful of children were born to my grandparents after reaching the New World. Unfortunately, his eldest son, John, drowned. When the youngest child, was born, they also named him John Carruthers after his eldest brother. Thus, he was ever after referred to as 'John C.' to distinguish him from the older John. They say that was a common practice in those days; if one kid died, they named a succeeding child after him/her.

My cousin was feisty. All her life Trudy had wanted to have a university degree. So-when her husband died in his sixties, she decided to enroll at the University of Victoria and study genealogy. I believe she was given reduced fees for being over sixty-five when she registered. She did extensive computer research and fieldwork into our family history as part of her course assignments. She traveled back East to the places where our family entered the New World, visited old family homesteads and graves, and even the Mormon houses of records at Salt Lake City. She graduated with a full degree in about 1975 when just over seventy! That was quite a feat in those days.

Another story my Dad used to tell was of the massive fire his family survived. He used to describe it as the famous Fire of Miramichi (New Brunswick), circa 1825. However, my family had not yet come to Canada at that time. So, it must have been another, but lethal, forest conflagration. Supposedly, my great-grandfather and his family were one of the few, if not the only humans, who survived it.

One day Great Grandpa was out in the yard working his homestead. The screeching of birds, and steady progression of animals scurrying past his farmstead alerted him to danger. He bundled his wife and all the children into their buckboard and raced to the nearest slough. Before leaving, he had thrown as many empty grain sacks as he could into the wagon. As soon as he reached the shallow water, he and his wife soaked the sacks and covered the youngsters. Then they crouched underneath until the torrent of fire passed over. (I expand on this intriguing pioneer story in the children's book I have also written entitled 'The Story of Roger Hardfoot.').

About the 1880's, I am guessing, my grandfather contracted with the government to 'prove up' a quarter section (160 acres) near Rossendale, Manitoba. That entailed ploughing and planting a certain percentage of the arable land and putting at least one outbuilding on it. When that was done, he would be entitled to purchase the land for only one dollar per acre. Soon after, he married and they had six children-four boys, and two girls. All are now deceased. Unfortunately, my grandmother died at age forty-six of so-called 'female trouble'. Probably some form of cancer brought on by the stress and hard work of raising six kids, running a huge farm, and assisting my energetic grandfather in his business and political endeavors. For years he ran the general store in town and was head of the school board.

However, according to my Dad, his own children didn't always go to school. This was common for farmers at the time. Although literate, Dad said he attended school only briefly. I guess, in those days, the mothers educated the children when they were really small. He said he attended school for only four Summers as he was needed in the Spring to plant and in Fall to help bring in the harvest. Winters, it was too cold to slog it the several miles to school.

Another impediment was that, at about the age of eight, he had suffered a serious accident. In the 'Story of Roger Hardfoot', one of two major children's books I have written, a theme is pioneer hardship. Many suffered terrible injuries yet had to 'buck up and carry on' along with their able-bodied fellows. So did my Dad. In my father's case it was an enormous wagon and massive team of oxen that hit him. It might have been a Conestoga with the big white canvas top also known as 'schooner of the prairie'. The pioneers could literally remove the top and use the box-like wooden bottom to ford rivers and lakes. However, this made the wagons heavy and dangerous.

He didn't know whether it was a Conestoga or heavy buckboard that hit him, the huge team that stepped on him, or both. All he knew is that his right side, leg and arm hurt like Hell and had been badly crushed. But he received the typical remedy of the time. In those days, the treatment for a severe crushing injury by the local 'sawbones' (as my Dad referred to him) was simple.

'Put him to bed and if he crawls out in the Spring, ye'll know he's gonna make it'.

In the Spring, he did crawl out, all but paralyzed on his right side. His right arm and leg grew, but were noticeably smaller and weaker than the left. His right leg never did work quite right. His right shin, the few times that I saw it, was a sickening and permanent dark purple from scarring.

Subsequent to that, Dad contracted rheumatic fever and spent another few months in bed. I suspect the fever episode explained the chronic heart trouble that also plagued him the rest of his life. But his disabilities never stopped him from putting in a hard day's work and certainly had no effect on his off-beat sense of humor or penchant for outrageous story telling. However, they later kept him out of World War I (and World War II also, for that matter). But, in the Forties, he did work at the Boeing aircraft plant in Vancouver with the 'midget girls' as Dad called them. The midgets, so his story went, were the only adults small enough to crawl into the wing openings on the aircraft. They held the wing while he welded it into place. He said he had a real ball working with those little girls, all of whom were feisty women with great senses of humor!

As an adult, his right arm was still noticeably smaller in circumference. Luckily, he was a 'south paw', but unfortunately the persnickety school marm had bound his left hand behind his back and forced him to write with his disabled right. He always did have atrocious handwriting!

So, much to the family's relief, my Dad did crawl out of his sickbed in the

Spring and was finally able to attend a few sessions of school.

'School days, school days,
Dear old Golden Rule days.
Readin' an' writin' an' Rithmetic
Taught to the tune of the hickory stick'....

School Days, Cobb and Edwards, 1907

It was a typical country school house, small and cramped with a wood burning potbelly stove for warmth. There were no black boards according to Dad, only hand-held slates. Chalk was often in short supply. And-horrors - (for a former school teacher, like me) up to eighty children in attendance in the Spring.

Years ago, my Auntie Audrey, a retired Grade One specialist, gave me a list entitled: Rules for School Teachers, Circa 1872. Some of the rules included orders for lighting the coal oil lamps and the wood stove before class and hauling in a bucket of water (to keep beside the stove in case of a fire). I don't know what the kids did for drinking water in those days. She was also expected to spend time before class sharpening the quill pens and filling the inkwells. The rules also stipulated that if a female teacher married, she would not be permitted to continue teaching. They only accepted 'virginal' unmarried schoolmarms in those days. Some of the girls 'graduating' from their one year of normal school (or teaching straight out of high school on a 'letter of permission') were as young as sixteen.

My Dad said that the only way the teacher could handle such a huge number of students was to have her desk up on a high platform at the front of the room and a bevy of little ones, called the 'Primer Class', directly in front of her. I guess those were the young students who were learning to read. I believe he said that the older students did have desks and that they were joined together in rows by metal rails.

Both the cane and the dunce cap were liberally used. The dunce cap, to the best of my recollection, was a pointed affair that she placed on the head of an uncooperative or non-progressing student. He was invariably, a large, overage farm boy according to my father. He would sit there for a specified period of time, the object of as much ridicule as the littler ones could get away with. Then, he would be returned to his seat in the back row to be further ignored by teacher until his next transgression. 'Out of sight, out of mind,' seemed to be the rule of thumb for learning disabled students in those days.

I now suspect that many of those overage boys suffered from dyslexia* (see Appendix) or had a mental 'difference' and learning disability we now know to be ADHD* (Attention Deficit Disorder). Several of my male relatives and a couple of females suffer from it. Thank goodness we are finally starting to recognize and treat it today. I was so thankful when, in the 70's, Eileen Daly, a courageous NDP Minister of Education, removed the strap from B.C. public schools. Educators eventually learned that most of the recipients of such inhuman treatment were learning disabled in some way, usually hyperactive boys with ADHD. Now these tortured little souls get help instead of punishment.

And next, the government needs to abolish the practice of Child Apprehension by the Children's Ministry. But that's a story for my next book(s).

In spite of Dad's physical difficulties, he and his three brothers were expected to run the farm, especially when his father was absent in town. Dad was taken out of school every Spring and Fall to plant and then bring in the harvest. Maybe that is why one of his favorite hymns was 'Bringing in the Sheaves':

> *'Bringing in the sheaves, bringing in the sheaves,*
> *We shall come rejoicing, bringing in the sheaves.'*
> Bringing in the Sheaves, Knowles Shaw, 1874

I know that in those days hay, still containing its grain, was hand-bundled into sheaves and stacked into stooks. At one time they had had to be hand-threshed. I think they used flails and that boring task often fell to the women. The later arrival of the threshing machine was a Godsend.

However, in the brief time that my father attended school, (three Summers, said he) he learned all that the little local school marm could teach him. Of course, his literate and scholarly mother had taught her children to read well before they started school (at seven or eight in those days; not age five as they do today). So, my father was largely self-educated. Ironically, he was an excellent student of Shakespeare and could recite nearly every word that Rrrrobbie Bbbbbburrrrrns (always pronounced with an exaaaggeerrated Scots accent) ever wrote. He also loved the poems of Robert Service. His favorites were: The 'Shooting of Dan McGrew' and 'The Cremation of Sam McGee.' I can still recite large chunks of those poems, much of which I learned from my old Dad before I toddled off to Grade One at the tender age of five.

For my recollections of huge chunks of the English epic poems, I must thank my finishing school educated mother. 'Horatius' by Lord Macaulay and 'The Charge of the Light Brigade' (Tennyson) are but two of which I can still remember multiple verses. Most I memorized long before I was old enough to know the meaning of the words. But like many young children I was soothed by the cadences and found the colorful language stimulating. For example, the beginning of 'Horatius':

> *'Lars Porsena of Clusium, by the Nine Gods he swore*
> *That the great house of Tarquin should suffer wrong no more...'*

What more intriguing name than 'Lars Porsena' could be chosen to conjur up romantic images in the mind of a small child? I told you more about my mother's incredible memory for verse and facility with languages previously. 'The Shooting of Dan McGrew', I blame on my father. Now, if I could just remember where I put my spectacles!

I think it is indeed a shame that memorization of poetry has largely gone out of the public schools and the homes. My parents' teaching of long reams of verse was a wonderful bonding activity. I'm sure it trained my brain for later memorization challenges in high school and at university.

Dad was also a Biblical scholar. He could quote chapter and verse of scores of Biblical passages, having read the Bible in its entirety several times. In spite of protestations of atheism in later life, he had a knowledge of the Bible that would rival that of most preachers. He said that was due to his Baptist mother dragging him to Sunday School with the other children for years. She also encouraged him to sing a wonderful high tenor in the church choir. So, the result was that both my brother and I were exposed to liberal amounts of memorization and singing as young children growing up at Stratfords Crossing. And, as my future university professors would probably attest, it never hurt me one darn bit!

> *'And I'll cherish the Old Rugged Cross*
> *Till my trophies at last I'll lay down*
> *And I'll cling to the Old Rugged Cross*
> *And exchange it one day for a crown....'*
> -The Old Rugged Cross, G. Bennard (1873-1958)

Dad's favorite hymn. My little son and I went in to his bleak hospital room and sang it to him just before he died. Little Lane, about seven or eight, climbed up on the bed. I stood beside to lead the singing. The old man, with tears in his eyes, said he was 'ready to meet his maker.'

Although he always said that the only thing he had liked about church were the Sunday School picnics. That because he got an enormous bowl of hand-churned vanilla ice cream served in a real glass dish, for only a nickel. Christmas concerts at both the school and church provided Winter entertainment. My Dad must have been the Recitation King. He sure knew enough of them. Reams and reams of Biblical passages, but also some naughty rhymes, too. Probably memorized just to torture his long-suffering mother. One of the cleaner ones went:

> *'What're ye lookin' at me fer,*
> *I'm not so very tall.*
> *Yer thought I was goin' te say a piece*
> *But I'm goin' ter fool y'all.'*
> -Anon?

Supposedly taught surreptitiously to his youngest brother. Used it to scandalize the parson one day when he and his wife and other dignitaries came for tea.

> *'Waltz me around again, Willy,*
> *Around, around, around....*
> *The music is dreamy*
> *Oh, peaches and creamy*
> *Now don't let my feet touch the ground!'*
> Waltz Me...composer unknown, sung by D.M. Appleton, Youtube, Jul/2011

Local dances. Usually held Saturday nights at the school. Dad and his buddies peppered the dance floor. The hall cleared inside of five minutes. Said some of the local girls were too poor to afford pantaloons. Ouch! Dad said he got the hiding of his life for that one. But I don't think, generally, my Dad was too much of a cut-up. Credit for that went to his brother, Graham. Family black sheep and scapegoat. He was the uncle who later tried to abuse me, but his ploy backfired. Graham probably had A.D.H.D.* for sure.

My pop had, at times, an acid wit and always a great sense of humor. Loved to poke fun at authority figures. Was not averse to swearing when it would spice up the story. Witness one poem, I suspect he wrote himself:

> 'The Pope, the Pope, the old son-of-a-bitch,
> I hope that he dies with the Seven Year Itch.'

My brother and I recited this stuff as children; even before we knew what a 'pope' was!). In his early years, in the mines and logging camps, Dad had learned additional rude verses and songs from which my mother often had to protect our delicate ears. But, as with most bright children, we soaked up Dad's smut like sponges! (I give more verses in the following section about my brother)

One was called 'The Inquisitive Kid' (see beginning of next chapter). The 'Hey, Dad, don'tcha know?' was repeated liberally throughout the piece. I can still remember most of it. I did, however, have to inquire years later, of my elderly Auntie Audrey (in Victoria) the meanings of words like 'pie can' and 'jay'. It seems they were definitely derogatory.

I have not been able to find the song's lyrics on the Internet, either. Maybe it was another one that my father or one of his cronies made up. I recently sang 'Clancy's Wooden Wedding', my Dad's Irish favourite, for a cousin's twenty-fifth wedding anniversary. It was quite the affair. Over sixty attended and I was one of the 'guests of honor'. At midnight, she and her husband came out waltzing. They were definitely elegant, wearing his fancy tuxedo and her hand-made wedding dress they had worn on the original day. Recently heard they got divorced about only a year or so later! She is now remarried. Go figure.

Someday I might publish a booklet of many of these funny old songs. Others, quoted earlier were 'When Father Painted the Parlor, and 'Georgie.' So watch for it, just in case….

As was Dad's wont, he told us a rather improper, but true, story about his penchant for reading. This episode occurred when he was yet a teenager (although 'teens' were not recognized as such in those days). I am not sure what his old farmhouse looked like, but it seemed there was a darkened loft wherein my Dad slept. Against his father's wishes, he would often read surreptitiously with a hidden candle into the wee hours (well, as much as you could hide a candle without starting a fire!).

One night, when Dad was about fourteen, his father climbed up the ladder to the loft expecting to find him illicitly perusing some scholarly work. He discovered him in bed, not with a classic tome, but with the hired girl!

My father had a particular dislike for religious people, especially Catholics and Jehovah Witnesses. Probably because he knew my mother had been raised by the nuns. He was similarly disgusted when she converted to Mormonism just before she died. I think he told nasty stories about Catholics in general and the Pope in particular, just to torment her. He thought all religious figures were incredible hypocrites!

He had little use for Mom's hoity-toity and well-to-do cousin, Geoffrey. He was the High Anglican Archbishop of New Westminster. (I later learned that High Anglican was very similar to Catholicism.) A nice man, though. When I was a child, mother took me to visit him and his wife a couple of times. We had tea with them. Very prim and proper. Dad wouldn't go near the place, or the church, either. The feeling might have been mutual as I don't remember Geoffrey and his cultured wife ever coming to visit at our home on the Island. I'm sure they could well afford it. Probably thought that my mother had married beneath her.

Back on the farm in Manitoba, a few years after finishing at the local school, Dad got the travel bug. May have been the result of an argument he had with his older brother, may have been just restlessness or a thirst for new adventure. Anyway, he told us that his eldest brother bought out my Dad's share of the farm and off he went. Seems he travelled West across the Prairies till the age of about thirty-eight, making major stops in Winnipeg and parts of Saskatchewan. Finally ended up in the little Northern town of Flin-Flon, Manitoba where he met his 'Waterloo', my mother. He has been doing a little ice fishing, fur trapping, etc. in the Winters.

Told us that at one point he built and operated the only wood-framed diamond drilling rig in the North. In this early 20's photo, the rig isn't showing.

Note the snowshoes stored handily on top of the tent. Not sure what they were drilling for, but Dad said it was the first time diamond drill bits were ever used. He was always intrigued by new technology and, years later, in his seventies, told us he wanted to live long enough to see 'men on the moon'. He did that and then some! He died in the Cowichan area in December of 1981 only three months short of his ninetieth birthday. A ripe old age, then.

As I said, sometime around the time of the Great Depression he met his match. My chubby, but diminutive mother, Millicent. He was over one foot taller and seventeen years older than she. One story goes that she was waitressing in one of the local cafes. Another story, that she was 'pushing pills' in a drugstore. She had, after all, graduated early from the Catholic finishing school in Winnipeg and done her Europe stint before entering nursing college. She may have either finished or flunked out and that was all the training she probably required to work as a pharmacist in those days (1929-30). So, the confirmed bachelor of thirty-eight finally bit the dust.

My Dad's name was Sidney. Mother always called him 'Jack'. Said, when they were both living in the far North near Flin-Flon, Manitoba, Dad had an old friend. An old friend with a lisp. Couldn't pronounce the 's' in Sidney, so he dubbed my Dad, Jack. My mother, ever-after, did, too.

Yep, Dad liked the Buxom Babes. I have an old photograph of him standing on a snowy street in Winnipeg, a chubby girl on each arm. Said he always liked them 'well-padded'. Told us he had a girlfriend from back home who weighed over two hundred pounds. He also said that he had two great aunts who were both about six feet tall. One weighed in at over three hundred. Said they'd go out to work the fields with the men and, when they rolled up their sleeves, they had arms like ham hocks. Neither really fat, just 'big' and muscular. I guess I 'come by it honestly.'

Supposedly, they'd work from early morning baking bread by hand, often with a baby suckling or on hip. They'd prepare enormous meat and potato meals to be served to the 'thrashing gang' in Summer. Usually on immense outdoor tables which they had to set up and break down daily. Then go out in the afternoon and fork and stook hay with the men till late. They'd make supper and do clean up into the wee hours. What's changed? A lot of mothers today have to get up early, feed their families, get their kids off to school and then go out and compete in a barracuda work force. Then come home late afternoon and put in another full shift of meal preparation and housework! The lot of women hasn't changed much over the centuries. Same toil, different methods.

He also told us stories of fur-trapping for many years in the far North and 'shacking up' with a plump 'squaw' for the Winter. Said many trappers did that in those days. The Hudson Bay Company dubbed them 'country marriages.' I read that they actually recognized those liaisons their, invariably male, employees had. They even gave pensions or cash settlements to the squaws and resulting children if her man left and went back to the Old Country.

The men made good use of the girls' cooking, sewing, and tanning skills. On those cold Winter nights, they also made good use of her body heat. Seems the friendly tribes also did not mind the girl's sharing in the wealth of the trappers. Somebody else could feed them for the Winter. I don't know if any little papooses resulted from my father's liaisons. When asked, Dad would only stipulate the following;

'I've had two children, well, only two that I'll admit to, at any rate.' Kind of neat to think that my brother and I may have a half-breed, half-brother or sister out there somewhere.

> *'Ha, ha, ha you an' me,*
> *Little brown jug don't I love thee...'*
> -J. Winner, 1869

Also confessed he decided to go Up North for a couple of years in order to 'get away from the booze'. Said he had taken to drinking too much when he was in town and headed for the snowy mountains with no bottle. That was an early method of detox in those days. For all the years that I knew him he would rarely take a drink or a smoke. And that only on Christmas or New Year's Day. Liked the hard stuff-whiskey or rum. One cheap cigar, usually at Xmas. Once in a blue moon, a cigarette. But, basically said they tasted like sh---!

> *'In the big Rock Candy Mountain*
> *Where they never change their socks*
> *And the little steams of al-co-hol*
> *Come a tricklin' down the rocks...'.*
> Big Rock Candy Mountain Folk song recorded H. McClintock, 1928

Got ripsnortin' drunk the night my mother died, though. Mom had been sickly for many years. After numerous hospitalizations she was finally put in a care home in Victoria. There, she languished.

As I said before in 'Millicent'..., she sank into a terrible depression and stopped eating. Died of Parkinson's so they said. I now think it was mental illness that made her so depressed she decided to starve herself to death.

Dad knew a German couple, poor and with several children, who lived about three miles from us. Only a day or so before, Dad had heard the news of my mother's death. He took us out to visit and achieved some solace in drinking some of the family's infamous potato wine. Wow! I remember the scary drive home. Dad was so polluted that he 'listed to the left' in a precarious manner as he drove. He insisted that all the telephone poles were 'crooked'. My brother did most of the steering on the drive home that night. That was the only time I ever saw Dad really drunk.

My pop, especially on the rare occasions when 'in his cups', liked to tell stories or sing or both. Some of his favorites (as I mentioned before) were: 'Clancy's Wooden Wedding', 'The Inquisitive Kid', 'When Father Papered the Parlor', and 'Somewhere, Someone is waiting'. The last had been soloed by him, he insisted, at the prairie wedding of Agnes Shatinbar (sp?), circa 1910. Part of it goes as follows:

> ' *Somewhere, someone is waiting for you, you, you.*
> *Somewhere, someone is waiting whose heart is true.*
> *Sometime you'll find a someone to love you too,*
> *Somewhere, someone is waiting for you, you, you.* '
> Somewhere -composer unknown, c. 1910?

Lovely tune, too. Had my brother solo it for my second marriage held in a little church in Cowichan. Gary sang like Pavarotti, yet a rich baritone. Could have sung for the Met (Metropolitan Opera). Did, in fact, sing in local Music Festivals and an operetta when growing up. When he sang 'Somewhere' for my wedding, he dedicated the song to 'all the single ladies in the congregation'. There wasn't a lady with a dry eye in any of the pews (whether single or married!).

> 'O, Dem Golden slippers, O, dem golden slippers
> Golden slippers I's g'wine ta wear, becase they look so neat.
> O, dem golden slippers, O dem golden slippers
> Golden slippers I's g'wine to wear to cross the Golden Street....'
> O, Dem Golden Slippers minstrel song -J.A. Bland, 1879

Dad thought organized religion was, basically, bunk. Knew Mom had been a devout Catholic when he met her. Had a whole repertoire of 'Pope jokes' just to torment her. Used to send the Jehovah Witness ladies racing away, red-faced when he would open the door in his underwear, or even less! I once heard him argue with a 'minister of the cloth' his theories of early sexual intercourse among the primates. Even that learned prelate gave up, stuttering.

When, just before she died, Mom converted to Mormonism, Dad was, at first amused, then disgusted. Found out that people often were pressured into donating a large part of their estate to the church. Remembered that my grandmother (my mom's mother) had left much of the legacy from her husband to the Catholic church. That left her and my spinster aunt nearly penniless in later years. Dad thought that organized religion was the biggest scam going.

So-whenever the Mormons would come to visit, Dad would be 'laying' for them. Little did they know that his mother had dragged him to church every Sunday for years back on the Prairies. His knowledge of the Bible would rival that of any ordained minister. He would get into such heated and convoluted arguments with them that they left, either with 'their tails between their legs' or shaking their heads. His favorite ploy was reciting all the sexier Biblical scenes and giving his own spicy interpretations of them.

However, I do believe that for all his protestations of being an atheist, he was really an agnostic*. He had an 'I'll believe it when I see it attitude.' To many things, not just religion. And I do know that he was asking a lot of questions about my belief in God just before he died. I told him that, by believing, he had nothing to lose.

I sang 'The Old Rugged Cross' to him on his deathbed. He seemed content. Said he had seen some little green men come the day before and beckon him from the foot of his bed. W.S. told him they were 'devils' and he was going straight to Hell. (for not becoming a J.W. and giving one-tenth of her estate to them as she had, of course).

I think he might have preferred to go to Hell rather than become one. (It was bad enough he was married to one mean enough to try to scare a sick old man on his deathbed.) Now I can see why. I was married to a 'disfellowshipped' one for a nasty three years (fodder for another book!). As my Dad would have quipped: 'He was so bad that even the Witnesses didn't want him!'

Some might say the little green guys were born of the effects of his deathbed medication. I say, not so. He was perfectly lucid. Even asked for a hamburger and fries the day or so before he died! My bro brought him one.

My Dad described the little green men in detail and I asked him what they were like and what expressions they had on their faces. He said they were friendly, smiled, and seemed to be waiting to conduct him to Heaven. For Dad with his love of all things scientific, little green men were preferable to angels. I have also heard of other people who have been conducted up to heaven by little creatures. I wish I could remember who told me! And I'm sure that the little men DID conduct my father to The Better Place. God would not keep out an old guy who had had as tough a life as he'd had. Or with a sense of humor as ribald and as 'off-colour' as my father's was!

CHAPTER III   OUR FAMILY (cont'd)   My Inquisitive Bro and Me

This was my brother and I x two!

The 'Katzenjammers'*

Years ago, in an old comic strip, there was a feisty family. The two little kids fought like cats and dogs. They were called 'The Katzenjammer Kids'. Today, the child therapy experts would be called in to deal with the 'sibling rivalry'. In those days, fighting was viewed as normal. As a matter of fact, if you DIDN'T fight, you were labelled a 'sissy' (read 'wiss'). In the strip, the kids were depicted as whirling dervishes-arms grabbing and legs flailing, a perpetual cloud of dust roiling around them.They were always at odds-if not physically, then verbally. Argue, argue, argue! That was my brother and me. To all this, my pragmatic father would merely shrug and say 'kids will be kids'. Nowadays, they'd call in Child and Youth Mental Health or a 'kiddie' psychiatrist!

I seem to remember the day the fighting finally stopped. I was in Grade Eleven or Twelve. Thought myself quite the sophisticated young miss. It was the early 60's, era of the fancy bouffant hairdos. I had probably spent over half an hour that morning dressing- working on my long, heavily backcombed locks and lacquering my hair with Sudden Beauty hairspray. Every hair was in place. So were my pristine, unladdered stockings. ('Nylons' we girls called them). Pantyhose had not yet been invented so I had hitched them on to my painfully razor-shaven legs with a fancy (and time-consuming) garter belt.

The 'nylons' which usually came to a few inches above the knee, were hitched on to the part cotton, part elastic, belt by little metal tabs which served as garters. About four per leg, a time-consuming and exacting business for a hurried student. Major catastrophe if you ever snagged a stocking, creating a nasty 'ladder' or run.

So, one fine Spring day, out the door I came. Not a stray lock, a run, or a wrinkle anywhere. Exquisitely quaffed and manicured- looseleaf full of books and requisite paper lunch bag all in place. Suddenly, whammo! I'm down on my face in the dewy lawn-school books, lunch bag, purse, (and, most importantly, the make-up) strewn everywhere. I try to get up. An immovable weight across the back of my legs. My brother. Pinning me down. I squirm and swear. I threaten. I scream. But, I can't twist around enough to get a good whack at him. He laughs uproariously, teeth with smart-ass grin, gleaming. But-what's even worse than the indignity of being knocked on my face is- I'm being observed. Observed by about thirty smart-alecky students hanging out of the school bus windows-jeering and giggling. Oh, the indignity! The humiliation!

Luckily, my father heard the commotion and came bustling out. I made my appeal. Dad agreed to drive us to school after I changed. He nodded to the driver who carried on with his load of kids. Dad took us inside and had one of his 'long talks' with my brother. But, this time, it actually worked. I don't know exactly what my father said to him, but my brother never attacked me again.

My bro was at all times impulsive and risk-taking. He found it impossible to organize his life. However, he had some rather ingenious ways of coping. Vis a vis his schooling-he usually made it to the bus 'just by the skin of his teeth.' (to quote Dad) Usually running out the door, bare-chested. Dad would jam a piece of toast in his mouth and off he'd run, throwing on his shirt. Long-suffering Dick or Ernie would have invariably been sitting in the bus honking for a good five minutes. I, of course, was normally ready on time or early. I know my bro was always jealous of my ability to organize myself and my belongings. I could always be 'on time' whereas he couldn't. I think that had a lot to do with the sibling rivalry/jealousy he felt for me.

How, you wonder, did he organize his clothes, laundry, etc? Well, one trick I remember was how he dealt with a dirty school shirt. Just turned it inside-out and wore the clean side! And he had the most incredible memory of just about anyone I've ever met. He may have had a photographic mind. Never studied a lick, but often excelled. To wit, his Grade 11 History exam: The year before, I had attended every class and took copious notes. He, on the other hand, often 'skipped' and never took a note. However, he wrote 98% on the final exam. How- says you? He merely stayed up most of the night before and memorized the History text book!

The following novelty song that my Dad used to sing describes my hyperactive little brother to a tee:

The Inquisitive Kid*

*My youngest son is of a very inquiring turn of mind
And the answers to his questions sometimes trouble me to find.
I was on a tram the other day when with anger I turned red
The passengers all smiled aloud when my young kiddie said:
"Have you spent the tuppence mother gave you?
Ain't that lady's face like our dog, Nell's?
Why are you always wearing whiskers? Mother never does, pray
Daddy tell...*

*Where did mother first discover you, Dad? Was it in a Barnum-
Bailey show?*
*How did you come to be my little Daddy? Hey, Dad, don'tcha
know?"*

My daughter Jane's been on the shelf for years but found a Jay
And so to see her married we all went to church today
But that darn kid started howling when I tried to kick him out-
He crawled beneath the family pew and this began to shout:
"Is it true that sister's found a pie can?
Does he know he'll meet an awful fate?
And does he know I'll visit often as I can,
Just to see that things are going straight?
Does he know that sister's leg's a corked one?
I wonder if she's ever told him so?
And do they know that mother's going to live with them,
Hey, Dad, don'tcha know?"

My rich old sister MaryAnn is worth some LSD (British pounds)
And in her will a year ago, she left it all to me.
But since I took that darn kid there, I'm cut off with a bob
He crawled upon my sister's stairs and this began to sob:
"Is that dried-up old rake my Aunt Mary?
Does she know she looks just like a guy?
And do you think that she talks thru her big, long, nose
To keep her teeth from wearing out, or why?
Is it true that you'll get all her money, Dad,
When she kicks the pail and goes Below?
And is it true you're gonna grease the stair, Dad,
Hey Dad, don'tcha know?"

I Googled this song, but can't find lyrics anywhere. Perhaps my Dad wrote it. Therefore, words quoted are from memory only. I can still sing it and have sung it at Open Mikes in the Cowichan area in recent years.

Gary

My little brother was a character. Talk about the original 'Inquisitive Kid'! A greater understatement was never made. I could easily write a whole book about him alone. He was bright, talented, and funny, but he was always getting into scrapes. Was he just a kid that was (what they called in those days,) 'accident prone'? Or was he a 'little imp of Satan' as my tormented mother often dubbed him? To my elderly Dad, he was just a bright, rambunctious lad, 'full of piss and vinegar'. I'll tell you a few of the high jinks he got into and let you judge for yourselves.

The first I can recall occurred even before we got to The Island. My brother was only two and I was probably about four. At the time, we lived in Marpole, a district of Vancouver in a medium-sized house my father had built. It was right next to a large 'rooming house' which my dad had also built and owned. He rented the rooms and was, in effect, a landlord. He also worked as a laborer for the City of Vancouver until his sixtieth birthday. According to my father, he had had the day off one Sunday so decided to take us little children to a local outdoor park. He wanted us to enjoy the day in the sunshine. I don't know whether my mother was there or not.

Unfortunately, the park also had an outdoor swimming pool. I have some vague remembrance of my dad telling me to 'keep a close watch on your little brother.' I remember us sitting splashing our feet at the edge of the pool. I also remember following my father's dictum to the letter. I did keep a 'close watch on my little brother'; I watched him all the way to the bottom of the pool! I remember how interesting he looked floating face down on the bottom.

I swear I can still remember the huge splash and expletive that I heard beside me. Suddenly, an enormous black blur appeared heading for the bottom of the pool. The water was roiled and much activity ensued as little Gary was dragged frantically from the bottom of the pool. The dragger turned out to be a minister of the cloth heading home from his morning's preaching. He was, according to my father, still clad in all his Sunday finery-best black suit, white collar, shiny black shoes. He ruined his outfit but saved my brother's life. Years later, I can still remember asking my mother why she kept a rust-stained, faded grey blanket, rough and tattered. We never used it on any of the beds. My mom told me that that was the blanket a kindly 'bum' sleeping in the park had given them to wrap my baby brother in.

So-my brother survived long enough to accompany us to Vancouver Island with only one other noteworthy episode while we were still living in the big city. A potentially life-threatening sojourn out of the yard.

I guess I, too, was quite an active and inventive youngster. Realizing this, my father had built an enormous and he thought, impregnable wooden fence around the yard. Tall, vertical slats, a la Tom Sawyer, I assume. The particular design of the fence required that it be supported on the inside by two-by-fours. Unfortunately, these boards bisected the fence at a fairly gradual angle from ground to top. It was easy for me to take my little brother by the hand and drag him up the fence. How I got him over the top and down the other side in one piece, my father never figured out. All he reported to us was that, one afternoon, (not even suspecting that his children were missing), he received a surprising phone call from the local ice cream parlor owner.

It seems my little brother and I had appeared in his shop at the foot of our street and quite a distance from our home. I was attempting to buy ice creams for the two of us using 'plug nickels' or 'slugs' as they were also called. My father had probably dropped them when doing some electrical work. He told the understanding shop keeper to give us the ice cream and he would pay for it with real money when he came down to pick us up. I, again, received the scolding of my life -this time for hopping the fence. But it is difficult to convince a four-year-old that she is doing something wrong. Even way back then, my love of ice cream was getting me into trouble.

And I have an interesting theory on this. My mother, as you will have surmised (if you read 'Millicent, her Legacy'), was profoundly mentally ill. But, of course, none of us knew it at the time. That was back in the days when no one knew what mental illness was and would never have spoken of it if they did. People like my mom were labeled lazy, uncooperative or 'eccentric'. In writing this, I am coming to realize how many accidents and other unfortunate events my brother and I both suffered because of my mother's difficulties with parenting. A clue was given to me when my father, years later, commiserated with me on my ongoing efforts to diet.

My dad had always been 'robust', but never down-right obese. My mother was and, I, by the age of two, looked like I was following suit. Dad stated:

'You will likely always have difficulty losing weight because, as a child, your mother plied you with sweets. I remember the time I came into the room when you were only about two and I had to grab Milly's arm. She had fed you the better part of an entire box of chocolates. You were so sick from the sugar that you had set your teeth together and she was trying to force yet another chocolate between your lips'.

He told me that he had also found her, in previous times, loading up my bottles with teaspoon after teaspoon of Karo corn syrup (substitute the word 'sugar'). Bingo! What is ice cream, but sweetened milk in another form? Hence, my lifelong choice of that incredibly fattening delectable as No. 1 Comfort Food. And an irony is that my mother, who had some nursing training, DID know what comprised good nutrition. In later years, she would even lecture us about the Canada Food Guide. Yet, she, herself, would continue to stuff with sweets. Merely a craving or self-medicating her depressions with the only 'upper' readily available?

I think in her youth she drank. I have one picture of her, probably in her thirties and possibly in some exotic clime. She was wearing a pretty sophisticated-looking dress and saluting the photographer with a glass of wine. However, I never saw her take a drink all the time I was growing up. It could have been because of all the pills she was taking. My father only rarely took a drink. But-he got ripsnorting drunk the day she died. And cried, and cried, and cried. As I did.

We'll never know exactly what problems my mom had when we were infants and still living in Vancouver. But I do know that I have a heck of a lump on my right collarbone. They always told me I broke my collar bone at the age of two. I fell off my mom's fat stomach when she was lying in bed. She either shook so much from the Parkinson's that she couldn't hang on to me or she fell asleep. (or both!)

Just recently a cousin 'way over in Alberta confided to me that her mother, my Aunt Jessie, had come numerous times to the Vancouver house to visit. There, she found my mother zonked out in bed and me in the crib. I was in a bad state, according to my aunt. Often unfed or inappropriately fed and covered in poop. She said she cleaned me up herself on several occasions. But then she told my father she couldn't continue to care for me because she had two children of her own at home, one a toddler.

So that was why my father, when we were infants and toddlers, was forced to hire help. My baby brother, Gary, had been born in 1949 when I was only fifteen months old. Soon after, a lovely girl by the name of Lena was looking after us. I don't know if she lived with us or just came for the day and went home at night. I know it had been very difficult for my elderly father. I have one of those tiny, brownish Kodak 'Brownie' camera photos of us. We, as babies, are lying propped on pillows and blankets placed carefully on the lawn. Dad is standing above us hanging diapers on the line still clad in his work clothes and heavy work boots.

We still have one picture of Lena. A dark-haired girl of unknown ancestry, but possibly black or Spanish blood. I remember her slightly and with fondness. As far as I know she took good care of us till my Dad moved us out to Cowichan in 1952. She, perhaps, saved our lives. Lena, our 'hired girl'. I guess my dad soon realized that we children could not be safely left alone all day with my disturbed mother.

All my life I have battled obesity. I believe it was somewhat caused by my mother's inappropriate feeding of me as an infant. I started actively dieting when only in grade two. Luckily, by late teens and college age, I discovered the benefits of aerobic exercise. I became a runner and weight lifter, lost about fifty pounds over a period of five years and have kept most of it off ever since. My brother, too, became a weight lifter and actually got into extreme lifts. He became massively strong. But more about that, later....

Dad later told us that, while living in Vancouver, he made good money working for the city. He also collected considerable rent money from the rooming house he had built. However, by the time he moved to the Island, he was practically broke. He had spent over two thousand dollars for two Caesarian sections to get us kids into the world. There were additional monthly bills for my mother's extensive doctors' visits and medications. No MSP in those days! Paying the wages for the necessary help for my mother, further took its toll of the family finances.

My mother had a penchant for oftimes lavish and uncontrolled spending. This made it almost impossible for Dad to build up any savings. I'm not sure exactly why my Dad chose to move us to the Island. It may have been to get Mom away from her old haunts, and also to try to achieve a simpler, less expensive, lifestyle.

But, anyway, back to my kid brother. My brother, for years, had a black finger. And I don't mean purply-black, like a bad bruise. I mean, black-black, - an incredibly bad burn. For months it would seem to heal up and then, bingo! Black and sore again and full of white pus. Dad would have to take Gawaine in to the local 'sawbones' to have it lanced and drained. The poor kid really suffered with that finger-until well into his teens. Every year, we were afraid it would have to be amputated.

You ask, how could a kid's middle finger, left hand, get to be in such a sorry state? Well, first you need to know that nearly everyone in my family is a leftie-'southpaws' they used to call us. And one fateful day (possibly while we were still living in Vancouver) my brother decided to stick that finger where it didn't belong! Unfortunately, it wasn't just the finger, but an errant bobby pin he had picked up off the floor. Yep- bobby pin, finger, and all right into the old light socket. A good zap later and the kid was lying on the floor howling and well-stunned.

A visit to Vancouver General hospital. The finger wrapped and bandaged. And the whole bandaged, infected finger scenario repeated every few months for years. More medical fees for my patient and long-suffering father. Incredibly, that finger, by the time Gary was in his twenties, seemed to have substantially healed. Anyone else would have had to have it amputated. My brother is now over sixty himself and, as far as I know, still possesses the finger! I once read somewhere that burns, especially burned bone, heals very slowly and from the inside-out.

Unfortunately, the above scenario illustrates a fateful character flaw my brother possessed almost from birth. He could not (and possibly still can't) take 'no' for an answer! If my Dad told him 'no, don't do it or 'no' you can't do it, guess what? The 'it' was the first thing he'd try. It was probably not long after we got to Somenos that my little brother discovered the neighbour's chickens. I believe my dad said that Gary was about eight when the next catastrophe occurred.

Putting Your Nose where it Doesn't Belong

Our neighbours, the Smythes, lived just down the road. At least once a week, if it were a fine day, my mother would walk us down the road to visit her dear friend, Myrtle. My mother was a semi-invalid and the walk comprised her much-needed daily 'constitutional'. It also gave her added opportunity for the socializing she craved. It was a lovely walk. Out the gate, past Larry's acreage on the right, and Ol' Mick's on the left. We saw dairy cattle in Mick's field and enjoyed the many colorful flowers and plants along the roadway. Delicious wild yellow plums, strawberries, and blackberries lined the route to Myrtle's. Those sweet plums formed a goodly portion of the three hundred or so jars of fruit we preserved every year. Until the road crew cut them down sometime in the Seventies!

In early Summer, the right-hand side of the road was loaded with the fattest, sweetest yellow plums you ever tasted. Mother used to make them into pies and 'plum cobbler' (plums on the bottom, scratch cake batter on the top and a delicious hot caramel sauce on top-super fattening!) We picked them by the bucketful and preserved jar after jar. Eventually, the road crew cut them all down. Said they were 'impeding the view of the traffic and constituted a road hazard'. So much for poor people being able to get nutritious food to eat!

Soon, we arrived at Myrtles-hot, sweaty, and hungry. While Mom and her friend visited, Myrtle prepared our usual fare of cake mix cake and fruit-flavored Freshie (which we kids, by the way, thought a real treat and a welcome change from Mother's 'scratch cakes'). Once in awhile she'd have bakery-baked cake doughnuts, not the greasier but nevertheless yummy bread doughnuts our Mom used to fry. We'd feast at Myrtle's. And my mom's friend kept a huge chest freezer on her porch; a real rarity in those days (but probably a necessity with nine kids!). From it, often emerged other savories. A trip to Myrtle's was always a cause for celebration-except for this day…..

My little brother had been severely warned- 'you may play in the yard near the house, dear, but don't go over to the pens near the creek.' My mother's repeated, dire warnings of vicious birds and animals did nothing to dissuade my ever-adventurous kin. In fact, I think they only piqued his interest further.

So-one fateful day, against even my warnings, my eight-year old brother shot like a bolt of sheer inquisitiveness down to the chicken pen. In those days the old chicken wire mesh had pretty large holes in it. Easily big enough to slip in a small finger or even a whole hand. Never did we suspect that a large part of a little face would also fit in there. You guessed it, little brother had a stick and was unmercifully poking and otherwise tormenting the chickens.

Unfortunately, he chose the wrong biddy to torture….. A peck and a yowl and here came my brother racing up from the creek. He was holding his eye and blood was noticeable between his fingers. Lucky the chicken missed the pupil. I guess Dad took him to the doctor, but I don't know for sure. I don't remember him ever wearing a bandage or eye patch. In those days, unless you had an obvious broken bone or were pretty well dying, you were not taken to the doctor. If things (such as bleeding eyes) seemed to settle down, the philosophy used was 'just leave it alone and let nature take its course.' However, to this day, if you look closely at his eye, you can see a noticeable scar on the white part near the pupil. A luckier sod never walked the face of the earth.

Putting Your Arm Where It Doesn't Belong

Grrr! Groowwll! Howl! Scrape! The terrible eruption of a roar. Coming from the darkened area behind the Smythes. Sounds of scurrying and a body slamming against the walls of the pen…

Myrtle had nine children. Tall, rangy chaps-her five sons were all good hunters and outdoorsmen. Especially, Delbert, the eldest. Their old man had been dubbed by the neighbours: Cougar Smythe. I think in those days, there were government contracts made with the locals to hunt and eliminate the big cats. Exactly why, I do not know. Today, we need some of them to eliminate all these problem deer on the Island! Those little scroungers eat everything in sight and need to be checked, in my opinion. Obviously, then, the opposite view held sway. The farms abounded with talented hunters, lethal 22's and 303's and BIG hunting dogs.

Delbert kept a vicious hunting dog named Jake, or, more correctly, Big Jake. I have no idea the breed of the brute. But because he was huge, short-haired and reddish in colour, I suspect he was a 'hound'. (half blood hound, half devil!) That dog didn't bark; he bayed. His bay was a mournful, blood-chilling howl you could hear all over the neighbourhood. Designed to strike terror and freeze a deer, elk or bear in its tracks.

Big Jake hated being confined in his pen. He was a dog bred for action. Whenever we visited Myrtle, we could hear him pacing and jumping. I don't know if he was chronically agitated or just craved exercise. Probably a combination of both.

Well, on that fateful day, Mother again admonished: "Remember children, do not go near Big Jake's pen. He'll rip your arm off!"

That was good enough for me. I only once saw that red devil out of his pen. The huge beast was snarling and fighting the rope that held him. Even the tall Smythe boy had trouble forcing him back into captivity. And he had also warned my brother- "Don't go near Jake's pen!"

On that one occasion, it was a quick peek and then a run back to the safety of my mother's ample bosom. I never got a good view when he was in his pen, either- too scared! Who had the guts to venture near with all that snarling and growling? He was almost as big as my little brother. I kept a wary distance from his pen at all times. I even avoided sneaking any further peeks to see what the huge brute looked like.

Not so little frere. Luckily, often when we visited, the vicious animal was not there. As I said only once did I witness his return being unceremoniously booted back into his pen. He must have been a good hunter, though, because the Smythe boys were reputed to have cleared all the local mountains of cougars.

Somebody told us the animal ate only raw meat. No sissy doggie kibbles for that lethal beast! I was terrified of the brute and so was my bro. But that didn't stop him....

Mother was sitting on the porch helping Myrtle peel potatoes. (or more than likely talking to her as SHE worked) The banging noises turned into ominous growls. Suddenly, a succession of snarls and a snapping of teeth. Then, suddenly a scream, but not from the hound. My mother was not a good runner, but she ran that day.

She somehow managed to extricate my brother's bleeding arm from between the slats before Big Jake tore it off. Blood poured from his arm socket. My poor, long-suffering mother tore off strips of his shirt as Myrtle ran for the water jug and tea towels. Teeth marks-big and ugly-mid-bicep and right up into his armpit. Big scraped patches, bleeding profusely. I don't remember exactly how badly Gary was injured, but it was lucky for him my mother had nurse's training.

"It's a wonder the boy didn't get his arm bit right off!" Myrtle clucked as my mother treated the arm. Myrtle helped her wrap the wound as tightly and neatly as possible. Myrtle probably didn't have formal nurse's training but was just plain practical-minded. Kept her own nine alive and fed for years.

"Yu'd better watch that wound close fer signs of infection; that there errysipilus can be deadly, ya know. I'd say if the boy gets feverish or that arm ain't right in a day or two, ye'd better take him to the doc in town."

Mother nodded and rushed to borrow Myrtle's phone. (No cells in those days!) She arranged for my elderly father to drive down to pick us up. In a week or two my ever-adventurous bro was right as rain and off to see what further mischief he could get into.

One of my aunts said Gary 'must have had an angel sitting on his shoulder.' He should have been dead about five times by teenage. A cat has nine lives; he had about a score! Needed them by adulthood. Mother had an old adage saying something about God watching over fools and small children. That, to a tee, was my bro. As far as I know, the horrible wounds healed with nary a scar. However, he never again ventured near Jake's pen. Like I said earlier, a luckier sod…..

The Case of the Murdered Chickens

The next 'accident' happened when Gary was about eleven. As I might have mentioned in 'Pioneer Dad' my father struggled, retired and in his Sixties, to eke a better living from our modest acreage. At one point, he raised chickens himself. And not in any small way. He ran no less than twelve hundred Leg-Horns- all white as I recall. To do that, he constructed two or three extra outbuildings at the back of the property. One was dubbed simply 'the chicken house'. It was a large wooden structure with a wooden floor covered with straw. There the huge flock of chickens resided when they weren't out in the chicken run, a wire-fenced area that ran down the slope to the creek. There was a large open space in the middle where the chickens were fed grain and watered in little troughs ranged along the side. Along each wall ran rows of nesting boxes wherein they laid their eggs. I often got the nasty job of reaching under a nervous biddy to rob her of her coveted egg.

I also had to pluck the 'eating' chickens and prepare them for dinner. To do that, I grabbed each carcass by the legs and immersed it in a bucket of boiling water. That loosened the pin feathers for easier plucking. Luckily, I didn't usually have to gut them. My Dad or brother did that job. A few years later I wanted to be a surgeon- but was too squeamish to pull out chicken guts? Maybe that had something to do with why I became a teacher instead. My brother, when he reached his teens, was given an even nastier job which I will tell you about later.

We had an egg candling shed just below father's immense vegetable garden. In there, we would shine a light through each egg. I think it was to make sure they had not been fertilized and there was no embryo inside. Imagine the shock of some plump, well-to-do housewife in town if she cracked an egg and a baby chick plopped out!

As I said, my father, when he was a chicken farmer, had a huge number of hens (and a rooster or two). Most of our neighbours also had chickens but, luckily, not in the large quantity of my Dad's. I think it was about this time that Gary got a bright idea. He decided to learn how to shoot Dad's small rifle, a twenty-two caliber. I would often hear him out in our extensive back yard shooting robins and other small birds. I think he usually only shot when Dad was away. He even tried to get me to shoot a robin one day. He showed me how to hold the rifle properly and sight on the target. However, I just couldn't bring myself to shoot that cute, plump, little robin redbreast! Gary was disgusted.

A few days later, Dad had an unexpected visit. It was our new and immediate neighbour. The neighborhood was in an uproar. Seems about half of Larry's flock had been shot (probably during the night). They were lying, dead, in his backyard. He had called the police, but they had no clues. Larry was going around questioning the neighbours to see if they'd heard anything. My Dad noticed a funny expression on my bro's face.

Later, he questioned him. Sure enough, my little brother confessed. He had used the chickens for target practice. My elderly Dad, mightily disgruntled, toddled over to the neighbour's, apologized, and paid him for the deceased hens. I heard the yelling when he got back as he took my brother out to the woodshed and admonished him sharply:

"Don't you ever go near any of my rifles again! I'm locking them up where you can't find them, so don't even try."

My brother spent the entire week hunting for those rifles. He finally located them; I don't know where. Then he went back over that night and shot the rest of the chickens! (I'm sure glad he didn't undertake to kill all of Dad's.)

However, when he became a teen, my inventive brother found another use for the egg candling shed. He had been a runty, skinny, kid. When he turned thirteen, he decided to do something about it. My brother's initial attempts to build a Charles Atlas body were commendable. His primitive weight lifting equipment comprised a huge cement block attached to a heavy rope and a chinning bar. Many's the time he tried to cajole me into lifting the unwieldy thing, and I sometimes did. But the mastery of the chinning bar (which was attached to the doorway at least a foot over my head) forever eluded me. Also, in those days we believed that girls who lifted weights or excelled in any kind of athletics would invariably grow up to have big muscles and small boobs. I did anyway in spite of my early efforts to avoid athletic activity.

Disaster!

My brother was only about fourteen when he started 'bugging' to get his driver's license. In those days, you could get a Learner's Permit at age fifteen and then drive for a prescribed period of time with an adult. If that time passed and no infractions, you could get your permanent license on or before your sixteenth birthday. Horrors! Most normal teens are impulsive and distractible enough without giving them the added temptation of death on wheels.

My brother learned to drive on the steep trail leading up Mount Prevost. My father chose to teach Gary there because there were 'no cops around' and the twisting turns were 'good steering practice'. I remember my brother being able to drive quite well by fourteen. He made a lot of illicit trips up the mountain with Dad, especially when they were working the mining claim. I suspect he often drove the old man down. And, you can't really blame my father. He was pushing seventy-five, his vision was going and it was a big help to have a young lad who could drive.

So, the very day he turned fifteen found Gary standing impatiently on the steps of the licensing office. Predictably, he passed the initial test and they gave him his permit that day. Soon after, he used money he'd saved up from his succession of part-time jobs and bought himself a hot rod. I have to admit, it was a beauty. A two-tone bright pink Ford with black trim; you could see it coming a mile away. '55, I think; the year they did the small fins. The rear window revealed a fake fur-covered back seat, white with large black spots. The inevitable white fur dice with big black polka-dots swung from the front windshield mirror.

During the last three months of my Grade Twelve year, I remember often being squired to school by my one-and-a-half years younger brother who had just got his permanent license. Me, I had no interest in driving at the time. As a matter of fact, I was quite terrified at the thought. It wasn't until I came home the first Summer after college and got a job in town that I forced myself to learn to drive. I was eighteen. In contrast, my brother loved driving –the faster, the better-and squired me around whenever one of us could afford the gas.

And gas, in those days, was dirt cheap. But-so were the wages. I remember my bro driving into the one gas station nearby and throwing a two dollar bill at the attendant. That pretty well filled the tank in the old Ford. There was no 'pre-pay' policy, no gas or bank cards. I doubt Mastercard even existed in the Fifties. Most people even shied away from mortgages and paid mostly cash. But, then, the average wage was only about two dollars an hour. Also, there were no seat belts. People would have laughed at the thought, and downright hooted at the idea of air bags.

Unfortunately, my brother always chose to hang with the 'problem' boys. It was that fact that lead to trouble one dark night on the roadway. He was probably just beginning Grade eleven when the accident happened. ……….

I don't remember being around at the time, so I may have already graduated. But, I heard the story from my dear ol' Dad, and a much-lengthened version of it from The Bro. Seems my Dad was asleep in bed in the wee hours one Sunday morning or sitting up waiting for my usually-late bro, I forget which. A call from the King's Daughter's Hospital in town. They had my brother. He had been in a serious car accident and was in bad shape.

Dad rushed down Somenos Road as fast as the old puddle-jumper would take him. Only to find my smart-ass brother sitting up in bed, his torso heavily bandaged, but complaining because they wouldn't give him any food. Also, he hated being in the hospital; it was too boring. He begged Dad to bring him a hamburger. Said he had been lying on the roadway half the night and was starving.

The doctor came in. Explained that Gary had sustained a serious puncture wound to his abdomen and he was ABSOLUTELY not to have anything to eat. The doctor was waiting to x-ray to see whether or not his stomach had been perforated. Dad waited a while then went out and got the hamburger. Obviously, The Bro was supposed to wait till the doctor gave the O.K. before he ate it. But 'waiting' was never my brother's long suit. Since Dad had left for home, he ate the burger and got into trouble with the nurses.

Later that night he roiled the nurses again. Caught him smoking in the can. As soon as the shift changed, he climbed out the bathroom window and hitch-hiked home. Never went back to the hospital. As far as I know, never got the x-rays done. Has been packing away huge quantities of 'growlies' with no problem that I know of ever since! Again, an angel sits on that guy's shoulder.

In due course, the gorey details were revealed. Seems the three boys had been speeding on an exceptionally dark, rainy night. All were sitting in the front bench seat. My brother was not driving and, luckily, was on the outside edge. They went into a skid on the wet roadway and headed straight for a telephone pole at the side. My brother flung open his door and jumped out. He cleared the car but landed on his face in dense bush. Unfortunately, the road crew had just been through and cut the brush. It was all sticking up in sharp spikes. One or more of the shards pierced his stomach.

As he told it, he pulled himself off the sharp spikes and crawled out of the ditch and up to the highway. He was quite angry that neither of the other two boys came up to assist him. He stopped a passing car and the driver somehow got them help. He cried when he told me later that his pal who was in the middle, died. I don't know exactly why. The driver sustained a badly broken nose (from hitting his face on the steering wheel) and other injuries. As far as I know, he survived.

Death Corner

Just a mile or so north of Stratfords Crossing, there was a serious bend in the highway. It was on the railroad side of the Cloverleaf*. Several bad accidents occurred there during the time that I was growing up. One of the worst, I will now describe;

It was a weekend and almost nightfall. I don't think it was black dark yet or my father would not have let my brother go. We heard the crash and Gary made a run for it. I don't know why I didn't. Maybe I had to stay back with my ailing mother. My father probably headed down the road, too, but would have taken time to get the old Austin out of the garage. Gary simply ran to the Cloverleaf*. My fleet-of-foot bro got there first. A horrifying sight assaulted him. At that time, it formed a three-way pattern. Today, the road to Westholme has been blocked off.

I don't remember whether the highways department had finally put up a guard rail. Today there is a low-lying cement wall of some kind. However, I think the car had cleared the low barrier and smashed on the tracks below.

My brother shinnied down the sharp incline. He said he almost puked at what he saw. A young man, conscious, but impaled on the steering wheel. He said 'the wheel had broken off and the post was right through his guts'. He was bleeding profusely. I think my brother knew better than to pull him off. I don't know how long the guy stayed conscious. My brother attempted to talk to him and keep him quiet until help came.

I think that, shortly, my Dad and some of the other neighbours must have arrived. It was an unspoken rule, that if the neighbours heard a crash coming from the Cloverleaf, all ran to see if they could help. All I know is that my brother came back, white-faced, and said he thought the young man had died. My brother was about ten at the time. We later dubbed that lethal bend in the road–Death Corner.

However, a 'happy' accident subsequently occurred. Again, but late-afternoon this time, we heard the smashing, grinding sound of a vehicle overturning on the highway. Many of the dads were at work so it was mostly the neighborhood children who appeared.

To our delight, there lay a bread truck, on its side, its contents strewn all over the highway. I think the driver was O.K. and was standing by his vehicle. He didn't seem to object when we started grabbing handfuls of delicacies-raisin bread, doughnuts, small pastries, anything we could quickly tuck under our arms and make a run with. I guess he knew the stuff could not be resold anyway. Many of the packages had burst open, but we didn't care.

To us, in those days 'store-bought' baked goods were a colossal treat. We could have crappy old home-baking any ol' time. But to get 'real' store bought goodies was an incredible stroke of luck. Like those yummy cake mix cakes thick with icing Myrtle used to make. We grabbed the goodies and ran home to feast…….

There were many serious accidents sustained by teens (or young men barely out of their teens) in the Cowichan Valley in those days. It was largely accepted as a matter of course. Many loggers died, some with young families. The Island at that time was almost totally dependent on the acronym industries-Fi-Lo-Mi-(fishing, logging, mining). They were all dangerous. I know of at least one fatality at the local pulp mill. Seems the chap got his arm caught in a machine and he didn't survive the trauma. He had been a school chum of mine. Another fellow student died on Bell McKinnon Road when still in his teens. Thank God that highway improvements, new workplace safety standards and the use of seatbelts and air bags have improved greatly on those statistics.

Me

So-who is this Cowichan Kid', you say? Again, I'm not quite sure how to do a character sketch of myself. Perhaps I should get one of my friends to do it. I wonder what they'd say? I wonder if they'd have the same opinion of me that I have of myself? Trouble is, if they had too many negative things to say, they might not be my friends anymore! Guess I'll just have to write this one solo.

I was a bright, highly capable child. Relatively happy. Except for 'teenagerus miserosa' (to paraphrase Queen Elizabeth). But-I think most of us are miserable during our teen years. And that was when my mom died. I always took my family responsibilities very seriously. Not so my 'scattered' brother. I think my mother's state of health had a lot to do with my self-image as 'woman of the house'. Thus it was a severe blow to me when, shortly after my mother's death, W.S. (Wicked Stepmother) took over.

Yes, I was pretty serious about most things, especially my school work, but I did have my Dad's wry old Scots humor. I think my rude introduction to Grade One with the kids pulling 'hangdog' faces and me howling uproariously was evidence of that. (see 'Stories of Somenos School', following).

I was a friendly kid and had many girlfriends. I never got 'into boys' as I was a serious student and headed for college 'come Hell or high water'. I had also witnessed a couple of neighborhood girls suffer teen pregnancies. I pictured their lives as ones of drudgery and thankless toil. I wasn't falling into that trap. And, in the Pre-Pill Era, if that meant staying strictly away from boys, so be it.

However, it didn't mean that I didn't have the usual complement of teenage crushes. I did. But- I didn't really date until I had completed my requisite two years of college.

I was never a 'joiner' and didn't align myself with any particular crowd. I was just me. I didn't really envy the snobby-nosed 'city slickers' of angel blouse fame. However, I was friendly, if indifferent, to those girls and they seemed to like me, too. I was very much my own person- independent and opinionated and have remained so to this day.

In elementary school, I had the usual complement of female friends, most from around my neighborhood. I held 'tea' and crafts parties at my place and we girls, walked, swam and rode our bikes together. We were skipping, marbles, and Red Rover aficionados. I became a competent baseball player, catching for my brother and playing with the kids up on Mickey's field. We used dried cow pies for bases.

One Spring I broke my pinkie and ring fingers 'catching burners' for my All Star brother. He played in Little League all through school and was an excellent pitcher and catcher. I did not because there were no 'Little Leagues' for girls in those days. I also skated a little and swam a lot. In high school, I became a competent field hockey player (we called it 'grass' hockey). I played center half as I couldn't run as fast as the front-line Wingers. I found playing defense too boring. Thus, I improved my running stamina somewhat and lost weight.

I never was into the teenage Rock and Roll music popular at the time. Singers like Jerry Lee Lewis, Fats Domino, even early Elvis, left me cold. I didn't really appreciate the Beatles until I was in college. In short, I was a 'square'. However, I did enjoy music. I sang in the choir for many years and played in the school band. However, because of my overweight, my self-image was tenuous.

I had always loved the heavy brass. In Grade Ten and Eleven I played the large, mellow, baritone horn (also known as euphonium). It looked like a smaller version of a tuba, but was higher-pitched. However, in order to play it, I had to somewhat puff out my face and chest. Also, to quote Mammy in 'Gone with the Wind', I had feared that it "just ain't dignified, it ain't dignified". However, in Grade Eleven, I scored a personal coup which almost made up for my puffed cheeks embarrassment.

We were scheduled to play the theme from Swan Lake Ballet by Tchaikovsky in the Mid-Island Music Festival. It ended with three very distinct, yet quietly played notes. Guess who had to solo? Yep, the euphonium. I practiced those three notes till my lips were raw. We had had a 'practice run' in front of the whole school. It went well. Most of my friends knew I had to carry a lot of the melody at the end and play those three notes. Then came the big day. We were up against two or three private schools as well as the junior secondaries. The big moment came. I was shaking, but again performed impeccably. We won the Festival. It was rare for us to beat out the larger, more well-funded private schools. I was a bit of a heroine among my circle of friends.

However, in Grade Twelve, I switched to clarinet. I, by now, felt the appearance of me playing that heavy brass instrument to be too 'unladylike'. I had tried to get access to one of the two French horns (a more delicate-looking and sounding brass instrument), but they were already taken. The clarinet looked nicer, but, to me, sounded wimpy. At the time, I regretted the switch. However, learning to play a reed instrument proved to be a lucky happenstance. A few years later, when teaching elementary school, I was able to use the same fingering to give recorder lessons to my music classes.

The boys, behind my back, called me the Ice Princess. I found that out years later. Felt quite flattered, actually. I didn't think they had noticed me at all! A boy I had barely noticed, but who had been in several of my classes, later spoke to me. I remet him at my stepmother's house about ten years after high school. Seems he had had a mad crush on me for years. I told him it was too bad he hadn't told me at the time! (He had made some kind of an overture to me and I was totally unaware.) Thus, he and his pals had dubbed me 'The Ice Princess.'

I guess, at times, some of the boys had made attempts to get my attention. Hence the overture (pardon the pun) made to me by the overly-friendly trombone–player who stood directly behind me in the band. He often delighted in poking his slide into my torturously coiffed 'Beehive' hairdo and messing it up. I guess that, from a teenage boy's point of view, was a token of 'interest'. To me, it was annoyance.

I was mildly horrified when, in my Grade Eight or Nine school annual, the song title they chose for me was 'The Great Pretender'. I don't know if that title had any reference to my non-existent love life or not. I didn't know if it held any serious significance or, in fact, who had chosen it for me. Perhaps it had been Rod, the kid with the crush!

In senior high school, which I attended in town, I added to my repertoire of local girlfriends. I was able to laugh along with the best of them. Usually, I was also able to laugh at my own foibles. But there was one time when I was not able to laugh about my own, rather rotund, exterior:

Our little town had, I think, a pretty commendable children's and teens arts program for its time. My brother and I were in our early teens when we began singing in school choirs and operettas. My bro had an unusually mature voice for his age-sounded exactly like an Italian opera star. An early Pavarotti.

We were fortunate in having the opportunity to act and sing with a local teen operatic troupe. We had had some previous experience, me acting in several major school plays and singing in a girls' choir. I had played Mrs. Cratchit to the local dentist's son's Scrooge in Dickens' 'A Christmas Carol'. Our girls' choir won the local music festival twice with renditions such as 'Greensleeves', 'Where be Ye Going' and the 'Twenty-third Psalm'. Who picked those selections, anyway?

'Where Be Ye Going ?' went something like this:

'Where be ye going to my dear little maiden
With your red, rosy cheeks and your black shiny hair?
I be goin' a-milkin' kind little man, she said:
'It's dabblin' in the dew makes the mild maids fair'.
Unknown (could be a takeoff of John Keats 'Devon Maid'?)

Those selections were pretty boring even for the late 50's. But we sang well and outdid the hoity-toities from the girls' private schools.

My brother distinguished himself with the lead role as Narrator in the Mikado*. I still have a lovely sepia photo of him in full Mikado regalia-long robe with fur trimmed sleeves and fancy school-made, but effective, headdress. However, his junior secondary school's choir performance bombed and bombed badly in spite of him singing a wonderful, short solo. I believe my brother was in Grade Eight or nine. They had a new, young music teacher. And, I mean, 'new'. I think it might have been his first year of teaching. He chose a very difficult piece for his students to sing. I know it would have been a challenge even for a senior secondary choir.

It was entitled: "Go Down, Moses".... ('Way Down in Egypt Land"):

Go down, (Go-o-down, Moses, Moses!)
Waa-ay dow-own in Egypt land!
Te-e-ll ol' (repeat 'te-e-ll ol',) Pharoah (Pha-a-roah)
To let my people (let my people) go!
Go Down Moses Jubilee Songs 1872

The parts in brackets were sung by two or three other groups of kids who had to echo the melody. Very difficult for Grade Eight students.

The teacher attempted to have the students master four-part harmony. And some of it in a 'round'. One section would start first, then the others had to come in later and harmonize as well. Disaster! Nothing was coordinated, they sounded awful, and it was embarrassing to listen to them.

Right before the choir started, the young teacher had stood up and announced to the audience that he feared his choir was not prepared well enough. But-he decided to let them try, anyway. Lousy incentive for a group of young neophyte singers! To everyone's chagrin, they fulfilled his prophesy and were given a rating of six (an unusually low score) by the adjudicator. However, he commended my brother on his well-delivered and inspiring solo. Thus, my bro was definitely an acknowledged talent.

We had both enjoyed two seasons of operetta in a teen group started by an elderly Arts-loving couple. The husband had written a longish homespun production entitled "Prince of the Forest". In it, I played Mother Tanya, a witchish, gypsy woman. My brother played a dashing officer of the Crimean War and his swordplay was really pretty good for an amateur stage production. I remember we both spent hours practicing-me a convincing mid-European accent and he, the swordplay Every song was to the tune of a Tschaikovsky classic. It had been both written and scored by our somewhat elderly choir director. I realized years later that he had been a 'frustrated composer'. Some of his pieces, especially the lyrics were 'God-awful' and some of it, not too bad. Example of 'Gawd-offul':

'Quickly, quickly, quickly quickly- let us start the day so quickly,
Even tho' we're fast asleep and feeling kinda sickly.
Hurry, hurry, hurry, hurry-there's no need to woooorry-wooorrry....'

You catch my drift? That particular song had a really dumb tune, too. But some of the better lines:

> *'This time of year I think of home*
> *This time of year, I long to roam*
> *Before I grow too old to go*
> *And memories melt like April snow....'.*

This one had a beautiful, lyrical melody. I would certainly give credit to the composer if I could remember his name. He is probably long dead now.
And one to a famous segment of Tschaikovsky:

> *'Ah, but the forest to my eyes has shown*
> *Beauty that daily like a flower has grown,*
> *Shown us a treasure, words cannot measure*
> *Knowing I long for it to be my own.......'*

My Dad was thrilled that my brother and I were in an operetta and dutifully sat in the audience after driving us to every performance. My Dad had also instilled in us the importance of finishing anything we started. I was no quitter. No matter how tough the going became in school or in life, I had always 'hung in' and given it my all. Except this time.......
The production successfully finished in late Spring and we were all look-ing forward to starting a new one in the Fall. Early October we received the

phone call. The elderly director and his wife were anxious to have us back. We had a casting call scheduled for the following week. Dutifully, we showed up in the little hall in town that they always rented for rehearsals. But-to our chagrin, not to be cast for the parts which, by virtue of seniority, we thought we so richly deserved.

We attended one or two rehearsals and each read at least two parts. The play was to be either Cinderella or Snow White, I forget which. I thought it was a given that my brother would be cast as the prince. He had, far and away the best singing voice among the youth, possibly of anyone in town. Though dark-haired, he was also well-built and handsome. I also read and sang for the female lead, secretly hoping to win it. But I didn't really hold out much hope of getting the part because of my low alto voice and overweight figure. I was quite pretty, but even I would concede that both Snow White and Cinderella should be slim.

Shortly after we auditioned, in walked the dentist's son-late. The very kid that I had acted with in the Dickens play. He was not terribly tall, rather skinny, and had non-descript brown hair. Even more tardy, another new kid, a girl, also from a prominent family, arrived. She was short and not terribly attractive, but vivacious and sang an O.K. soprano. She was definitely from the 'right side of the tracks and of the 'angel blouse' crowd. The dentist's kid had a good speaking voice, but was pretty skinny and couldn't sing well. Both had the audacity to show up late for practices.

At the second or third casting rehearsal I was availed of my fate. The new girl was given the female lead. I was to, again, play an ugly old crone and – insult on insult-my brother, rather than playing the Prince, was to play some lesser (and villainous) soldier role. Guess who was to get the male lead? Yep, the well-to-do dentist's son who was definitely Lincolnesque in looks (and voice? However, he probably fit the costume (as my brother was quite muscular) and read well. Now, I'm not suggesting there was any discrimination going on, but…..

So- in typical fashion, I soldiered on. We both completed the rehearsal and went home. However, the parts we had been given definitely didn't sit well with us. I either phoned the directors or spoke to them at the beginning of the next rehearsal. I told them I was very unhappy with the casting of my brother and that he should have been given the lead. (Especially since we had both been loyal for about two years and the other two were merely upstarts.) No way, Jose! The director's wife told me that her husband had chosen the parts and that was that. The Old Man had spoken and his word was law.

So-I grudgingly accepted our fates (or thought I did) and went to the next rehearsal with my brother. I remember I reluctantly started reading the part of the Witch and the lady came over to me. She thought I wasn't sounding 'witchy' enough. She started coaching me on how to do a 'cackly' voice. I remember, after a few attempts, I burst into tears and ran for the door. I was trying to be 'dedicated', but my heart wasn't in it. I didn't wanna be a witch!

On the way out, I flung a comment or two-none too complementary- at one or both Leads and perhaps even the choir director. I yelled at my brother to follow me and, without protest, he did. Seemed he was just as disgusted with the way things were going as I.

So-I headed home in high dudgeon, my brother upholding me. We complained mightily to our sympathetic father and vowed never to return to that 'hokey' production. However, being a basically good kid with a respect for authority figures, I soon felt the prick of conscience. After all, I had left the rehearsal precipitously and was quite insulting to crew members. I debated and stewed for a few days. On the one hand, I HAD been rude to two fellow players and showed an uncharacteristic disrespect for the elderly directors. On the other, they had a Hell of a nerve casting those No-Talent Upstarts and callously ignoring our months of toil and loyalty. However, the embarrassment of my blatant rudeness won out.

With great trepidation and 'swallowing my craw' as my Dad would have said, I phoned the director's wife. And I don't think my Dad had urged me to do it, either. He usually possessed the remarkable talent for keeping out of other people's business and letting them 'settle their own disputes'. The wife was sympathetic, but unwavering. To my chagrin, she made little or no effort to entice us back. However, I had been adamant with myself that no threat of punishment or sugary inducement was strong enough to force us to go back (unless they recanted and gave Gary the lead.) She offered neither. So I quickly made the briefest of apologies and hung up the phone.

Even though I was but a teen at the time, I realize now that that was about the most difficult and humiliating thing I have ever had to do. It was also one of the few times I ever quit a 'job' without completing it. (Although there were times when, for the sake of my own health, I probably should have quit.) With one exception- a run-in with some scary steers- which I write about in the chapter Our Work-Outdoor.

Well, that's probably enough to give you an idea about my family and, as to me, more will be revealed as my saga progresses…….

Our Pets: Boots, Little Peep, and Others

At Stratfords over the years, we had a rag-tag assortment of low-cost play fellows and companions. I don't think there was such a thing as an SPCA in our area yet, so we just scrounged pets wherever we could find them. We had tiny pets and we had big pets. Everything from baby chicks, salamanders and turtles to large dogs. Tadpoles and salamanders we commandeered from the creek each Spring. We 'visited' the neighbours' cows and goats. In the Spring, we'd catch tadpoles in the creek and bring them home in jars to see how they would grow. My mother, who was very soft-hearted would make us take them back to their natural habitat 'poor things'.

We tried keeping turtles in a dish on more than one occasion. The only pets we ever paid for. I think they cost a whole twenty-five cents each at the pet store in town. The glass bowl to keep them in cost about a buck. It had a fake palm tree in the center and a fake rock. We added more of our own and a few 'weeds' to make it more homey for the turtles. In spite of all efforts (even feeding them the recommended bits of hamburger from time to time), they all developed 'soft shell' and died.

When he was about six or eight, my brother had a tiny pet. It was a chicken. Or rather a chick. 'Little Peep', he called him. He had been rescued from the pecking hordes when the mother hen threw him out of the nest. Animals and birds, especially of the domestic variety, can be vicious. Any fellow creature they perceive as 'weak' or 'damaged' and, thus, a burden to the flock, they try to eliminate. This wisdom came from my Dad who, in our eyes, knew everything. Peep's legs were twisted and he dragged his fluffy butt when he tried to walk. My Dad said he had the chicken's type of muscular dystrophy. He could flop around a certain amount when encouraged, usually by placing a few tasty grains in front of him. However, he always looked inebriated and, because of his unusual gait had been pecked out of the nest. "Survival of the Fittest", my father declared.

My dad judged him to be a hopeless case, but my brother tenderly nurtured that little chick-fed and watered him and patted him till he nearly rubbed all his feathers off. My dad had warned him not to handle him so much or so often. After a month or so, the inevitable happened. My brother and I buried him in a wooden match box in the garden after holding a simple funeral. Little Gary blubbered uncontrollably. I have never since seen my brother grieve so over man or beast. He didn't take on as much when his beloved dog, Boots, died on the highway (or so we surmised) a few years later.

I don't remember exactly when we got Boots. I think we were pretty small at the time. A Heinz 57 my mother got for us on the Indian reserve. Probably from her good friend, Mrs. Johnny. Of indeterminate parentage, but mostly Black Lab, he was a loyal companion, but dumb as a rock. A more stupid mutt never walked the face of the earth.

It may be indelicate here to tell you how he got the name of 'Boots'. It wasn't just because he was solid black in color. Suffice it to say that, when he was in an amorous mood, he found our black rubber boots most enticing. We were constantly kicking him away at certain seasons of the year. He was too dumb to know the difference between a friendly female or a piece of footwear. Or, because no female was available, he was willing to settle for second best.

But, as I said, he was a loyal companion (if absolutely unable to learn even the most rudimentary of tricks), and followed us everywhere. I can remember in Summers lying for hours on our large lawn studying the scudding clouds. Boots would lie right beside us, our guardian, our pal. He even accompanied us on long treks to the creek or river. It was great; we didn't have to bathe him much in Summer.

He was an outside dog. Dad didn't believe in having animals in the house. He would make disparaging comments about his many 'poor' neighbours growing up in Manitoba who had shared their homes with goats and pigs. Or who had a sort of divided house-the cows and other large animals stabled on one side, the humans on the other. He said the stench was unbelievable! One thing about me ol' Dad, he was always scrupulously clean.

Perhaps this is a good time to tell you about my brother's dogs. I don't know why the dogs were always considered my brother's. I guess Minnie, the Cat, was unofficially mine. The first dog I can remember us having was Boots. I'm pretty sure my Dad got him from Mrs. Johnny down at the Reserve in Duncan. That's where all our dogs came from. I think Boots had had a predecessor, but I can't remember him.

Boots, as I said, was dumb as a rock. As a matter of fact, a rock may have been smarter 'cuz it at least has the good sense to stay put. He was also untrainable. Not that my brother ever tried very hard and my overworked pater didn't have the time. Boots would roam the neighbourhood at will, annoying the cows and scaring chickens and other livestock. I'm amazed that the neighbours put up with him. Luckily, we had few.

When we first moved to Somenos in '52, our nearest neighbour, except for the McAvoys across the road, was a good half-mile away. So- there weren't too many people around to care what our animals did. The one big draw-back, though, was that we lived only a half mile from the 'Cloverleaf'. That was where Somenos Road crossed the highway. I guess it was considered a four-way crossing, hence the 'cloverleaf' analogy. From time-to-time, usually late at night, we would hear a horrendous 'smash' up at our place. That usually meant another unfortunate had missed the turn to Somenos and gone off the train overpass and down onto the tracks. If he were lucky, he would just miss the turn and end up in the shrubs and trees to the right of the highway. About that time, the highways department put up a two-foot guard rail. It still didn't stop all the fatalities and serious injuries.

One time, when my brother was a teenager, he insists he ran down to an accident there. As I mentioned earlier, he heard the screams and insists he found a guy, in agony, impaled on his broken off steering wheel. We had already phoned the police or the fire department or whoever it was we phoned whenever we heard the crash. I think poor Boots met a similar fate down on the highway.

The next mutt after Boots was Juno. Also a Lab-cross. Probably also from the Indian reserve. Imagine my brother's horror when he discovered that it was also a boy dog but he had given it the name of a Roman goddess! Chico came along much later and was the cutest little pup you have ever seen. Totally different from the other two who had come to us as adults. I don't know if little Chico was a boy or a girl. It was brown and roly-poly and had interesting black and white markings on its broad little face.

I have a nice photo of my mother, by now severely incapacitated and sitting in a chair outside. She was holding the little pup. She loved that puppy so much. I don't remember what ever happened to him (her?), but assume it, too, died on the highway. Mom didn't last too much longer, either. My beautiful mother died in 1964. Eventually Dad forbade us to have any more dogs.

Minnie

Minnie had to be Cat Mother Extraordinaire. A fat, fluffy, beautifully marked old feline, she was rarely without a kitten or two following behind her.

She had the colorful brindling of a Norwegian Forest Cat (I just looked 'Domestic Cats' up on the Internet). But she was short-haired rather than shaggy. Almost fuzzy, actually. I don't know where Dad got her from or if she just appeared one day. Her coat consisted of a pleasant rainbow of colours- browns, reds, white, even some streaks of black. Her paws were pure white, fat and pleasantly fuzzy. I loved to rub them along my face-when she'd let me, that is. And she had the softest fur. My bro and I, when we were little, would spend hours stroking her. However, not if she'd just thrown another batch of kittens. Then she would be impatient and cross and prone to scratching. Thirteen or fourteen unruly kittens were more than enough for her to handle. She couldn't or wouldn't tolerate the unsolicited ministrations of a couple of pesky kids.

She was a well-padded cat. Not one of those skinny, boney show cats that eat only a low-fat Alpo diet. She was a good mouser. Many's the time we'd see her, hiking across the Back 40 with a fat mouse in her jaws, often as a protein snack for her latest brood. At times, she had the patience of Job. I guess she had to with as many as fourteen or fifteen kittens crawling all over her each Spring and Fall.

I remember in Junior High being relatively petless except for old Minnie. I guess my mother was too ill to help us look after pets and needed help herself. I don't remember when Old Minnie died, but remember her as Cat Mother Extraordinaire. She must have had more than fifteen huge batches of kittens over the years. Sometimes as many as fourteen at time.

We never knew who the fathers were. I don't know whether spaying hadn't been invented yet, or Dad just couldn't afford it. But I remember that often we kids would hover in the doorway while Minnie jumped up on the roof of our adjacent porch. She'd climb in a little window Dad had put there for her, kitten in mouth. She would, one at a time, when she was ready, bring her latest brood onto the porch roof for our inspection. It was almost as if she seeked our approval for the fine job she had done and wanted to introduce each kitten to us. Usually, in fine weather, Dad made up a bed for her on the porch roof. That way, we kids could go out to inspect and play with her brood daily.

When she became elderly herself, she would eat all but one. Perhaps she realized by then that Dad would drown them if she didn't dispose of them herself. Or perhaps just some instinct that comes to older cats when they know they won't have enough milk. I don't know how she made the difficult choice of which kitten to save. Maybe that fact was the inspiration for the poem I quoted earlier!

Dad said there were a few neighbourhood kids that HE would have drowned at birth if he'd had the chance! I think I was in about Grade Ten or Eleven when she died. Or just went away. One day, in between kitten batches, she just disappeared. When, after a few weeks, she didn't return, we questioned my father. He said:

"Well, she was getting pretty old and grey around the muzzle". She couldn't really look after her kittens any more. She knew her time had come. So-she probably just crawled out to the forest somewhere to her favorite spot to die. That is an animal's way of going back to Mother Nature."

Although my bro and I hunted for her carcass for some time, we never found any evidence of her demise.

So-that's the unhappy story of my brother's pets, apart from the succession of salamanders, frogs and other pond life brought up from the creek. None lasted very long.

But, then, there were the neighbour's pets. The Nilssen's next door, fine Swedish people, had goats. Three or four shaggy little beasts that ate all the grass in their back yard and left it looking muddy and denuded. I never played with them although my brother did. By the time we had an immediate neighbour, I was in high school. The Nilssen's didn't arrive until the early Sixties. Guess by then I thought I was too sophisticated to play with goats.

Our neighbours across the way had a cow. Needed to, with seven skinny kids to feed. I don't remember if they had any other pets (other than the usual cat and dog, which, in those days, didn't count.) It was lucky they did or their kids might have starved to death. The dad wasn't much of a provider. Had a bad leg injury, probably from W.W.II and wasn't able to work much. The mother, like most moms in those days, stayed home to look after the kids. I remember I always envied those girls their slim figures. Years later, I remet the youngest daughter in town and she confided to me that they weren't purposely slimming- they never had enough to eat!

Yet they were quite generous with what little they had. I remember several times going over to visit and being treated to a squirt in the eye from 'Ol Bessie, the Cow'. Well, the eldest boy, who was in charge of her usually aimed for my mouth, but often missed. You have never tasted good milk until you've had it, Bessie's milk-warm, straight from the udder. Sweet, creamy and so--oo-oo good! Tasted nothing like the watery, pasteurized pseudo-milk we get from the stores today.

In the Eighties, when I lived in Mill Bay, we could still buy milk from a local farmer. (As long as we went to his door to get it). Sold it to us in those glass bottles or large gallon 'milk jugs' you never see today. Milk stored in plastic or even waxed cardboard just doesn't taste the same. Pasteurization also alters the taste. This milk was unpasteurized and oh-so-delicious. I figured the farmer's kids are drinking it and they don't get sick, so why can't we? After only about a year, however, the government (in all its wisdom) shut the little farm down. They were no longer allowed to sell unpasteurized milk to anyone.

I remember from time to time, Mrs. McAvoy would send over a bottle of milk if she had some to spare. Dad would reciprocate with generous amounts of garden veggies and eggs in the Spring and Summer. In those days, the barter system, not Mastercard, was used. No one had any cash, but often had spare goods or services to provide. You'll hear all about the neighbour's horse my dad borrowed to pull a stoneboat a little farther along in my story. But that horse, although a pet, was a working member of the family.

Most farm animals in those days were there to do a job or perform a service (such as guarding one's property); they were not meant to sit around and be admired—or molly-coddled- as they are today. My Dad would puke if he saw some of the pampered canines being toddled down our street in Winter, tiny bells ringing on jeweled collars to match their cutsie little Xmas sweaters. And some off those tiny, skinny little brown dogs, the darlings of the Senior set, he would have called 'glorified rats'. The likes of Mrs. Pumfrey were probably unknown to my father's generation. On a farm, every creature, great and small (pardon the pun) pulled his own weight. Even old Minnie the Cat kept our basement and storage areas free of annoying rats and mice for many years.

'Mrs. Pumfrey' was an endearing character written about in 'All Creatures Great and Small, a comical British story. It was penned by James Herriot, a veterinarian. He often talked about his utter frustration trying to deal with the rotund and wealthy Mrs. Pumfrey.

Her pampered little Pomeranian, Trickey-Woo, was often the bane of his existence. Trickey's main health problem was that he was overfed 'people' food instead of proper dog food by his ever-generous mistress. Herriot would often be called out in the middle of the night merely to attend to 'doggie indigestion'. Mrs. P. so personified the unfortunate creature that she would send the vet cards for Xmas and on his birthday signed inappropriately" "Your son, Trickie" (or words to that effect).

Her long-suffering chauffeur hated the spoiled pet and often mimicked of booting it through the air as if it were a soccer ball. Such was his opinion of such a pampered and useless creature. It would have been dad's opinion, too.

CHAPTER IV   **OUR WORK – Indoor**

Riding the Dust Mop

'Tee-hee, hee!   Ha Ha!' Ha Ha Ha!'

Squeals and shrieks of delight. Excited howls and giggles emanating from the front hall. All in the high-pitched tones of little kids. Anyone entering our front door would be met with a hilarious sight. My chubby, diminutive mother hauling her two little kids around on the dust mop.

The dust mop was not quite like the Swiffer jobbies we see today. For one thing, it sported a full-length handle and a terry cloth cover. The cover was about eighteen inches long and oval in shape. It was definitely heavy-duty compared to todays' models. And it wasn't just used for dusting furniture. My mom also used it to dust and polish our hardwood and lino floors. I can still remember us looking forward to 'floor cleaning day' with joyous anticipation and vying to see who could be first to jump on the mop head. My mom would scoot around from room to room alternately pulling and pushing the mop as fast as she could. She would be laughing with glee right along with us.

When my bro and I were really small and still living in Vancouver, we could both sit on the mop. But one had to be on each side of the handle. However, by the time we got to Cowichan, I was almost five and very rotund. I doubt if I was even allowed to ride it solo by then, but my ever-skinny brother probably was.

My mother said our added weight prevented the mop from riding up and gave the floor a better 'polish'. And we had a great time, poking and screaming-exerting supreme effort to keep our feet from dragging on the floor. Maybe that accounts for the fact that today, many years later, I'm still told by the trainers at my gym that I have extremely strong abdominal muscles.

Sad Iron, Sad Story

As soon as I got big enough, I did most of our cleaning. In the early years, back in Vancouver, we had a 'hired girl' to help Mother out during her down times. At those times, Mom cried a lot. We kids thought it was just her Parkinson's. But I have since met many people who have advanced Parkinson's and they don't cry. Not 24-7 like Mom did, anyway. These depressive bouts invariably interfered with her ability to do housework. After about age six, I did most housework and a lot of the cooking. 'Poor little you', you might say. Au contraire, my ability to do household chores and manage a farm from a young age probably helped to make me into the strong and capable person I am today! Our motto in the fifties was 'Hard work never hurt anybody.'

For years on the inside of my left arm, I bore a nasty scar. About three inches long, it was volcano-shaped with a white line running through it. Luckily, I have no recollection of the accident. However, I have been told that I was about three. That means that the accident happened when we were still living in Vancouver, my father was working, and my disturbed mother had primary care of me.

My Dad, by now almost sixty, worked long hours as a laborer. His employer was the city of Vancouver, so I assume that it was steady employment. Someone, I don't remember who, later told me that my father (in spite of a bad heart and weak right arm) worked like a trooper. He laid cement sidewalks, dug ditches and performed other heavy labor jobs as part of the crew. He later told us that he either 'retired from' or was let go from the job when he turned sixty. That is when he sold the big rooming house he had built and managed. We moved to the Island.

My Aunt Vina later told me that, while Dad was away working, my mother did not take very good care of me. She overfed me sweets, often left me wet and poopy in my diaper too long and, when I was two, fell asleep with me on her stomach in the bed. I rolled onto the floor, breaking my collarbone. All I remember of that event is the vague 'feeling', not a conscious memory, of being taken away from my parents.

As I was later told: my Dad had come home to find me crying on the floor. He rushed me to Vancouver General and I remember the terror I felt when a nurse put me in a wheelchair and callously wheeled me away. Dad said I set up quite a howl. I don't know if they subsequently allowed my parents into the examining room. I also seem to have a memory of coming back out of the scary room sporting a cumbersome and confining shoulder sling.

The volcano-shaped scar was the result of another unfortunate accident I sustained while mother was looking after me. In the old days, there were few, if any, wrinkle-free fabrics. Everything that had unsightly wrinkles had to be ironed. Some of the housewives even ironed their cotton sheets. Mother said all the mothers on the block competed to see who could have the whitest laundry on the line. Many even added 'bluing' to their white items to make it look even whiter. The mark of a 'good housewife' in those days was blue-white and wrinkle-free laundry.

I guess one day I climbed up on my little stool beside the wooden, built-in ironing board my Dad had made. I was going to help my mother. If you have ever seen an old 'sad iron', you'll know that they were: one piece of solid metal, not hollow as most are today. I'd say that ours weighed at least five pounds, maybe more. A heavy load for a little kid to heft. After sitting on the top of our roaring woodstove for an hour or so, it became red hot. So hot in fact that mother 'tested it by first spitting on her finger. If the spit sizzled with the right amount of noise, she knew that the iron was ready for use.

The clothes to be ironed had usually been 'presprinkled' with the sprinkler. The clothes sprinkler was usually an old beer or pop bottle with a rubber end on it. The rubber end was punctured with numerous holes through which the water inside could 'sprinkle' out. I don't know if the punctured ends were actually purchased at a store, or if it was something my dad rigged up. I can remember spending an hour or more presprinkling clothes and household cottons for ironing before the days of wrinkle-free polyesters and other man-made fabrics.

Unfortunately for me as a mere toddler, the old sad iron was extremely heavy and I didn't really know how to use it. For some reason I started ironing my arm instead of the garment. I can imagine the screaming I must have done on incurring such a serious wound. I don't know where Mother was or if I was taken for medical help. Often, for burns, they just rubbed some Vaseline on them and hoped for the best.

I also remember that we didn't think much of it at the time. Kids were always 'having accidents', was the tenor of the times. Fusses were not made over every childhood injury the way they are today. At least, not by my family. Therefore, I didn't think very much of it myself, although it must have been a heinous burn to leave such a large and long-lasting scar.

However, I distinctly remember that even into my forties and fifties, that scar was prominent and angry. It is only now, in my sixties, that the ugly blot has started to fade (or is slowly being obliterated by the ever-wrinkling hide?) I think it was just subsequent to that, and probably on the arrival of my little brother only fifteen months after me, that Lena appeared. I still have a vague remembrance of Lena, our 'hired girl'. And one sepia 'brownie' camera photo.

Lena was tall and slim, of some 'foreign extraction, according to my mother. In the photo, she seems to have very muscular arms. I can understand why, packing us little kids around and doing all Mom's housework. One of the aunts, I presume, later told us that my mother often spent many hours lying in bed, sometimes crying. I believe it because, after we moved to Cowichan, she used to sit in her upholstered rocker, similarly crying for hours on end. We kids just surmised it was because of her Parkinson's disease but I now know that, at those times, my mother was severely depressed. When not depressed, she strongly exhibited the euphoric moods of full-blown mania. She was probably Bipolar. Of course, the term was not even coined in those days. It probably would not have been openly talked about if it were.

In my thirties or forties, I had vaguely heard the name 'Manic-Depressive' assigned to Bipolar persons. I think it actually described the situation better. However, back in the Forties and Fifties, such things as bullying, sexual abuse, spousal abuse, Gay/Lesbian issues, and the like were considered 'hush-hush'.

So, thank God, my father was able to hire a young worker to look after us. I don't know if Lena lived in or went home every day. I do think she was with us pretty constantly till my Dad sold out and left for The Island.

In later years, he confided that he arrived 'broke' because of us kids. My mother's two Caesarian sections had cost him over two thousand dollars in medical bills, a fortune in those days. To wit, he bought our acre of land and small, but usable house at Stratfords for only a thousand in 1952. Lena's salary, too, must have cost him plenty.

Why he decided to sell out and leave the big city, I never really knew. I don't think us kids ever thought to ask him. However, I presume that, because he had been raised on a large farm in Saskatchewan at the turn of the Century (20th, that is), he preferred 'country' life. He had 'batched' up North for years, running a trapline and fishing the frozen lakes. I am certainly thankful that he moved us to the (then) quiet, countrified island I grew up on.

When my mother met him, he was 'living rough' near Flin Flon, Manitoba. The forty below Winters didn't daunt my father, but eventually did my mother and they moved to Vancouver where her sister and mother resided. Her mother also owned a rooming house and my aunt inherited it when my grandmother died. I don't know if my mom inherited some of the proceeds but, if so, that may have helped to finance the move to the Island. Also, my Dad had a dream of mining for gold at or near the old Tyee Mine site on Mt. Sicker. Hence our big move in 1952 to Stratfords Crossing...

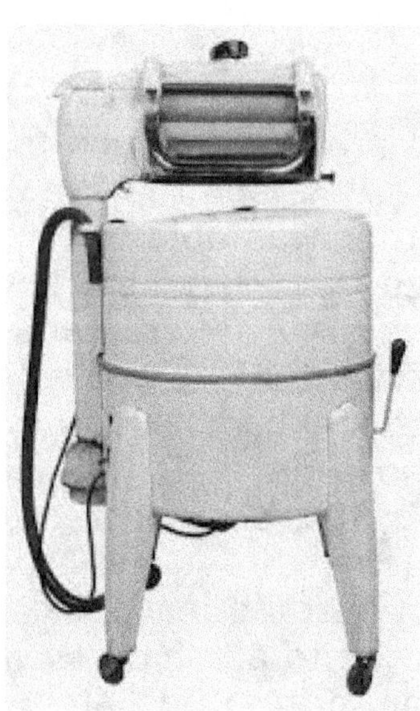

My Old Nemesis (Wringer Washing Machine)

'She got strangled to death, you know. Wearing a scarf around her neck. Her neck broke before her mother could release the rollers'....

A dire warning from my mother. Just what I needed to hear when I'm hauling a gimongous bucket of clothes down the creaky old basement stairs. My naughty brother of course, had to remind me of the cautionary tale my mother told us nearly every time I pulled laundry duty. I guess she thought it would ensure that we were careful whenever we were near that potentially-lethal wringer. It did. I had nightmares for months obsessing about this helpless little kid-sucked blue-faced by the neck into the giant maw.

The WRINGER-yeah! That, innocent, creamy-white, virginal looking gizmo that squatted above the huge mechanical washtub. The first thing my mother did was show me how to release the cumbersome safety catch at the side of the old monster. You actually had to bang it rather hard with the flat of your hand to get it to release. There were two wringers. Looked like two giant rolling pins stuck one on top of each other. But, believe me, you didn't want to get your finger (or any other part of your anatomy) stuck between them when feeding in the clothes! Every Saturday, for years, I was a victim of:

THE LAUNDRY PROCESS

1. Fill the gimongous tub with hot water from the large stoneware sink on the wall. Add detergent.
2. Press the large lever on the side to set it spinning and mix up the soap.
3. Separate the 'whites' from the 'darks'. Set heavily-soiled work clothes aside.
4. Add the clothes and replace the round-shaped, rubberized lid. (for safety; it also wouldn't be nice to get an anatomy part wrapped around the imposing agitator in the middle, either)
5. If a load of 'whites'. Add bluing (which supposedly gave the whites a bluish glow signifying that yours were 'whiter' than anyone else's). Let clothes agitate for twenty minutes or so. (I don't remember if the tub had a timer or if I just stopped it when I felt the clothes had 'cooked' enough.)

6. Set it to 'drain' (a 'reverse' process wherein the water was sucked back into the hose and down the sink drain) Refill tub with cold rinse water. Let it swish around some more.
7. Drain again.
8. Find the big, old heavily-stained wooden spoon standing in the corner. Use it to lift out the clothes one, by one.
9. Feed them (instead of your finger) into the wringer and between the huge rollers. (If you missed on first attempt, the item fell back into the tub and had to be retrieved again).
10. Pull clothes out the back and throw into the waiting laundry basket. (If, perchance, you feed more than one item in at a time, the rollers will go 'bumpity-bump' and you'll have to smash the safety release. Remove the offending items and throw back into the tub. You'll need both hands to reset the wringers and reclasp the release catch. Start over.)
11. When all is finished, drain the washer out through the hose, then wipe out both the washer and the laundry sink with the convenient (and often smelly) rag hanging on the sink for just that purpose.
12. Push, pull, or drag the loaded basket up the steep basement stairs (unless you could bribe or threaten little brother into doing it).
13. Haul out onto the back landing and peg onto the line one-by-one with wooden clothes pegs. (Pegging clothes on a line has become a forgotten art which I won't go into here). Pray that the day is not too windy or you'll be out at night picking them out of the muddy garden plot.

In Winter, or on rainy days, I had to hang the sopping clothes on a rather unique 'overhead' drying rack as well as a wooden, stand-up one.

On the basement ceiling hung a large wooden rack. It possessed the unique capability of being able to move up and down. This feat was accomplished by means of a long cord which hung at the side. I think it was a double, 'oblong' cord which, if you pulled it from the back, lowered the rack. If pulled from the front or in the opposite direction, it raised the rack back up into the dark recesses of the ceiling.

How it worked was this: I would carry the heavy basket of wet clothes over to the rack and lower it by means of the cord. After hanging the items carefully on the four or five rack runners, I would pull the cord again and the rack would return to its nest in the ceiling. Once the clothes were dry, I'd lower it again. A rather ingenious innovation my father had for drying laundry above the hot furnace on wet days.

The whole process took up my entire Saturday morning for many years, especially if there were more than one washtub full. Unless it was an exceptionally fine day and we could convince my dad to let us troll the highway for pop and beer bottles. I'll tell you more about these 'pop bottle picking' mornings in a succeeding chapter.

MOM'S FAVOURITE RECIPES

Apple Fritters, Hog Jowls, and other Yummies

Of course, other than house cleaning and laundry, the job that took up the most of our time was cooking. In those days nearly everything was cooked or baked from 'scratch'. I cannot remember us ever purchasing a cake or cookies from town. Not even doughnuts. Mother made her own. She had a huge deep fryer which sat beside our combo wood and electric stove. I don't know if either exist today. If they do, they're probably both fossils.

However, that deep fryer made the best 'melt-in-your mouth' apple fritters, doughnuts and dumplings you've ever tasted. For fritters Mom would melt left over lard or shortening and get the fryer started. I'm not sure if it plugged into an outlet or was somehow hooked in to the old stove. It would take a while for the fat to start to sizzle. I think she used lard which, in those days, came in small tubs. Hence, I guess the phrase 'Tub of Lard' for a fat person who ate too much greasy food. Unfortunately, that label was given to me by the school bullies a time or two.

While the fryer heated up, she prepared the batter. I guess it was similar to pancake batter, but with a little sugar and flavoring added. Then we helped her peel and slice up the apples. One-by-one, she coated them with batter and carefully plopped them into the sizzling fat. Soon the yummy aroma of baked apples filled the room. In just a few minutes, the batter would form a crispy, delectable-smelling crust and she'd take them out on a 'drainer spoon'. The deep fryer, of course, was verboten to us little kids. We could only view its treasures from afar.

'Be careful, don't get too close. That sizzling fat can fly and take your eye out!'

(A horrible accident that, supposedly befell my great-grandmother when she 'took her eye out with a sewing needle'.) After an hour or so, she'd have a huge platter of gold-encrusted apples ready for the final step. Sugar-dusting! We'd squabble to see who got to perform that coveted task. Because, of course, the kid who got to spread the sugar got to lick the sugar off his fingers. So-Mom would reach for her old flour/sugar sifter.

The sifter was a medium-sized, barrel-shaped metal cylinder which had once been painted white with a red floral pattern. The flowers had long-since faded to a dull pink and the paint was well-chipped, but it still worked. Inside, it held a thick, curved wire which, when the handle was turned, forced the flour or sugar through a bottom sieve. There it fell onto the food in intriguing clouds of white. Just right for little licked fingers to poke, first into the sugar, then into the mouth.

So-whichever kid's turn it was to dust the plate did so and, if we'd been 'good', we got to sample one or two. However, if it was close to supper time we had to wait. The waiting was excruciating. Usually, when biting into the succulent tidbits, we'd discover one apple slice. However, from time-to-time, there would be two or even three trapped inside. We'd vie with my Dad and Mom at the dinner table to see who could find one with multi-slices.

Unfortunately, by the time supper rolled around, the fritters would be cold or, at least only lukewarm. They were still yummy, but not as delectable as those fat sizzlers fresh out of the fryer. Mom often cooked them in the early afternoon so we could sample the hot delicacies and not 'spoil our supper'.

A similar method produced delicious 'bread' doughnuts, sometimes chocolate ones and covered with icing, coconut, or other handy toppings. I don't think 'sprinkles' had been invented yet. If they had, we would have considered them a luxury too dear to purchase!

Brown Beans and Hog Jowl

This was another delicacy, a staple actually, I wish all kids today could sample. The recipe consisted of kidney beans (raw in the bag, not canned), molasses and hog jowl. Hog jowl was sliced from the cheek area of the animal; it was tender and succulent after simmering for a few hours in Mom's recipe. First, she'd soak the beans overnight. Then the next day she'd drain them, refill the pot with fresh well water and boil them until tender. She'd add a cup or so of the good black strap molasses. None of that sissy 'baking molasses' for her. Then a tablespoon or two of dark, demerara sugar (or golden yellow if she had to substitute). Lastly, the hog jowl, preboiled and cut into cubes. Then she'd simmer the mixture for an hour or so, spoon it, piping hot onto our plates and yum! yum! Hot tip (pun intended!): It tasted even better on the morrow after sitting for a day.

I could tell you interesting stories of the many afternoons we spent cooking and baking with my mother. There was definitely a reason why I was fat as a kid. I now believe that singing, cooking, and playing with us were my mom's 'raisons d'etre'. Her 'chocolate cake in a pan' was to die for. Usually covered in plain white butter (in our case, margarine,) icing and sprinkled with either walnuts or shredded coconut.

She also made 'finger foods', the iced delicacies she'd learned to bake in France. I think (but am not sure) that they were a type of bar or square, baked and then iced with colored icings. She'd top them with variations of walnuts and coconut or sometimes tiny silver-colored candy beads. I'm not sure if she used chocolate chips; they may not have been invented yet.

Her Hot Biscuits, titled 'Baking Powder' biscuits in the recipe books, were basically a flour paste leavened with baking powder. She'd throw in one egg and a teaspoon of sugar 'for flavor'. They were often served with an egg or bacon for breakfast. For variety, she'd add shredded cheese or raisins to the mix before rolling them to about half inch thickness and cutting out with a floured water glass or large cookie cutter.

I'm sure that the incredible fudge she also made took out at least a couple of my teeth. For what is fudge, after all? Basically, butter and sugar. I don't exactly remember how Mom made it but I know it entailed boiling either butter or margarine, 'golden yellow' sugar, and Pacific canned milk on the stove. When it reached the correct consistency, she'd pour it into a square pan to cool. As it cooled, it hardened. She'd sometimes add Fry's cocoa from the yellow can (to turn it into chocolate fudge) or top with whole walnuts or coconut.

Her Johnny cake was basically a muffin recipe with equal amounts of flour and heavy cornmeal. When served with Rogers corn syrup or, better yet, the 'real' maple syrup she sometimes got from Old Man McGonagal—yum!

We lost a few teeth to cavities by the time we were in our late teens. I blame it also on chewing Wrigley's spearmint gum (no sugar-free in those days) and mom's homemade candy-especially the taffy-which stuck to our teeth like glue. The sugary home baking probably contributed, too.

I'm not sure exactly what constituted the taffy. Probably brown sugar and milk or water with vanilla flavoring. I remember we had to heat it on the stove till the carmelized or 'candy' stage. If you overcooked it, you ended up with flavored cement. For 'pull' taffy, we only made it when it was snowing. I think we somehow kneaded it first, then 'pulled' it. I can't remember if the 'pulling' occurred before or after we threw it out in the snow to cool to a rubbery consistency.

I remember us kids competing to see who could stand on one end with mother on the other as we pulled it to soften it and add air for lightness. Mom's taffy was melt-in-your-mouth good! So you can see why controlling my weight was a real challenge while I lived at Stratfords!

A few of Mother's favorite recipes:

Quick Spaghetti

Note: My mother's 'Quick Spaghetti' wasn't really spaghetti at all as it was made with egg noodles….

Only required four ingredients: a pound of lean hamburger, a package of egg noodles, a large can of tomatoes, and a large onion.

Preboil a package of egg noodles; add about a tablespoon of oil or lard if worried that noodles will stick. Brown the hamburger and chop it up with the spoon as it's cooking. Add finely chopped onion right away so it will soften with the hamburger. When hamburger nearly cooked, and onion soft, add the can of tomatoes. Then dump in the pre-cooked noodles. Keep stirring. Today we'd probably call it 'supper in a dish'.

'Anything' Fruit Cobbler

Mom's versatile cobblers were our dessert staple during berry season. You could simply line a square or oblong bake pan with any kind of fruit (berries of all types, cut-up, pitted plums, apples, rhubarb, etc.). Put a couple of tablespoons of flour and sugar each in a cup. Sprinkle over. For apple cobbler, we also sprinkled cinnamon over the apples. Rhubarb you'd have to add a little extra sugar or mix half and half with berries which were a lot sweeter. Otherwise the rhubarb in the pudding would be too sour.

Then you'd whip up a vanilla scratch cake or plain biscuit dough and pour over top. Bake for 40 minutes to an hour and voila-instant dessert. To make it almost festive, mother would top it with one of her pudding sauces-usually vanilla/caramel or lemon.

Mom's Easy Pudding Sauce

Melt a dollop or two of butter or margarine in a saucepan on low heat. Turn up the heat and add about an eighth cup brown sugar and an equal amount of flour. This could probably be thickened with corn starch instead, but Mom never did. When almost boiling, add water or milk to desired consistency and stir like crazy remembering that it will thicken more as it cooks. In only two-three minutes it would thicken and be ready to serve. To prevent lumping, put flour and water in small Mason jar with lid. Shake like crazy and then add to recipe.

To turn it into lemon sauce, just squeeze in lemon juice to taste, probably two-three teaspoonfuls. The sauce could probably be turned into chocolate sauce by adding cocoa or melted Baker's chocolate, but I don't remember Mother ever using chocolate sauce, not even on ice cream.

However, Mom's baking days were probably over by the time I was nine or so, and she ceased teaching me any other recipes. I had taken over most of the cooking chores and probably all the house chores, by the age of about ten.

Sometimes, for dieting inspiration, I'll watch those 'extreme weight loss shows on T.V. They show morbidly obese people weighing, in some cases, over six hundred pounds. That's to scare the bejesus out of me so that I'll stick to my self-imposed diet and exercise 'regimen' and not eat so much of my Mom's fattening recipes!

'Her Finger is Caught in the Sewing Machine!'

That was Mom, dutifully trying to fulfill her role as 'perfect' mother. In those days, being a 'good mother' was enough. Today, we seem to expect a lot more of women. (Or do women expect more of themselves?) However, with her Parkinson's she shook so badly that, from time to time, she'd have a nasty accident with the sewing machine. Like many housewives of the day, she had an old singer treadle model. Would probably be worth a small fortune in antique shops today.

In those days, you didn't take out the knee of your pants and then run to Wal Mart or the thrift store to get another cheap pair. You patched. Mother would keep flat chunks of denim from our 'too small' or 'damaged beyond repair' pants to use as 'patching'. She'd line up the offending hole (often after having basted a suitable patch over it first) in the machine. Then she'd have to turn the fabric to stitch around the patch.

Unfortunately, some days her hands shook so badly that she'd impale a chunk of her finger on the rapidly descending needle. She'd scream and, at first, Dad would rush in to rescue the digit. As we kids got older, one of us would have to do it. However, one day, she drove the needle right through the bone. When Dad came in from work and found her hysterical in her chair, that was the end of Mom's sewing. I suspect that I then had to take over the additional job of sewing and mending.

I howl at the teens today buying expensive designer jeans. They then cut the knees out and append multitudinous holes throughout the legs, or buy them that way for some ridiculous price! If mother had seen those on us, she would have made us cut them up for cleaning rags! My ex recently told me that one enterprising youngster bought a whole slew of old jeans from the local thrift shop for two bucks each. Then, he/she cut big holes in them and retailed to other kids for up to fifty bucks a pair! Now that's entrepreneurship for you. (Wish I could do that with my book sales….)

How times have changed. Years ago, no one wanted to 'look poor'. Now the 'grunge look' is where it's at!

Mother was a good knitter and an expert crocheter and tatter. She had, in the Forties, spent four years meticulously crocheting two huge bedspreads out of ecru thread. Then she knotted in literally hundreds of hand-made tassles. I remember that one bedspread was a double size and comprised probably a hundred or more large maple-leaf-like designs. It was completely bordered by the rich-looking, yet fuzzy tassles. A work of art that would be priceless today.

When I was away at college, W.S. used them as couch covers. She then washed them in the washing machine after letting her immature, yet hard-working male boarders sit on them. In those days, they still affected the 'Elvis' hairdos and had ratting combs sticking out of their hip pockets. The long stick-like combs tore gaping holes in the gorgeous fabrics.

A few years later, I was able to 'bribe' W.S. into giving them back to me even though she said they were headed for the garbage. Unfortunately, she was right. I even took them to an older German lady in Mill Bay, a well-known, experienced crocheter. She said she could not repair them. Unfortunately, as a crochet project is made, it's all of a piece. It is impossible to crochet 'patches' (even if one could obtain the original pattern and she said that would be dicey). She deemed it impossible to stitch them back in after-the-fact. I nearly cried when I had to take the sad tatters those gorgeous pieces had become and throw them out.

A job that was, just generally, not-my-favorite was sewing. I can still remember sweating over 'bound buttonhole' and zipper samples in home ec class in high school. Mending pants and putting up hems wasn't so bad, but actually producing a whole garment was, for me, sheer Hell. More about the dreaded sewing classes towards the end of this book…..

Just generally, then, our indoor work consisted of cooking, cleaning and sewing. Clothes were handed down, recycled, patched or cut up for dishcloths and cleaning rags. My folks would laugh out loud to see in today's cleaning aisles, the neat boxes of cleaning cloths. They would never have thought of paying money for such things. That would be as silly as actually paying for bottled water! Recycling? We invented it! In those days, you didn't have to be taught how to recycle -you just had to be 'brought up poor'!

OUR WORK- OUTDOOR

'Chicken with its head cut off!'

There were a couple of other good stories associated with chickens. As I might have mentioned in 'Pioneer Dad' my father struggled, retired and in his Sixties, to eke a better living from our modest acreage. At one point, he raised chickens himself. And not in any small way. He ran no less than twelve hundred Leghorns, mostly white, as I recall. To do that, he constructed two or three extra outbuildings at the back of the property. One was dubbed simply 'the chicken house'.

It was a large wooden structure with a wooden floor covered with straw. There the huge flock of chickens resided when they weren't out in the chicken run, a wire-fenced area that ran down the slope to the creek. There was a large open space in the middle where the chickens were fed grain and watered in little troughs ranged along the side. Along each wall ran rows of nesting boxes wherein they laid their eggs. I often got the nasty job of reaching under a nervous biddy to rob her of her much-coveted egg.

We had an egg candling shed just below father's immense vegetable garden. In there, we would shine a light through each egg. I think it was to make sure they had not been fertilized and there was no embryo inside. Imagine the shock of some plump, well-to-do housewife in town if she cracked an egg and a half-formed baby chick plopped out!

However, when he became a teen, my inventive brother found another use for the egg candling shed. He had been a runty, skinny, kid. When he turned thirteen, he decided to do something about it. My brother's initial attempts to build a Charles Atlas body were commendable. His primitive weight lifting equipment comprised a huge cement block attached to a heavy rope and a chinning bar.

Many's the time he tried to cajole me into lifting the unwieldy thing, and, occasionally, I did. But the mastery of the chinning bar (which was attached to the doorway at least a foot over my head) forever eluded me. Also, in those days we believed that girls who lifted weights or excelled in any kind of athletics would invariably grow up to have big muscles and small boobs. I did anyway in spite of my early efforts to avoid athletic activity.

The worst and 'nastiest' chore associated with the raising of chickens was getting them ready for the stew pot. To do that, someone had to butcher them.

That task, T.G., usually fell to my father and, later, my teenage brother. If a hen became too old to lay or we had an extra young rooster in the flock, it became supper. However, the task of getting the free-roaming bird from the yard to the pot was onerous.

First, you had to catch the son-of-a-gun. It took quick wits and even faster feet. My brother, luckily, was lightning quick. I wasn't. Give me a skipping rope or a bike and I could go for hours, but fast sprinting was never my long suit. Dad had rigged up some short poles with looped snares over them. If you were lucky, you could get one of the loops around the chicken's neck, then grab her, hugging the body tightly to your chest. (And hope you didn't get pecked in the eye while doing so!)

Then the bird was carried firmly to the chopping block. If not carried firmly, she could flap you very painfully with her wings. The block was a large round of log set up in the backyard. Its top was always stained pink with chicken blood. With the bird in one hand and the axe in the other, the executioner would slap the chicken's head firmly down. Holding the axe overhead, he'd make like a human guillotine. If the blow was clean, with enough force applied, the head would roll free. Dad wouldn't let Gary butcher till he was strong enough to make a clean cut almost 100% of the time. He felt it was cruel to make the chicken suffer the trauma of a partially-severed head and a second cut.

So-a quick slap and the head was plopped onto the ground beside the block. Then, the chicken was released. Many times the bird would not simply die and hang limply. Often, it remained alive for a minute or two. Then, I'd hear my brother yelling from the backyard: 'Chicken with its head cut off'. That was the cue for me and any neighborhood children who happened to be visiting to run to the backyard and provide an audience. We'd stand in a circle, some giggling, some shocked. The frantic bird would run madly in all directions as if it could regain its missing head somehow by rushing to look for it.

The next stage of chicken-to-table chores fell to me. I'd boil a huge pot of water on the old woodstove and haul it out to the front stoop. Grasping the, by now, lifeless bird by its legs I'd upend it in the water. This was to loosen the heavy pin feathers so that it could be plucked. After about fifteen minutes of hard 'elbow grease', the hen was ready to be gutted. A job I also hated. My brother, being rather gorey-minded, kind of liked it. During his senior high school years, Gary worked part-time for a veterinary surgeon across the highway. He, at one time, had aspirations of becoming a vet. I guess the gutting procedure was good preparation.

He'd make a central incision from neck to groin and pull out the steaming entrails. I'd caution him to take care with the heart, gizzard* and liver. The liver was a particular delicacy for me, especially if fried quickly in grease in the fry pan. The gizzard and heart, which tended to be tough, tasted better boiled and softened in a small pot.

I'd make a stuffing of leftover bread crusts, melted margarine, onion, and spices, (a combination of bread leftover from school lunches and old, tough crusts carefully frozen in the top of our old Westinghouse fridge). If a tougher old 'stew hen' or young rooster (that wasn't needed to perform his fertilization duties on the hens), it would be boiled. Again, we'd add potatoes, onions, and carrots, stewing slowly on the back burner. In a couple of hours, we'd have succulent chicken stew or 'supper in a pot'. As far as I know, electric crock pots had not yet been invented. Had they been, we probably couldn't have afforded one, anyway. But, mind you, Pop's old hen stews were better-tasting than the supposedly fresh young birds we get in the supermarkets now!

Dad always made sure that his birds had a modicum of fat on them. Not for him the tough and stringy veggie fed 'health' birds of today. They boiled up juicy and succulent, filling the house with a delicious odor by suppertime. Rarely have I experienced anything so tasty as those plump old hens my father expertly raised back on our little truck farm at Somenos.

Stoneboat Basement

"Grab her head, kid, and hang onto 'er. Don't drop those reins! Gotta get this boat turned so she'll pull 'true'. It's a heavy son-of-a-gun. She's getting crooked, again. Here, stop ol' Bessie while I straighten her out. O.K. Pull, girl, pull. That's it; almost made it………."

In the Spring of '58, I had the worst back pain I have ever experienced in my life. My Dad, as I told you earlier, decided to get rid of the Stinky Oil Stove. So-he devised a plan to dig a huge hole under the house, cement it in and put in a partial basement to house his (largely home-made) furnace. My brother, being only about nine, was too young to be of much help. So-the unpleasant and lengthy task fell to me.

In order to do the work, Dad had to borrow or rent the neighbour's stoneboat and an old horse named Bessie. The stoneboat was a cumbersome wooden affair made up of planks and logs. The planks were hand-hewn and very thick. They formed the base. Two huge canoe-shaped logs comprised runners and had pointy ends. The inside was hollow for dirt-filling. Thus, the thing could be dragged by the horse along the ground giving least resistance.

The plan was to hand-dig shovelfuls of earth day-by-day, load up the stoneboat and drag it to the back of the property for dumping. It was arduous work. Initially, there was only a small hole under the house where Dad had stored vegetables. The work required constant stooping and it was hard to get any 'swinging' room to throw the dirt into the stoneboat.

After a few days of hard digging, there was room to stand and we progressively extended the hole. I also started to have Hellish back pain. By the end of the day, my spine would be so bad that I'd cry when trying to lie back in bed at night. My dad would come in, hold me by both hands and lower me slowly into the bed so I wouldn't scream. I don't think I complained enough to be taken to the doctor just then. I do remember complaining later.

In those days you didn't go to the doctor for every little 'ache and pain' as people do now. You had to be bleeding uncontrollably or half-dead before anybody bothered. And then, you'd better have a darn good story to tell the old sawbones or there'd be Hell to pay.

"Why did you waste all my time and gas money driving you in here when there's nothing wrong with you? I could have put in another half day's work instead of hauling you around."

And they didn't practice much 'preventive' dentistry back then, either. I was lucky that my dad usually took us to the dentist every year or so for a check-up. Most kids didn't get taken till the toothache was so bad that they had to have an extraction. In spite of check-ups, I had quite a few of those by the time I reached adulthood. One time, the old dentist in Nanaimo even caused a small split in my upper jawbone because the molar he was pulling was so solid. I heard the nauseating crack! But-that's another story.

So-I soldiered on, back pain and all. I remember lying on my back on the grass to rest it when the pain got unbearable. And-Dad and I would 'spell off'. First, he'd dig for an hour or so and I'd manage the old horse. Then, I'd dig and he'd haul. Eventually, I remember being taken to the doctor to have my ongoing back pain checked out. All I remember him saying is that I was having 'growing pains' and that's 'totally normal'. Luckily, after the hard work of pick-axing was over, my back pain largely disappeared for several years. It recurred with a vengeance when I was in my early twenties.

Then, years later, when my severe scoliosis* was diagnosed in Victoria, I went back to that old M.D. in Duncan. (or wrote him a letter, I forget which). He was shocked to discover that I had back trouble. My whole family had been patients of his for over twenty years and he never diagnosed my back problem. The specialist I was seeing in the Big City said it would be helpful to get any previous spinal x-rays. There were none. It turned out that the spine had been 'growing' all right-growing crooked!

So, we soldiered on and after about a week of hard digging, had a sizable hole under the house. We spent another week or so deepening the hole and placing a makeshift door to 'keep the night critters out'. Then my dad began the laborious process of setting forms and pouring cement. He was determined to make the basement deep enough that he could stand up in it. Since he was six feet tall, that took a lot of digging.

By the end of the month, we had a huge hole, freshly poured cement walls on at least two sides, and a cement floor. Or partial cement floor as I know he reserved a dirt-lined area under the stairs for a 'root cellar'. He then proceeded to 'invent' a stove. He procured a heavy old rusting boiler from somewhere and converted it to a firebox. I think he had a welder cut a hole in the front for a door, but he may have torched it himself. Eventually, the furnace was finished. When he stoked up the son-of-a-gun, it really roared. He cut vent holes in the floor of every room in the house.

He attached homemade wooden grates. We were pretty toasty once the old thing got going. We could even dry laundry and wet boots over the hot air which shot up miraculously every morning. And my dad had plenty of dry wood available. Most from the demise of the old maple which had been lying, nicely 'seasoning,' for a few years.

Everybody except my brother thought that the home-made furnace was a great innovation. He was the poor sod who had to get up just after five every morning and get it started. He also cut most of the kindling for it. I don't remember having to start or stoke it very often. I think I was afraid of the flames and my dad let me beg off. I had to make the breakfast and dress my mother instead.

'You can't go home again….'

In the early Nineties, long after I had graduated college and the house had been sold, I had a shock. I had been living out-of-town for sometime, but often enjoyed leaving the highway and detouring down the side road to check out our old property. It had changed hands once or twice since I had lived there. I remember, in the Eighties, I had stopped in and knocked on the door. My Dad had died in '81 so he had probably sold out about 1975. W.S. had insisted he move back into her crappy little house in town. A youngish woman with two or three kids answered. I told her that was the house I had grown up in and asked her if I could come in and see if it had changed much. It had.

The basic layout was still the same-rooms still in the same places, but it had all been redecorated. It was barely recognizable as the eclectic, forties-style ranch house I had once lived in. I thanked the lady and left. I never went in it again, but looked at it many times in succeeding years as I drove by. I showed the old property from the road to my young son and many friends. But-one day about 1998 or so I drove by and only the chimney was standing. And it was blackened. Uh-oh! There had obviously been a fire which had taken down the old house. A few months later, there was nothing but a gaping hole.

Then, a while after, a new house emerged. Much larger and more modern, with a huge attached garage in front and pinkish, vinyl siding. I hated it. The house was so huge and ungainly that it dwarfed what had once been a generous front lawn. The wonderful old orchard had disappeared, ditto the cherry tree. The landscaping was all changed. The fence and tea roses were gone. The old dirt road to the back of the property was grassed in. Next to the neighbor's property, a huge hedge had appeared. I hardly recognized the place and felt a pang of sadness every time I drove by in the future. I guess most of the good things in our lives must end sooner or later. I feared that the old boiler Dad had converted to that makeshift furnace, had been the culprit in the housefire!

Bovine Hellions

(Or perhaps I should call this section 'Learning Your Limitations.')

It was the very beginnings of feminism. Or maybe I was one of the original and perhaps, unintentional instigators. It was late Spring of my grade Eleventh year. I had been working every weekend for a month or two at a local farm-berry picking. I was pretty good at it. But, the pay averaged about sixty-five cents per hour, a lousy wage even for those days. I deeply resented that the fact that, for college money, boys had much better chances at a good-paying job than the girls had.

The raspberry picking wasn't too bad, as you could mostly stand up, but strawberry picking was Hell. Even then, I had a bad back and it would ache ferociously by the end of the day. Also, for the low strawberry bushes, you were crouching all day in the hot sun. Whereas, with raspberries, there was at least partial shade. I was a fast picker, but on this farm, we were not paid by volume. We were paid by the hour. I later picked on a farm near Chemainus and often earned eight or ten dollars per day. There, I was paid for number of pounds picked.

Over the few weeks I had been picking since nearing the end of my Grade Eleven school year, I had observed two or three 'farm boys'. Their chores didn't seem to be much more arduous than mine. However, they bragged that they earned a whole dollar an hour. I wanted that dollar. So- I finagled the elderly farmer into giving me a chance at 'men's work. He looked at my hands and cautioned me that he 'didn't think I'd be able to handle it'. But, he agreed that, if I could do the same work as the boys, I would get the same wage.

The boys usually worked ten hour days, so I had the potential to earn the princely sum of ten dollars per day. If I worked a six-day week that was sixty dollars or $240 per month. I could put at least $200 of it into my college fund. $200 in those days, would buy me enough books to last at least a term if not the whole year. Since early childhood, I had been determined to get to college and become a teacher. I saw education as my only ticket out of poverty and as a ticket to 'freedom'. I was right.

Much to my brother's amazement, I had been saving money in my piggy bank (and later in the 'real' bank) since early childhood. I had had a number of part-time jobs and always squirreled away a goodly portion of my earnings. To his surprise, I even saved a certain percentage of my poker winnings whenever I played with the family. In later years, he'd tease me about how 'cheap' I always was. I would set a limit for the game for how much I could afford to win or lose. Once I had either won or lost to my limit, I quit playing. He, being impulsive, could not set such limits and stick to them.

From about age twelve to seventeen, I babysat every chance I got. If for 'cheap' parents, I was paid thirty-five cents per hour. If 'richer' ones, fifty cents. I suffered through some truly horrible babysitting jobs which I may tell you about later.

My worldly-wise mother, as I have mentioned earlier, had friends of all nations and all ilks. One of them was a French lady named Blanche. She made pretty, painted handkerchiefs. They were lovely; always flowers-oil-painted on colored silk squares. They were really quite well done. Years later I figured out that they had no real practical value. The blobs of oil paint in the center were pretty thick and non-absorbent. No one would want to wipe their nose on them. Their only value was in their intrinsic 'prettiness'. (I wish I had some of them now; they'd be conversation pieces if not down-right works of Art.)

I guess she, like Mother, had grown up in an era wherein ladies didn't use handkerchiefs to wipe their noses on. They were merely used to project an aura of 'elegance'. Ladies held them in their hand for 'emphasis' and waved them around to get people's attention.

So, for several years, every chance I got, I flogged the hankies door-to-door. Eventually, I flooded the market in our immediate neighborhood. Later, my father took up selling Raleigh's products door-to-door. He sold from his little car and went as far afield as Sooke. When my Dad gave up the Raleigh products business, he rarely went to town. Maybe once every two weeks or once a month. Unless we had a school concert or something. So I couldn't hitch free sales rides with him. But, by this time, selling hankies was not a very reliable source of income anyway.

So- for a better income, I had to attempt the job of field hand. I think I lasted three days. Maybe a week, but I doubt it. It was the scary steers that did me in. Grubbing in the dirt behind the tractor for potatoes along with the other boys was arduous. But I didn't see it as dangerous. The next job the farmer asked me to do-was.

I had had zero experience with farm animals. Especially not huge farm animals like cows and horses. I spent a few days hoeing and weeding the extensive fields and grubbing for potatoes. Each night I'd flop into bed, spine aching and exhausted. I started dropping weight. I was too tired to eat much. Then, when I had been on the new job less than a week Mr. Mc came over and told me he had a new job for me-herding cows.

I had seen the size of those cows. Except, as it turned out, they weren't cows. They were steers! He intimated that I had told him I could do a 'man's work' so here was my chance to prove it. He led me to the cow pen, a fairly tall, split-rail affair which housed about eight or ten of the beasts. I didn't know if they were cows or bulls-but, the first thing I noticed was their long horns. And sharp hooves. The farmer handed me a long, sturdy pole and told me to go in and get the cows out of the pen. I hesitated. The beasts were enormous and shaggy and continually hurled their full body weight against the wood railings of the pen. The cattle were packed in there like sardines with little room between them. In spite of that, they managed to bash at each other, stomp and snort in an alarming way.

Not only was I terrified of the shaggy beasts, but I didn't have a clue how to do it. What DID you do? Poke them in the behind? I was afraid to aim for their head in case I poked one in the eye and made him or her really mad.

"But-but, how do I get in there?" I pleaded.

"Just climb the fence, Missy, climb the fence," the tough old fella replied.

It was taller than I! I don't think I'd climbed such a high fence in my life, but, with trepidation, in I jumped. Within a minute, I was trying to figure a way to jump out again. Luckily, the farmer stuck around to see if I could handle the somewhat dangerous task.

The pen was small and the beasts huge. As I tried to find room to heft my pole, the cattle crowded closer. All I could see were their huge shaggy heads and dangerous horns. The terror of being squished into a bullock sandwich overcame me. I started screaming and the old farmer reached over the fence to help me out. To give him credit, he didn't 'rub' it in. Humbly, I went back to my berry picking job and never again attempted to do 'man's work'.

Those were the only two times I can ever remember quitting something that I had started. In the ensuing few years, I had a number of difficult or even 'gross' jobs. Cleaning up drunken loggers' vomit in a hotel room, working a difficult day job and an exhausting night job (car hop) in order to get enough money for college. (Those were the pre-student loan days). But I didn't give up. I guess my Dad's good ol' pioneer grit saw me through.

Orchards and Egg Houses

My father, as I mentioned previously, planted and tended a huge truck garden every spring. He had, at the left side of our house, a small, but productive fruit orchard. Two each of plums, pears and apple trees to compliment the immense Bing cherry on the other side. I'll tell you more about the succulent fruits those trees produced and the labor involved in 'putting down' more than three hundred jars of prime fruit in the chapter entitled 'Seasons-Fall.' We also made cucumber pickles, chutney, and sometimes my mother even canned salmon or venison which she obtained for free. My father would howl if he knew how much money I spend buying fruit today. In those days, we just picked it in or yard, along the roadway, or up on the mountain,

However, the 'poultry project' was ongoing. We had to tend the chickens no matter what time of year (or time of day, for that matter) it was. At one time Dad ran twelve hundred leghorns and a few Rhode Island Reds. For several years, the proceeds from the eggs were our main source of income. I don't know if Dad actually sold some as meat birds or not, but he must have done something with the old hens when their laying days were over. I do know that we ate an awful lot of eggs and chicken in those days, however.

In order to raise so many birds, he had to construct a huge chicken house and an egg candling shed. The immense chicken coop's floor was lined with straw which required changing at least weekly. Then, there were the floor-level watering troughs and feed troughs. Some were ingenious devices Dad had rigged up and which virtually watered themselves. I think at some point we had to fill the feed troughs from a huge sack, however. Finally, the daily chore of gathering the eggs.

Ranged all along was wall were the broody 'cubby holes'. These were square-shaped boxes set into the wall and partially open to the outside. In it the hens sat when they were ready to lay their eggs, especially if they were 'brooding' over a batch of fertilized eggs. The back side of the hatches contained strips of thin wood holding down burlap squares which we could lift from the outside to get at the chickens. Perhaps this is where the term 'boobie hatch' originated. We soon learned the personalities of a lot of the hens. Which ones would let you reach under their bottoms to glean their oval-shaped treasures and which would not. Many's the time I've been pecked on the hand by a 'broodie' who did not want her nest disturbed.

Once the two hundred or so eggs were gathered into large wire baskets, we had to take them to the egg candling shed. There we meticulously shone a light through each one. I think it was to check to see if the egg had been fertilized or had any flaws. Imagine the shocked face of some unsuspecting housewife if she opened an egg and either a bloody embryo or a baby chick popped out!

When the eggs had been washed, processed and put into cartons by hand, they then had to be transported. Dad had a contract with several of the little stores in town, particularly the 'Chinese groceries.' Often, we'd see an old wooden truck come toddling down the dirt track at the side of the house. One of us would run down to the candling shed to load up the grocer with how ever many dozen eggs he had ordered that day. I don't know how Dad regulated production vs number of orders to avoid wastage. I DO remember, however, that, in those days, we ate a lot of chicken! Raising chickens on a small truck farm was a tremendous amount of work. I think we only raised them for a few years until Dad realized that the effort was not worth it. He then decided to sell Raleigh Products.

There he was-in those days an 'old man' in his mid-sixties. He'd load up his English puddle jumper early every morning and head out on the road to sell. He tried to coordinate his working hours with the hours we were at school. His territory ranged from North Cowichan to Sooke. I remember that, when I was still young enough to share a room with my brother, (what later became) my bedroom was The Storeroom.

At least two of the walls were covered with (homemade) floor-to-ceiling shelving. They held an intriguing array of goods-spices, baking products, ground herbs and medicines. I think there were even cleaning supplies. The shelves were neatly stacked and labelled. In the corner stood a writing desk containing order books and other paperwork. We kids were always admonished to 'stay out of the storeroom; it's not for play!'

I don't know if Dad ever made much profit in the 'selling game', but he certainly seemed to have a lot of customers. He said that he did particularly well in Sooke and on the Indian reserves. I guess the customers there had difficulty with transportation into town and appreciated the door-to-door service.

However, by the time he was about seventy, he was having too many health problems to be able to continue to work. We had to exist on his meagre Old Age Pension combined with my mother's 'cripples' pension'. After she died, I know it was a lot harder for Dad to make ends meet. But, I was by then seventeen, my brother almost sixteen. We worked at as many odd and Summer jobs as we could to pay our own expenses. My brother, to this day, decries the fact that we 'grew up poor.' At the time, I didn't know any different. Most of the people living around us would be considered living in poverty by today's standards. Until I was into my mid-teens, I just accepted that that was the way it was.

Pop Bottle and Other Huntin'

When still too young to work for an employer, one of the ways we earned our meagre spending money was by hunting for pop and beer bottles along the highway. Nearly every Saturday morning, early, we'd each grab a feed sack and head for the road. Friday being a heavy drinking night in those days, proved lucrative for us kids.

When we were really little, we'd carry only one sack. I can remember spending the whole morning loading it up and helping my little brother drag it back to whatever rendezvous point my dad had set up. Boy, that was work! The resistant gravel, the exhaust fumes (no emission controls in those days), the traffic noise-all combined to make it a miserable job. However, on sunny Summer days if it wasn't too hot, we kind of enjoyed it. Either way, we had no choice. If we wanted to go to the Odeon Theatre matinee, we had to earn the dough. We'd hike along the deep ditches, heads down, searching.

Beer bottles, then, earned us the princely sum of two cents. I think one cent for pop. On a good day, we'd collect thirty or forty bottles before we heard Dad honk from the top of the road. He'd take us to whatever store was currently taking large quantities of bottles. Or we'd spread them out and go to two outlets. No Bottle Depots in those days.

Most often we'd take them to the Old Lady's Store. That was its official name among the kids of the neighborhood. I never did know her real name. Initially, the store stood at the corner of Somenos and Herd Roads. Later, the Old Lady moved it to the corner of the main highway and Herd Road. It was painted a garish white with bright red trim. It comprised what would today be termed a 'convenience store' and gas station. In those days, they still had the tall skinny white pumps with the handle hanging down at the side. They still had an attendant, usually the Old Lady herself, to pump the gas. You'd drive up to the pump, she'd pop your gas cap and give you a fill, you'd throw her a brownish-colored two dollar bill and off you'd speed.

Her policy of taking back a few dozen bottles at a time was a good one. We never took the money; we always exchanged them for candy. Usually, the dreaded Wrigley's Doublemint, which I'm sure caused the demise of several of my teeth. Or her magnificent ice cream cones.

Ice cream cost a dime. And she generously overfilled the scoop as much as she could. Usually, we could only afford a 'single'. But, if we'd had an especially good pop bottle 'haul', we'd treat ourselves to a big double cone. A single was only five cents. So, for ten, you'd get four huge scoops on a double cone (two single cones fused together by a little cookie-dough bridge. My all-time favorite was maple walnut flavor. But she also sold strawberry (with the big fat 'real' strawberries, not that fake pink-coloured stuff of today), chocolate, and vanilla.

The Matinee cost thirty-five cents each. The concession also sold candy. If we were lucky, and hadn't already spent it at the Old Lady's, we had enough money for more treats. Wrigley's spearmint gum-my favorite-was five cents. Ropes of black licorice were probably two cents. Unfortunately, it was the pre-dental floss days. We did a lot of damage to our teeth on those Saturdays.

In those days, it being the chauvinistic society that it was, the hunting and fishing was mostly done by men. However, I had occasion to accompany my brother on many minor fishing trips. I don't ever remember going on a hunt with my father and brother, though, as those mostly occurred after I had left home.

It was hard to decide which subheading to put this under-Work or Recreation because it was a little of both. Most times, it was fun ranging the mountains for game or accompanying Dad to the seashore to dig clams and oysters. However, many Winters, if Dad or Gary hadn't come home with a fine deer, bear, or 'eating birds,' our protein diet would have been pretty boring-hamburger, sausage, and chicken. My father, after my mom died, was a 'plain' cook-he didn't fancy his meats up with sauces or spices. The fanciest meat dish we ever got was 'hamburger hash'. He'd fry up some chopped onion and hamburger in the fry pan, add a little flour and water for gravy. He'd serve it over mashed or baked potato. That was it. Bachelor fare! And, luckily for my weight problem, he never baked (unless it was his famous 'breakfast bannock' or pancakes).

Occasionally we had elk meat which was given to us. I remember one Winter we had bear meat. I don't remember whether Dad shot the bear or the meat was given to him by a neighbour. All I remember is it was very dark in color and very 'gamey'. It had a beef-like flavour only much stronger. Since we didn't have much freezer capacity, we had to use it up. I remember being very sick of bear meat by the end of the week!

Seafood-yum! Although my father rarely took us to the ocean, my mother had a good friend in Ladysmith whom we saw occasionally. She happened to run the big oyster company there. Mother would sometimes be the recipient of the fattest, juiciest oysters you ever tasted. Salmon, mother would sometimes get from her native friends. The rich-flavored, reddish sockeye was the best. All the meats and seafood then and such things as coffee and tea were much richer flavoured than they are today.

In the chapter which talks about Mount Prevost, I go into more detail about those mountain creek fishing trips. As little kids, we also tried to fish the little stream (Myrtle called it 'the Crick') that ran at the bottom of the back hill, parallel to our house. Often lacking appropriate fishing gear, we'd merely cut and whittle a rod of wood, usually a small tree trunk or large branch. Then we'd find a chunk of fishing line somewhere and attach a bent pin if we didn't have a hook. Earthworms, dead flies, and other bugs made tempting, cost-free 'organic' bait. I don't think we ever caught much-the occasional rainbow trout. I remember being so proud one time because I had caught a 'seven-incher'.

But, in the meantime, my little brother and I enjoyed life on the farm and most especially…………………….

CHAPTER V   OUR RECREATION

The Steamboat Stump

'*Whaaaa-aaaahhhh!   Whaaaaaa-aaaaah!* (Noise of an old steamboat's whistle). *It's gettin' shallow! I see the shoals. 'Swing off to starboard there! Mark twain!'* (the linesman calling out the two-foot depth mark.

It indicated that the huge steamer was getting into shallow water)

At the back of our property lay the well-weathered corpse of the old maple tree. The immense stump, lying on its side looked like a giant spider. Or better yet, to us, Mark Twain's* paddle wheeler. It's trunk, lying prone, was remarkably smooth, probably worn so over the years by the rain (and by little bums sliding down it!). The trunk was elevated about four or five feet off the ground and sloped down into the tangled roots. It made a perfect slide for our little butts . At the top, a convenient, circular-shaped chunk of stump remained. We'd climb the roots and shinny up the shiny trunk. Grasping the rounded end in our chubby hands, we'd whoop and yell:
'Steady as she goes. Watch the depth in the shallows. Mark Twain!'
That old stump gave us hours of scope for imagination. One day we'd be a Missouri steamboat, the next Captain Ahab's vessel, or, in fact, the whale. When the neighbourhood kids came over to play, we'd vie to see who could be the captain. Much negotiation ensued involving 'who could be first' and 'taking turns'. As young children, we spent many hours 'plying the Mississippi' and reliving the adventures of Mark Twain on that old stump.

Cloud Watching

I was going to call this little subsection 'cloud gazing', but it wasn't really that. We actually 'watched' the clouds. Lying on our backs, on our Dad's huge lawn, we'd gaze and stare for hours. A wonder we didn't end up blind from sun exposure. We didn't have sunglasses in those days.
And we didn't just mindlessly watch the clouds scud. My brother and I would actually discuss the different shapes, colors, rates of speed, and amount of fluffiness in the clouds. We'd study shapes. Many were fluffy bunnies or blobs of cotton candy. But we also saw angry pirate faces and majestic Spanish galleons under full sail. Our cloud revelations were only limited by our imagination.
Later in school we learned the proper names for clouds-alto, alto-cumulus, cirrus and the non-official names such as thunderhead or anvil. We'd try to predict rain or wind or blaring sun. We could judge wind direction and the earth's rotation just from the movement of the fluffy scudders.
A rainbow was a major event. We'd explore colors by studying rainbows. We'd marvel at prism-like effects of light showers splitting the raindrops. Often, we'd be out on the lawn for hours, our faithful mutt, Boots, lying beside us. We'd take our boots off (so he wouldn't pounce) and lie there half the day. Until chores or darkness beckoned.
In Summer, we'd lie, bathing suit clad, and drowse in the heat of the sun. Today, a young mom would come running, sunscreen and sunhats in hand. Or tsk! tsking and rushing us back indoors. Or hazing us to a minivan for the interminable road and shopping trips. Those days, we were lucky if we visited the nearest town (Duncan) twice a month. A trip to Victoria, only thirty miles South, was a twice-yearly event. A trip to Vancouver maybe every two or three

years. Then, nobody worried about sunburn or skin cancer. If we didn't get at least one peeling sunburn per season, we weren't kids. By end-July, our shoulders and backs would come off in strips. By August, our noses were freckled and raw. Sometimes even our cheeks would become mottled as we peeled off the dying skin.

By the end of August, our feet were black. Even the almost-daily pot soakings and frequent dunks in the Chemainus River could not recoup the pale feet of Winter. Round about Xmas, most of the black and calluses would have worn off. Sunburn? Skin cancer? Peeling feet? Nobody cared. We survived. Today, our lifestyles (and even those of our children) have become hyper-scheduled and artificial. We are divorced from nature and burdened with hurly-burly. Our kids fall victim to our rushed-up lifestyles. How sad for modern youth that they rarely, if ever, get a chance to lie on their backs, 'veg out', and observe. And now, at seventy, I have fond memories of the good ol' bygone days when kids could just be kids.

The Comic Collection

In my bedroom, I had another dresser painted a delfin blue to match my mother's more ornate mirrored dresser. It comprised three large drawers. Each one, eventually, was stuffed with comic books. Most of them were mine, but some had been collected/stolen/traded by my brother. My favorites were the Classics illustrated editions: Tarzan of the Apes, The Hunchback of Notre Dame, Moby Dick, Oliver Twist. Classic authors from Dickens to Disney. Defoe ('Robinson Crusoe'), R.L. Stevenson ('Kidnapped')-all the greatest from history that would be of any interest to children. I had them all tidily arranged in the overstuffed drawers in perfect number order. Maybe had something to do with the fact that, in later years, I worked as a teacher-librarian.

The comics were a large drawing card to our house. Many a rainy day was spent lying on my bedroom floor, kids sometimes spilling out into the hallway, usually propped on cushions, enjoying those old comics. They opened to us a world of history, of adventure and romance. They were an education in themselves.

Sadly, when I came home from college a few years later, they had all disappeared. I think even the dresser had disappeared! I think W.S. had somehow done away with them. I never did find out what, exactly happened to ......the comic collection.

The Pop Bottle Club

When I was about ten or so, we girls formed a little club. In those days, the pop bottles were made of real glass and their crimped metal lids had little corks underneath them. All the kids knew that if you pried out the cork you could make a type of badge for your clothing. How you'd do it is this:

You'd pry out the little piece of cork and hold it inside your shirt or whatever piece of clothing you had on. Then you'd place the metal cap over it. When the piece of cork was pressed into the cap, voila, a badge.

So thus was formed: The Pop Bottle Club. A group of five or six young girls would meet at my place every month or so. Each girl had to don her badge before she could enter the sanctum of my bedroom. We even had club officers such as President, Secretary, etc. I think we even had a treasurer and a meeting cost of about twenty-five cents. We would engage in activities such as embroidery, knitting, comic book reading, and discussing the latest books we had read. A big drawing card for girls in those days was the Carolyn Keene Mystery Series, Nancy Drew. We, of course would also discuss things happening at school.

Ironically, I don't think we spent much time discussing boys. We weren't the type of girls to be 'boy crazy' as they called it in those days. We were all serious students at school, most of us hoping to get into a good college. Most of us did. And I think the fun, the fellowship and support we girls gave each other in the Pop Bottle Club was a contributing factor.

Dishes in the Creekbank

In those days most of us little girls had a set of plastic dishes. Tiny tea cups, usually white, with an attractive floral pattern, plates and a cunning little teapot. I kept mine all in a special box which I could access quickly. I and a girlfriend, often my friend, Flora, would take them down the road about a half mile to Myrtle Smythe's property. Like ours, her property sloped fairly steeply to the creek. I guess we chose a steep slope on her property because it was set in an open meadow. No trees, fallen branches or chicken runs to impede our play.

In the embankment created, we would gouge large holes to form a make-believe 'cupboard'. On Summer days, we'd play 'tea party' for hours. Sometimes my young brother would come along to provide the male perspective. The only fly in the ointment was the old bull.

In the neighboring pasture there were always a few cows. Unfortunately, the 'divider' fence was not very secure. Occasionally, the old bull would be in residence and he'd sashay over. The bull was a large, black devil and definitely possessed a nasty disposition. He felt it his duty to go after anyone who had the audacity to encroach on his territory.

So, the downside of this particular location was that we were constantly looking over our shoulder to see if the old son-of-a-gun would appear. Luckily, he wasn't in residence very often. If he was, we'd hear him stamping and snorting long before he left his other compound. It gave us just enough time to grab our little dishes, throw them into their special box and tuck it under our arm. We'd sprint for the road. In those days, we could always outrun him and reached the safety of the split rail fence before he could get too close behind us and prick us with his horns. However, there was one occasion when we were not so lucky:

Another time my brother and I were in that same field. Again, the bull saw us and made a B-line. Unfortunately, we saw that we'd never make the rail fence on the road before the bull got us. He was racing at us in full charge-horns menacing. We screamed blue murder as we headed for the road.

'Yaa, haa! Off there, off now, you devil!'

Cougar Smythe. I guess he'd climbed the high fence to get to us and was yelling at the bull. I'd never been so glad to hear an old man's voice in my life. The bull, of course, was still charging us, oblivious. Cougar was wearing his usual blue denim 'farmer's overalls. They had a small, red cotton band at the side which held an enormous hammer. He somehow managed to get in front of the massive animal and threatened it with the tool. The bull veered.

'Run for the fence, you kids, and don't you come back here. This old fella is just too dangerous'.

We ran. And we didn't go back. Thus ended the 'dishes in the creekbank' play.

The Reading Tree

Between the Horton's and McGonagal's cabin lay a hilly acreage, ill-tended and wild. The acreage was so huge that it spread clear over to the highway on the East side. And it produced the best apples I have ever tasted. We called it simply: Old Man Whitehead's Orchard. We kids spent many a Summer day picking the small and somewhat scabious green apples, eating a few, then filling our pockets to take home to mother for pie.

At night, and especially at Hallowe'en, the scraggly growths took on a ghostly appearance. The never-pruned trees were ancient and mossy, the moss and blight crusts hanging down like ghostly tendrils. No one (well at least no one under the age of about fifteen) dared go near the place after dark, but most especially on Hallowe'en night. We were sure that all manner of ghoulies and spirits inhabited the trees. They were just lying in wait for unsuspecting children whom they could torture and terrify.

But the aging orchard had one feature we always looked forward to with relish, especially in the warm Summers. I called it The Reading Tree. It was the giant of the lot and probably the oldest. Its leafy and spreading branches were dominated by one particularly large one which spread conveniently in a horizontal direction about four feet off the ground. A good shinnier could climb up and lie prone in less than a minute even with book in hand.

And, of course, that was the main purpose to which it was put-reading. I can remember hiking it the mile or so down the road, book in hand. I'd spend a pleasant afternoon, semi-reclined on my back in the welcoming splendor, enjoying such favorites as Heidi, Little Women, and Anne of Green Gables. Later-Tarzan of the Apes, King Solomon's Mines and other, supposedly, boys' adventure stories. The Reading Tree's leafy canopy was cool, moist and incredibly quiet except for the occasional trill of a bird. I remember experiencing a sense of peace and contentment I've rarely (if ever) experienced since.

I vaguely remember meeting Old Man Whiteside on one occasion. I don't know if my dad took us up to his big house on the hill, or if we kids ventured up there alone. I remember that he was quite hospitable to us and told us we could eat as many apples off the old orchard trees as we wanted. I guess you would have to categorize him as one of our 'rich neighbours'.

Cowpies 'n Catchers' Mitts

A controversy raged. Should we girls in the neighborhood play hardball or softball? Hardball won out on several counts. First of all, there weren't that many girls in the neighborhood. The boys needed us to 'round out' their hardball teams. My brother was in boys' Little League and needed me to help him practice. That necessitated learning to pitch and catch hardball.

After my younger brother had been in Little League for a couple of years, they formed a girls' softball team in town. (Girls were not allowed to play in the Little League). I tried the girls' softball. But-not only did it mean a lot of extra driving for my father to get me to the practices, I thought it was too 'sucky'. I had already been playing hardball with the boys for a couple of years. And I had been 'catching' for my brother. He was, unusually, not only a star pitcher but also an excellent catcher. So was I –catcher, that is. That is how I broke the two fingers on my right hand. Like my brother and my Dad, I was a leftie. Here is how it happened:

Nearly every day, my brother would practice his pitching skills by firing a hardball up against the side of our large garage. Dad was not too happy about that practice, as it was gradually destroying the boards. So my bro decided to use me instead. Thus, for many hours each week, I would stand out on our large lawn being a backstop/catcher for my brother. All had been going well, as he was an accurate, fast, pitcher. I knew how to make a good target for him with my mitt and could vary it depending on the 'pretended height' of the batter.

One day, I went racing out the front door, 'leftie' catcher's mitt in hand to join him. I didn't have it quite in place on my hand when he fired the ball at me. You guessed it, fingers on the, mostly uncovered, hand were bent back by the force of the blow. We heard the two small fingers crack. Yup, I was stuck in a cast and out of baseball for about six weeks that time.

I'll probably tell you how I broke my foot playing at Duncan Elementary School further on in the book.........

When we played hardball, we had our choice of two fields. The one opposite Capt. Grenfell's Mansion was the better of the two. Mickey's field was rockier and bumpier and had more wet cow pies. Yes, in those days we used dried cowpies as bases. (If you're not sure what a 'cowpie' is, just use your imagination). The Captain's field was drier and more level, so even though it necessitated a longer walk (about two miles from our place), we usually played there. The Horton boy had to come all the way down from Stratfords Crossing on his bike.

There were two girls who now lived next to us plus the six McAvoy kids - well however many of them were old enough to play at the time. My friend, Fay and her older brother. A couple of kids from the old road past Death Corner. Then a ragtag assortment of players sometimes joined us from Bell McKinnon Road. Once in a while the kids from south of Stratfords would make the journey. There were about four or five living at south Somenos.

So, on any given night we usually had at least eight or ten kids-of mixed ages and genders-enough to play 'Scrub' Baseball. Once in a while we'd have enough to play teams, but usually, it was Scrub. Scrub Baseball was played as follows:

All nine traditional positions were covered-if we had enough players, that is-pitcher, catcher, three bases, shortstop and three outfielders. It was really quite a neat game because a player would get to play each position within a relatively short period of time. How that happened was this: there would be at least two players 'up to bat'. If one got a hit, he ran the bases. When he made it to 'home', everyone moved 'up' a position: the catcher would join the batting line-up; pitcher would come in to catch, first base moved in to pitch, and so on until each player had come in to a new position. If the batter 'scrubbed' or was 'out', he had to go into the outfield. The rules of Scrub really kept the whole game moving faster than a traditional 'teams' game. I loved baseball with a passion and I'm sure those wonderful games up on the old cow pastures are one of the reasons I am so fit today.

Weights in the Candling Shed

As you know, at one time my father ran twelve hundred leghorns on our smallish acreage. He had constructed a wooden shed approximately ten feet by twelve. We called it the 'candling' shed. It was there that my bro, initially, set up his makeshift gym and weight room. Of course, he did not have or could not afford barbells or dumbbells. But he improvised -a couple of huge bricks with ropes wrapped around them sufficed. He made a makeshift inclined bench out of scrap lumber. Then over the doorway he installed a chinning bar. Often I'd join him to have a little weight workout in the old candling shed.

However, shortly after W.S.moved in with my father permanently, my brother moved into it. I was, by then, away from college. He said he couldn't stand her cooking or the way she treated him. So he took a sleeping bag and as much food as he could snitch from the house or somehow buy. The shed was unheated. I don't know how he managed to survive in that cold shed. But he did.

The Old Odeon Theatre

As I mentioned earlier, nearly every weekend we'd take our hard-earned pop bottle money to 'the show'. The shows happened at the old Odeon Theatre on Station Street, usually the kiddies' matinee. My memories of the beautiful old relic are a bit foggy. I don't even know in what decade they closed it, but I suppose I could look it up. However, I remember that the décor inside was gorgeous. As you approached the exterior, you'd see a glassed-in ticket booth with a real person inside. You'd purchase your ticket from her and then proceed through the main doors. An usher, usually dressed in a red velvet 'monkey' suit with gold braiding, would be standing there to take your ticket. On a fine, floral carpet you'd follow the line of patrons past a red velvet rope and to the double swinging interior doors.

Within, a gorgeous sight awaited you. The small theatre was all decked out in burgundy reds and golds. Gold flocked velvet paper covered the high-ceilinged walls. The rows of low, curved-backed seats were red corduroy. The seat bottoms could be lifted and held against the seat backs when not in use or to allow people to pass by. Above, at the back was a large balcony section similarly decorated.

But the crème de la crème was the huge, hanging curtain on the stage at the front. The rich velvet hanging draperies in multi-pleated folds dominated the scene. They were tied back with rich gold-braided ropes. At the back was a peep-hole glass opening through which the beam from the projector shone. They still used the big old reel-to-reels in those days. Just before the movie would filter down from the ceiling, a man would come out and stand on the stage. The owner, presumably. He'd introduce the movie, bow to the audience, and disappear.

Then the excitement began. The music would start. The huge curtains would slowly part to reveal the preambles. Often a news reel, then a cartoon. I remember watching the coronation of Queen Elizabeth in 1953 on that screen. To me, it was magnificent. My favorite cartoon was Woody Woodpecker, but I'm sure we also watched Tom and Jerry. I don't think Road Runner had been invented yet. And, of course the Disney features were superb-Fantasia, Bambi, Cinderella, and Snow White dominated.

The only problem with going to the matinee was that we'd spend half our time, especially before the feature started, dodging popcorn. If it got too bad and the air was becoming cloudy with flying missiles, the projectionist would turn off the reel. Somebody would yell at us to 'stop throwing corn or this movie is not going back on' and we'd cease and desist. I, being (according to my brother) a 'big Goodie-Goodie' never threw. My brother sure did. I'm sure that beautiful flocked wall paper was eventually covered in blobs of grease. Luckily, the theatre was usually so dark that you didn't notice.

PRANKS WE PULLED

Indian Tomahawk

'If you do that again, I'm gonna get out my tomahawk and scalp you.'

On hearing that, I started to shake, and slunk down even lower into the back seat of Dad's little car. We were sitting outside the small gas station at the Crofton turn-off. For some reason, in those days, bad things happened to me at the road to Crofton. I had been sitting in the back seat of Dad's puddle jumper eating a banana. My brother was probably bugging me (as usual) so I decided to just heave the large yellow peel out the window.

Unfortunately, I hadn't noticed that, parked right beside us on the other side of the gas pump was a huge 'Indian boat'. The native Indians in those days, mostly being poor, often drove the ten-years-plus gas pigs. It was mainly the whites who had the up-to-date vehicles. How the natives afforded the gas in those old pigs, I'll never know.

So, upon hearing his threatening words, I looked OUT my window and UP. There, high above me, in plain view, sat my bright yellow banana skin prominently displayed on his windshield. I could see why he wasn't happy. I slunk further down in the seat hoping he would blame it on my brother who was sitting next to me. However, that huge native's eyes bored into me. Then I saw the twinkle. My Dad exchanged a few apologetic words with the chap (who obviously had kids of his own). The banana peel was removed and, with a pleasant wave, we drove off. However, I quaked in my seat for over an hour till we made it back to the safety of Stratfords and home.

The Pulp Mill Fart

(This wasn't exactly a prank we pulled, but aunt Villa thought I DID !)

My snooty old Aunt Elvira was vicious. I often anticipated her annual visits with trepidation. I think she was either a Jehovah's Witness or had been raised very strictly. She definitely believed that children should be seen ………….

Aunt Vira and Uncle Ebenezer lived in Prince George. In those days, that was considered as far away as China. They didn't come to visit very often, but when they did there was usually trouble. Although Uncle Eb was a quiet, relatively benign individual; (he had to be, married to Elvira!), his wife wasn't. My aunt was loud, dictatorial, always had to be in charge. I also think she had no use for kids. (I feel sorry for the two she raised).

It was about 1959 and they were visiting. For some reason, Dad decided to take us all on a day trip out to Crofton. As most of you know, in those days there was an enormous pulp mill there which is still in operation today. Huge booms of logs would be brought to the lower reaches of the site, usually by tugboat. These logs were then somehow dragged up the beach and into the mill chutes where they were processed into pulp. During the process, bleach was used. Boy, did it stink. The worst 'rotten egg' smell you have ever smelled!

That day me, my mom, my brother, aunt and uncle were all crammed into Dad's old Austin. Aunt Vira, me, my brother and Uncle Eb were crammed into the back. (I think my little brother had to sit on somebody's knee). So-we proceeded out to Crofton and, I think, took the ferry over to Saltspring Island. We had a nice lunch there and my aunt indicated that she thoroughly enjoyed it. However, on the way back, she struck.

We were just driving past the mill and I was committing the unpardonable sin of speaking. I was told in no uncertain terms: 'children should be seen and not heard.' Soon after, my aunt interrupted us in a strident voice:

'O, my God, what a stink! Which one of you kids did that?'

Since I was the kid who happened to be talking at the time, I was the one blamed.

'Joy, did you let that go? Shame on you, you filthy child'.

Despite my protestations, she continued to blame me. And, for some unknown reason, I don't think my father spoke up to defend me. Usually, he did. Perhaps he hadn't heard her or misunderstood. I tried to tell her that the awful smell was coming from the nearby mill, but she retorted:

'What a story. Shame on you. Couldn't you hold it until we got home?'

She decided to open the window to let in some fresh air. I tried to tell her that would only make the problem worse. The awful stink was even more noticeable after she opened the window. She alluded to my transgression a couple more times on the way back to Stratfords. She ranted with words to the effect that a 'proper young lady' should not be so rude as to let fly in mixed company. I was mortified (and innocent!) For years to come, I was silently enraged with my Aunt Vira over the P.M.F.

'Boys Will be Boys!'

'Dad, Dad, there's eyeballs looking at me through the bathroom window!

Me-pants down, sitting on the toilet. Unfortunately, the only window faced the toilet and was also conveniently located over the low roof leading into our basement crawl space. Convenient, that is for two newly adolescent boys with curious minds and hormones raging.

'It's Gary and his creepy friend, Ray! Daa-aaa-aaa-ddd!'

And, with that I took off out of the small bathroom like a shot, ready to do battle. Of course, there was no sign of the boys by the time I ran out to the porch. I peered out the cat door which conveniently opened onto that little roof, but they were long gone. Mortified and red-faced I ran to find my father. Tears raced down my face. Whether from shame, rage, or mortification I didn't know.

My long-suffering father listened, as always, with a sympathetic look. He nodded his head at my accusations and promised to speak to the boys. He must have because, to my knowledge, they never spied on me again.

The Old Plymouth Touring Car

What can I say? It was big, it was red with rust, it was loud and ugly, yet it was the joy of my brother's heart. Procured by my father for the enormous sum of thirty dollars, it had once been worth ten times that much. I don't remember the year exactly but it was probably Forties vintage. It sported a powerful engine that roared with a vengeance you could hear all over the neighborhood.

It had rusted down to an unattractive red primer and I don't remember my brother ever trying to paint it. At some undetermined point in time, someone had added a pickup truck box to the back. Big and powerful and open to the road, it was the perfect vehicle for mountain travel as far as my bro was concerned. One of the reasons many young teens chose to drive the mountain road was because they were too young to yet possess a Driver's License!

I can remember one fateful New Year's Eve (it happened to be my birthday) when he took me, a couple of cousins, and a male friend or two up the treacherous Mt. Prevost Road. The old tourer was so powerful that it took even the Hairpin Curve in its stride. That notorious, paperclip-shaped bend in the road did a full 180 degrees as it sharply wound back on itself. We clung to the side of the box like monkeys in a tree. The steeper the road became, the more inclined we were to slide to the back. Some of us were lying in a jumble, being jostled side to side on the crazy ride up. I think he stopped a couple of times to pick up one of the boys who, somewhat anesthetized with beer, slid onto the gravelly track.

However, the ride back down was positively 'harum-scarum'. Before we even got back to that treacherous curve, the monster vehicle had picked up speed. I estimate we were doing more than fifty miles an hour when we hit the curve. Somehow my brother managed to negotiate it, the old car sliding and skidding, we girls' terrified screams and giggles filling the night air. We rocketed down the narrow track hoping against hope that no one was ascending either on foot or in a vehicle.

When, finally, we regained the safety and sanity of Somenos Road, we all breathed a relieved sigh. However, the experience of that harum-scarum ride was seared into memory, a memory so precious that I'm sure none of us have forgotten it over the years.

CHAPTER VI   THE SEASONS

SPRING   (My Favorite Time of Year)

Rototilling the Garden

This was, on our little farm, probably the first harbinger of Spring. As soon as the frozen ground was soft enough to be worked. When my Dad was still in his Sixties he could be seen, bare chested in late March walking behind our old fossil of a rototiller. The rototiller was like a miniature plough, possessing a (probably gas) engine, two handles and two large and lethal looking rotors which were capable of churning even the most resistant of soils. My Dad would spend several hours or even days going over and over our large garden patch to 'work in' the fallow soil, kitchen compost, and debris from last year's crops.

However, by the time he was in his mid-seventies, Dad had to give the job over to my brother. Gary, even as a teenager, was massively strong and well-muscled (used to lift weights in the candling shed among other things.) I'm sure that all the heavy work he did with Dad on the farm contributed to his excellent physique. In his later teens he procured a number of well-paying haying jobs.

'Haying' was extremely physically taxing. Not only were you usually working long hours in the hot sun, but forking the hay off the truck or pitching bales required a lot of physical strength and endurance. My brother possessed both. Each bail weighed up to ninety pounds. I remember being jealous of the good money he earned. While I was staying up late at night to earn thirty-five cents an hour babysitting or picking berries in the glaring sun for sixty-five, he was earning up to three dollars per hour in the hay fields.

I don't know what he did with all that money he earned, because he usually didn't have any. However, I suspect he used at least some of it to buy the Old Plymouth Touring Car I tell you about in the next chapter.

Planting the garden was also an onerous task. And my aging father was quite meticulous about it. After the garden was roto'd and well-smoothed by hand with large rakes, the stakes and garden string were brought out. For each row he intended to plant, a stake had to be driven into the soil at each end. Then a string was strung from stake to stake for rows that were 'poker straight'. Of course, such crops as strawberries and raspberries would have survived from the previous year. Weeding and fertilizing got them going again.

Fertilizer. Yeaaahhh! Dad, unfortunately, was a great believer in fish fertilizer-the smelly and liquid kind. He did use chicken manure when we had the poultry farm, and occasionally cow poo he mooched from the local farmers, but-as he became more elderly, I guess he found that fish fertilizer was easier to apply and manage. While manure had to be bagged, hauled, spread, and 'dug in', fish fertilizer could be merely sprinkled on the crops. Big downside-it stunk. At times in the Spring and early Summer, I'd be embarrassed to invite the girlfriends over because of the stench emanating from behind our house.

Blossoms and Tadpoles

However, the bright lights of the Spring season were the cloud-like canopies of blossoms covering all our orchard trees. I think the pear trees had a pink or reddish tinge and the apples a sort of a peachy tint. But, best of all was the enormous Bing cherry tree that stood to the right of the farmhouse. As little kids we'd stand under it and feel that we were in a marshmallow fairyland. As long as Dad didn't catch us, if we shook the branches, our heads would be covered in 'fairy snow'.

Another favorite thing-besides rushing around to enjoy all the new tree and shrub blossoms, was 'discovering' new growth. Watching the bud tips of all manner of plants grow day-by-day. First the snowdrops, then daffodils and flag irises and daisies coming into flower. Then down by the creek – the other wildflowers such as the tiny miniature field daisies and all manner of tiny grassland plants in the meadows and cow pastures—their little heads glinting in shades of yellow and purple.

The plants of the high fields and mountains I'll talk about more in Mountain Shenanigans. The precious 'Lady's slippers', now virtually extinct, lay hidden on the trails. The trillium, a purplish-white tricorn lily, now a protected species, also abounded.

Another favorite pastime of ours was wading the creek. As soon as it warmed up enough that our calves didn't ache too severely, we'd wade on in. Over the years, the little creek at the bottom of our rear slope had carved sides that were about three feet deep. Just deep enough for little kids to get a good soaking. When we were older, we'd pole makeshift rafts made out of ropes and old chunks of log. Often we'd wade all the way down to Myrtle's ignoring the pain in our legs from the frigid water. She'd usually help us dry off, feed us a snack and send us home via the road.

In late Spring, we'd enjoy the riches the waters offered—first eggs clinging to grasses and reeds, later tadpoles galore. Water skaters, mosquito larvae, snakes and all manner of little creatures abounded. Luckily, I have never been very afraid of snakes. Creepy-crawly spiders have always been my particular Waterloo. However, on one occasion, I had a run-in with a snake that almost changed my mind about certain slithering reptiles.

I was wading the creek, alone. Wearing only a bathing suit. It was probably late Spring or early summer by this time because I remember the day was quite warm. All of a sudden, I felt this remarkably cold, clammy feeling coursing up the inside of my thigh. I looked down. Ugh! A garter snake. Or at least I thought it was a garter snake. If true, it was about the biggest garter snake I'd ever seen in my life. It had somehow run up my calf and was twining itself up the inside of my leg and right into my crotch.

What a disgusting feeling! I was terrified. I tried stomping it down with my foot, but, by now, it was so high up the inside of my leg that stomping was futile. Screaming and stomping, I jumped out of the water and onto the high embankment. Grasping the ugly reptile by its slithery head, I somehow managed to rip it off my thigh and threw it with all my might into the air. It landed in the water and where it went from there I neither knew nor cared.

We Fifties kids were a tough lot. We were not easily daunted by a little bit of snow or cold water. Thus, we'd usually hit the river in late Spring- far earlier than the coddled tourists or 'city kids.' As soon as it was warm enough, we'd head for the river, bathing suits under our dry clothes. I can remember jumping into Hell's Gate when it was so cold that your nipples would remain hard all day. Of course, in late March and early April, we wouldn't exactly swim. We'd 'dip'. A quick run in, then an even quicker run out.

Even in the cold weather, we'd love to haul our oversized truck inner tubes up the road. Sometimes we'd lug them up to the river deflated and inflate them with the pump when we got there. Then we'd jump in them, butts first, and only have to get that part of our suits wet. Oh, the long-forgotten joy of jumping into a freezing river and not even noticing the discomfort on the long trek home!

Mountain Shenanigans

We kids would also think nothing of heading out in Spring or Summer early in the morning. We took nothing but a few eggs, perhaps some bacon, a fry pan and our fishing rods. The eggs and fry pan were in case we didn't catch any trout in the little creek that shadowed the roadway most of the way to the top of Mount Prevost. The hike along the gravelly old road was arduous. Steep and winding, it formed the infamous Hair Pin Curve about halfway up. The 'hair pin' of course, was a curve that turned back on itself on a steep section of rough road. Woe betide the novice driver (my bro eventually being one) who didn't slow enough to negotiate that devil!

But in those days, we were too young to drive so we hoofed it all the way to the top. The hike took about two hours if we didn't stop to fish. Quite often we'd catch one or two small trout and my brother would start a fire at the top. We'd cook our catch, eat anything else we'd brought, and head back down.

But I remember one memorable day when our trip up the mountain was not so uneventful. It was probably late Spring because I remember that we were barefoot, or at least I was. I had then and still do detest wearing footwear of any kind. We had made it almost to the top when, to my chagrin an enormous ice field blocked our path. I don't know why it was so mandatory that we get to the top but, for some reason we were determined. I remember that my then fifteen-or-so weight lifter brother picked up my considerable bulk and carried me across that field. I guess I had pretty frigid feet by the time I hiked it home.

It was then well-known that Mt. Prevost's main feature was a whitewashed stone cairn* that stood sentinel on one of its twin humps. The cairn was maybe fifteen feet high and we could just make it out when we stood below on Somenos Road. Our challenge to each other was usually to see who could be first to make it to the top and the cairn.

On one memorable occasion, my 'city' cousin, Gay, had come over from Vancouver for the weekend. She of the cautionary warning when she had once driven me to the Downtown Eastside:

"'Don't hang your arm out that window; there are drug addicts around here!" We were so green that we didn't know what a 'drug addict' was or why it was dangerous to hang our arm out the window. We were by then mid-teens, she two years older. We challenged her to race us to the cairn.

I have the feeling we drove partway to the top, not sure if this city slicker (who also smoked) could make the top without having a heart attack. I remember she saw it as an incredible feat and enthusiastically took up the challenge. She made it and I have an old Brownie 'black-and-whitie' of my brother and cuz standing triumphant at the foot of the old cairn. Her foot is raised on the rocky base in a triumphant pose similar to the lion killers in India. I must have taken the picture. Ironically, to her it was a huge accomplishment, but to a couple of country kids like us, it was 'all in a day's hike'!

The Old Tyee Mine and the Stratfords Crossing Connection

'There's a goldmine in the sky far away
We will find it, you and I some sweet day.
We will say 'hello' to friends who said good-bye
When we find that long-lost goldmine in the sky.'
Goldmine in the Sky   K. Charles and K. Nick   1938?

My memories of the old mine sites on the top of Mt. Sicker are vague. The main ones were the Lenora and Tyee mines. The Lenora mine was named after the owner, Harry Smith's, daughter. 'Tyee' of course was a native Indian word denoting a type of salmon. I did a bit of research and discovered that both gold and copper had been mined on the mountain, gold being the by-product.

The copper ore had been shipped overhead, via an aerial tramway, probably consisting of wooden buckets. These went to Stratfords Crossing where the ore could be efficiently loaded on the train. It turned out that the passenger service our family utilized for Winter shopping was merely an auxiliary service provided.

My father was always convinced that more gold still lurked on the mountain and was merely sitting there, ripe for the taking. That is why he established a claim which he worked every Summer for years. When my brother was old enough, he worked the claim with Dad and eventually took it over himself. In those days, you could get an income tax deduction for claim maintenance expenses and I believe my bro took advantage of that for several years after he became an adult and established a business.

My Dad had a number of other theories to support his enthusiasm for mining. Not only was he convinced that there was more 'gold in them thar hills', he had an idea of how to locate it. He believed that the atmosphere was made up of many different types of air waves, some magnetic and emanating from the North Pole. Supposedly, those waves, or rays were an indicator of large deposits of ore.

Enter the 'lipstick Geiger counter'. Each Spring, Dad would make an ingenious little device for sensing these magnetic waves. It was a tiny instrument constructed from one of my mother's metal lipstick caps (back in the days when lipsticks were made of real metal, not plastic). He'd somehow drill or poke a tiny hole in the top of the cap and thread a bit of string through it. Then, he'd walk over the ground on his claim, waving it gently in the air. It seemed to us kids to be a process similar to the well-witching people did with forked sticks in those days.

Seemingly, if the bob started wobbling rapidly back and forth, that's where the magnetic waves were concentrated. In practicality, I don't think his theory worked very well because he never did discover his 'gold mine' on the mountain in spite of over twenty years of trying!

In actual fact, I think he had been trying that mountain claim for OVER twenty years. The reason I know this is because he once showed us 'the sunken bathtub'. In the late Thirties or early Forties (I presume because it was before I was born) he came over to the island with my mother 'on spec'. I don't know if he had the claim yet or not. However, I think they camped near the top of Sicker for some time because my mother, determined to keep clean in spite of hardship, had him build her a bathtub.

My Dad showed it to us on more than one occasion. It consisted of a large rectangular hole about four feet deep by six or seven feet long. He had carefully lined it with wooden boards, probably cedar, because cedar was not so prone to deteriorating in the wet weather as were other woods. I'm not sure how he filled it; probably let it fill with rainwater or-in the summer drought, hauled buckets from the nearby creek. I can just picture my mother, singing and soaping, stark naked in the tub of a Summer's eve not caring who saw or heard her. She would be reveling in the natural canopy of nature all around her, maybe even mimicking the birds in the trees. I'm sure her antics often charmed my much-older father.

The Bear in the Blackcap patch

Another 'adventure' I had when helping Dad with his claim was one I could actually have done without. Years ago, the mountain abounded with berries of all types, including the rarer blackcaps. They looked to me like a species of salmon berry, very dark, almost black and with a bit of a licorice flavor. They were shaped like those little cloche hats the Twenties flappers wore. Small, but dark and shiny, they hung in tantalizing splendor from several bushes about a hundred yards or so from my father's claim. Because of their diminutive size, it took quite a lot of work to pick enough for the four of us to have a meal.

So, there I was one Summer's day, picking. My brother and Dad were quite some distance away, working the claim. My father usually kept one of his hunting rifles at his side 'just in case'.Thank God, my ever-pragmatic pater had given us full instructions on what to do if we ever encountered either a bear or cougar. I did. To my chagrin, I discovered that I was picking on one side of the large bush and a big, fat mama bear was picking on the other. I heard her lip-smacking and satisfied grunts before I actually saw her. And then, horror of horrors, I spotted the cubs. They were rollicking playfully nearby.

O-my–God! My father had severely warned us to always stay clear of a mama with babies (of any species). I was afraid to shout for my dad in case I scared the bear into attacking. Instead I took his former advice and slowly backed away. I kept my eyes on her (and she on me!) sweating with the knowledge that she could quit her munching and attack at any moment. Luckily, she didn't and I kept up my slow, backwards pace. However, as soon as I got within sight of my dad and brother, I turned around and ran like Hell for the safety of my father's arms.

Mountain Flora

The mountains abounded with flora of many types. In the Summer, near the summit we experienced an alpine climate. Colorful mosses in hues of green and reds covered the exposed rocks and were interspersed with dried, yellowy grasses. Of course, most of the mountain was covered with the typical West Coast trees-huge cedars, Douglas firs, hemlock, and the occasional (and now protected) dogwood—the provincial tree.

Near the creek, the flora was totally different. In early Spring, snowdrops, and tiny wildflowers in purples and yellows greeted us on our climb. In late Spring, if we were really lucky, we'd find a patch of the incredibly delicate lady's slippers in varied hues of maroon and mauve. I once read that they were actually a species of wild orchid. They were delicately veined and bulbous in shape, much like the glass slipper of the Cinderella story. In other locales, I have even seen them in shades of brilliant yellow. Trilliums, their stark white. elongated petals contrasted with the brilliant green of their leaves.

My father, of course, always cautioned us- 'don't pick the wild flowers or there won't be any next year'. Of course, being little kids, we did. We were anxious to bring a dehydrated and fading bouquet home to my mother. However, in later years when I hiked the mountain and went to the old orchid patches, I found no orchids. I have, since then, found a few patches on trails bordering the old highway in Parksville. So, hopefully this beautiful species on the Island will somehow survive. They are now considered endangered.

Several edible berries were also to be found on the mountain paths. We picked Saskatoon berries, similar to, but grainier than domestic blueberries. Blackcaps were rarer, but we knew of a patch or two up near the old mine site. My favorite, however, were the tiny, but incredibly sweet wild blackberries, their crawling tendrils usually to be found along the roadway. I write in 'Stories of Somenos School' later in the book about pitching pop balls we'd strip from the bushes at the base of the mountain road. In Spring the roadway would also be replete with the fuzzy grey balls of pussy willows. We'd rub them on each other's cheeks, pretending it was the softness of cat fur.

In the marshier areas, we'd discover tall reeds we called 'cattails'- fuzzy and brown. However, there was one area we always avoided. That was the marshy bottoms of the creek housing the bright yellow, cruciferous skunk cabbages. Their putrid stink would befoul the air all around us. If we wanted to be mean, we'd race to the bottom, grab a chunk of the stinky weed and 'menace' each other with the disgustingly smelly flower. I have not travelled that mountain road for many years. But I wonder how many of those wonderful natural plants still exist in numbers even close to those we enjoyed as children?

SUMMER

Tales of the Chemainus River:

Dewey's Pool/Slug Hollow/Hell's Gate

The first remembrance I have of the Chemainus River was being thrown in it. I was about six. Today, my father would probably have been convicted of child abuse. Luckily, my elderly father (who could not swim a stroke) had stood on the shallow bank and pawed his hands in a 'dog paddling' motion. I caught on immediately. My little brother was not so lucky, Unfortunately, rock-like, he sank. He was a non-swimmer for years. Eventually, he took swim lessons at a large rec center in Victoria and learned to swim after a fashion. I don't know how he managed to help me save a girl from drowning in the river, but, he did.

In those days, we thought nothing of biking it the three or four miles from our place down to the river. From there, we had a number of choices. We could stay in the area under the bridge or hike it through the bush further up the river. After we were about ten or so, the area under the bridge was considered too 'sucky' for older kids.

Next step was to hike it along the river's edge for about half a mile up to Dewey's Pool. I don't know exactly how it got that name. it was a beautiful roundish section of the river, bounded on one side by the cliff banks. It was fairly sheltered, being surrounded by trees and riverbank on one side and the cliffs on the other. The 'intermediate' swimmers favored Dewey's as the current was not very swift and there were a few 'gouge holes' in the cliffs that made convenient diving spots.

However, for more of a diving challenge, one could hie one's way a few hundred yards more upstream to a section called 'The Cliffs'. There the cliffs were higher and the diving more challenging. A part of The Cliffs was heavily sculpted from the surrounding clay. We dubbed it Slug Hollow for obvious reasons. The embankments hung with the enormous slimy creatures like huge gobs of snot. Obviously, no one chose to swim at Slug Hollow.

But the most challenging spot of all was Hell's Gate. I don't know how it got its name either, but it must have appeared to someone reminiscent of the roiling rapids on the Fraser River. It, too, roiled, especially in the Winter. We could see it clearly from the top of the huge cliff, the side of the mountain, actually, that one had to climb down (or slide down) in order to access it.

If we wanted a long and arduous hike, we could access it by proceeding up the river from Dewey's Pool or the cliffs. More often we would ride our bikes or get one of the dads to drive us up to an access road about a mile up from the silver bridge. After hiking down a short, beautifully treed, forest trail, we'd come out upon a small promontory. Beneath us, a gorgeous vista awaited.

Far below, lay the river. Directly below us it widened out to form a huge bowl-shaped pool. In the center of the pool stood a huge rock jutting about ten feet above the level of the river. The river was bounded on the far side by trees and mountain. On our side, the enormous cliff and rock formations. On the north side, the river entered the pool through a narrow, gorge-like formation. It exited via rapids which the most daring among us liked to shoot on inner tubes.

We'd exit the forest trail, stand on the rock and dirt promontory and decide whether we were going to run or to slide on our bottoms down to the rocky ledge above the pool. The rocky side was covered with a thick layer of soil and, over the years, little bums had molded it into a dirt slide. Running was faster, but dicey. Although for years there was a large fallen tree at the side of the ledge, it would not have broken our fall should we have 'overshot our mark' and slid into the pool. It would have been about a fifteen to twenty foot drop into dangerously shallow water. To my knowledge, in all the years we went to Hell's Gate, there was never an accident.

However, I remember one scary occasion when I was basking on the central rock. I looked below and there was a rather large girl screaming and floundering towards the shallows. Having no lifeguard training whatsoever, I jumped in to rescue her. Imagine my shock when she grabbed me by the hair and shoved my head under, trying, I assume to get on top of me and use me as a life preserver. I, too, was sputtering and floundering. Suddenly, a strong arm came over my head and grabbed the girl. I think my brother had raced in from the shallows on the other side of the pool and was able to grab her. Luckily, he did, or she would have drowned me! I later learned that I should have held a towel or pole out to her and remained on solid ground.

So, after we'd made it to the enormous level rock outcrop immediately above the pool, we'd spread our towels there and bask for awhile. When ready for a swim, we'd find the most prepossessing spot on the ten-foot cliff to climb down. The truly adventurous would dive over the side nearest the North gorge. However, the current flowed swiftly there and one risked either a broken head or being swept away.

Most of us chose to climb down the cliff directly in front of the pool. From there we'd 'touch bottom' on sand and then swim over to the huge rock. We'd scale its side and spread our towel or sunbathe on the bare rock itself. One fun activity was to throw glass pop bottles over the side of the enormous, central rock. Then we'd dive for them. The water was about fifteen feet deep directly in front of the rock. We all became pretty good divers plunging for 'sparkling treasure' in the azure water.

I've reminisced about how it might have acquired the name 'Hell's Gate'. I think it was because the swiftly flowing stream plunged through to the central pool much like the gates of Hell on the Fraser. I don't know who gave it that name, but I think it was very apropos.

After our active day of swimming and sunning was over, we'd look to the hill. There, at the top of the cliff would be one of the dads, his body halo-like as it was backlit in the twilight. If we hadn't ridden our bikes or were with a large group of girls, we always knew that either my Dad or Fanny's would be there to get us before dark. Sometimes my Dad would come to get us anyway and simply throw my bike into the old car's trunk. It was that continual assurance of the love and consistency of the male figures in our lives that, I think, contributed to us being the well-rounded, confident, women that we are today.

FALL

Preserving Our Bounty

End of September, early October, we'd start reaping the fruits of our Summer labors. Of course, we would have already gleaned from most of the Summer berry bushes and fruit trees. Strawberries came in about end-June, blue and raspberries, a little later. Blackberries were usually the latest of all.

Dad would make each of us a rather ingenious and cost-free 'picking can' (unless he had one left over from last year.) It was made out of a large metal coffee can saved for the purpose. He'd punch two holes in it, one on each side near the top. Through those holes he'd thread one of his old, worn out leather boot laces. He'd tie the ends to make a loop and, voila a can that could be slung over the neck leaving both hands free for picking.

We'd head to the patch ready to strip the ripe fruit. All the berries grew on our property except for blackberries. Those we'd hunt for along the road edges or on the neighbors' property. And I already told you about the fat, juicy yellow plums along the road in front of Myrtle's.

Fruit, we usually canned. We also canned some vegetables, such as yellow beans, but, generally vegetable canning was dicey unless one owned a pressure cooker. We didn't. I think they cost some outrageous sum like one hundred dollars, even in those days. We couldn't afford one.

There were two methods one used to can fruit-one a sort of 'fruit bath' method, the other 'water pack'. You could simply cook the fruit in the biggest pot with a cup or so of sugar. Then spoon it into the hot, sterilized jars. To sterilize them, we boiled them in hot water in a big canner or large turkey roaster. For the water pack method, one simply packed the cut-up fruit into the jars and poured in a 'bath' of boiling, sugar syrup. Once the hot lids were added (also heated to boiling in another pot or bottom of the canner) and sealed down with rings, we were done. We'd then place them on a board or rack on the counter to cool. Usually, we'd hear the lids 'pop' as they sealed.

Then the final chores involved wiping them down with a soapy cloth in case any of the sticky liquid had been dribbled down the side during the canning process. If any of the sticky liquid had dribbled, the jars would be covered in bits of mould by Winter. Finally, the trip to the basement to store on the big 'canning' shelf which took up an entire wall. One year we preserved over four hundred cans of fruits and vegetables.

W.S., after she invaded our place, would go into 'canning frenzy' every Summer. When she and Dad moved to her little place in town, she took what was left of last year's canning with her. She also canned a lot more. Shortly after she died, her nephew crawled into the dirt crawl space under her house. It had never been properly insulated. There he found jar after jar of rotted fruit. The lids were in many cases raised up due to the intense heat under the house in the Summer. Many of the jars contained green mould. I can remember the times when I visited at her house and heard suspicious popping sounds. That was the lids blowing off the fruit in the intense Summer heat under the house.

I often wondered why she would have been so wasteful. Then it came to me. She had been raised 'dirt poor', the second oldest of twelve children. She was always terrified of starving. I had noticed that the food cupboards in her house were always overstocked. Perhaps a protection against the time that she may be starving again. In addition, growing up in a remote area on the Prairies, meant people could not easily get to a grocery store for staples. They had to stockpile to get them through the winter. I guess she had learned to stockpile jars of fruit, too.

Vegetable preserving was a different story. Unless the veg could be pickled in vinegar and water and stored in jars, they had to be stored differently. The carrots, potatoes, or whatever it was would be carefully washed and dried (or left as-is depending on how much dirt was on them). Then they'd be put into burlap sacks and stored on the cool dirt ledge remaining under our basement stairs. We also had a bare dirt area near a crawl entrance which Dad utilized for any vegetable overflow.

Because my Dad's basement WAS properly insulated, vented or whatever, it was always very cool underneath. Yet the dirt didn't freeze in Winter. It was the ideal storage spot for veggies and boxes of store-bought produce such as mandarin oranges at Christmas.

Russell Farm Market*

As I said, we had no grocery stores in our immediate area, but in Summer, there was a handy farm market about two miles up the highway. Russell Farm Market was under (what was then) the silver bridge on the Chemainus River. I think it's since been painted a pale green color (or faded to that?) I don't know if Russell's was its original name, but know it has been called that for many years. It was named after Russell Stewart who owned and managed it till his death in 2017. Although we attended different elementary schools, (he at Westholme, I at Somenos) I knew him as a neighbour and from the market. The farm that supplies it was named Katie Farm after Russell's mother, Kate, who was a friend of my mother's.

For years, Russell could often be seen travelling incessantly back and forth, back and forth on his tractor. That was to make deliveries from his surrounding fields to the market where the fruits and vegetables he grew were sold. Often, he'd stop to chat with a customer or friend and, after they opened the deli, could often be seen having his meals there. I attended his huge memorial service at the Cowichan Exhibition Grounds on July 19, 2017. I can only wish to be mourned by half that many people when I pass on!

I believe his family also owned the Red Rooster Café which sadly also closed a number of years ago. I can remember as a child, Dad taking us on rare, special occasions for a meal. The old café was painted in bright, barn-like red and white and I believe sported, a rooster mock-up on the roof. (Or it may have been a rooster weather vane). I believe its interior was also red and white and had an old-fashioned counter with upholstered red 'bar' stools we kids loved to twirl around on. I believe it served good old-fashioned fare and was famous for its hamburgers and milk shakes. I wish it hadn't closed but- there is now a relatively new and modern incarnation of it at the gas station nearby.

For many years now, I've made an almost-weekly ritual of visiting Russell's farm. Often I'll take the grandkids and make it a 'Saturday outing'. We'll race around and fill the shopping cart provided, maybe even visit the deli, then take a much-needed break. I'll often order an inexpensive hot dog (all trimmings including two kinds of onions provided for 99 cents!), a cup of tea and, best of all, the biggest and cheapest ice cream cone on the Island. On a good day, they'll even have my favourite flavor-maple walnut and add a bit of chocolate to the cone for me. I think this policy of giving good value for money was actually started by Mother's good friend, Kate Stewart.

Then to 'make a day of it', I'll head up Mt. Sicker Road directly behind the market. In Summer, it makes a picturesque walk for a mile or so past numerous farms and fields owned by the Holmans and Stewarts. The flat, green farmlands, framed by rolling hills were particularly picturesque when Granny Holman's old farmhouse and barn still stood. However, the farmhouse disappeared a few years ago, although, I think the original barn still remains. In late Summer, the grandkids and I have enjoyed picking blackberries along this still-quiet old road.

But-now you have to hear about the best salesperson I ever met. When I knew her in the Fifties and Sixties, she was short, grey-haired and feisty. Kate Stewart- also one of the friendliest ladies ever. And boy, could she sell produce! When we walked into the covered area housing the marketing stalls, Kate could usually be seen, sitting on her chair. She'd give out free samples of berries to almost everyone who came along. Many's the time I have had a fat strawberry or raspberry plopped directly into my mouth with the exclamation:

"Isn't that the best strawberry you ever tasted? They're the best on Vancouver Island."

And you know what? They were. Then good ol' Kate would regale us with information about the specials of the day, how the produce was grown, why it was superior to everyone else's and so on. Invariably, I (and other customers I am sure) would end up buying more than we had originally planned to. But we didn't regret it.

When I was a young child, my little brother and I were often the recipients of kisses and head pats with comments on 'how much we had grown', 'how much we were starting to look like Mother (or Father)', etc. Yes, those Summer and Fall visits to Russell's farm were occasions to look forward to....

Cowichan Fall Fair

In September, we'd always attend the large Fall Fair at Cowichan. When we were little kids, we'd enter a prized vegetable, flower, or baked item. I can't remember if they had contests for dioramas, art work, and the like as they do today. I also can't remember whether I ever won or not. However, a few years ago, my granddaughter won two ribbons for her artwork.

The fair, in those days, was held on the Duncan fairgrounds near the highway. Outside, the 4H Club* held sway. We were fascinated by the farm animals-huge bullocks, 'moo' cows and horses. The enormous Clydesdales with their huge shaggy hooves were fascinating (and scary). The smaller 'pets: fat rabbits of every type and color; chickens-black, white and red, probably even ducks and geese. Goats, and other rarer creatures abounded.

The main exhibits, I recall were housed in a large building that looked somewhat like a skating rink. On entering the huge hall, what a cornucopia of sights met our eyes! I can remember always running first to gaze at the enormous eight or ten-feet-high sunflowers usually standing propped against the entrance. Droopy-headed and bright yellow, they overshadowed the brightly colored dahlias, daisies, chrysanthemums and other large flowers which dominated the colorful scene. And table after table of vegetable exhibits-squashes, yellow, green and orange- two or three pounds each; enormous cucumbers, beans, and potatoes. There were prizes for the 'weirdest potato' and the 'biggest veggie' in the show.

Miniature flower arrangements in teacups contrasted with the gorgeously colored large ones. Creative arrangements of all kinds by both children and adults. Handicrafts filled several tables and hung on walls-crocheted tablecloths, handmade garments of every type-both handsewn and machine-made. Stitchery creations: crocheting, knitting, tatting; some years there were even wool carding demonstrations- a specialty of the local native Indians.

We'd spend the whole day at the fair eating large feathery blobs of cotton candy, whole roasted cob corn and sometimes even hamburgers. What a treat! As long as I lived in the area, I can't remember us ever missing the Cowichan Fall Fair.

Addendum, September 2020: I can't resist going out of context to insert this one: In about 2015, my granddaughter (the very one who did the illustration of our old farmhouse earlier in this book) entered the Cowichan Fair kids' art contest. She won a prize for a colorful watercolor she painted entitled: Beach Cat. A pic of a funny, fat feline wearing sunglasses and lounging by the seaside. So-clearly sixty(!) years later, and although its location had moved to North of town, the Fair was still going strong. I think it a rotten shame that it had to be cancelled this year due to the Covid virus scare.

Ghosts in the Crossing House

But before I go on, I should give you a little bit of background to one of the scariest places we visited on Hallowe'en-The Stratfords Crossing House……

The picturesque little country road I grew up on was called Somenos* (see Appendix), a local Indian word. (In those days, we called natives or First Nations peoples, 'Indians'.) I assume it is Coast Salish, and means 'resting place'. About a mile down the road from us was Stratfords Crossing. That was the place where the railway tracks crossed Somenos and was marked by an old, red wooden 'crossing house'. This was where local people went to sit and wait for the passenger train from Victoria or Up-Island. As I mentioned in the prelude, the train had not been originally designed for passenger service. It was first used for bringing ore down from the mountain mines to be shipped. I don't know when exactly it had begun to be used for passengers. There is a huge controversy raging here locally as to whether or not the rail line should be reconstructed and reopened.

The Crossing House was a large structure sturdily constructed of heavy planks probably hewn, years ago, from local old growth trees. It was painted a rather bright, rusty red. It comprised two or three rooms and a bench outside for people to wait on in the finer weather. I recall that it was primarily an open structure but that could have just been because I only went there during the day when it was open. Perhaps they had large sliding doors which could be closed at night. But because of what I later learned about the Crossing House-I doubt it. I suspect that it was must have been open because of the high jinks that occurred there, especially at night.

The purpose of the Crossing House, of course, was to provide passengers for the E & N Dayliner a place to wait out of the rain and snow. Well-worn benches lined the interior walls. I believe the train ran twice daily. I think there was a ticket booth but don't remember us ever buying tickets there. I think that, by the time we were using the train, one could buy tickets on the Dayliner itself (from the conductor). We only took the train a very few times as my father could not afford the fare and usually our little English Hillman could get us to town to shop.

The Stratfords Crossing house, I hate to admit, was always filthy. Its back room was often littered with everything from old rags and newspapers to obscene strings of toilet paper, some of it used. The reading material that some of the kids left there at night definitely furthered my and especially my brother's, sex educations. Deteriorating copies of Playboy, Hustler and the like littered the floors. Of course, for years, I was too young to understand the purpose of the 'skin books.' I only knew that was what the naughty boys called them. I guess that litter and vandalism is why they closed the Crossing House about twenty years after I left the area.

And now to my last recollection of Stratfords Crossing. I had a close school chum from the age of about six. Her name was Flora. She was half a year or so older than I and definitely less naive. Her grandfather lived on a road which ran on the other side of Somenos, just in behind the Stratfords Crossing house.

One day we were late leaving his place and headed home. I don't remember how old we were. It was nearly dark. We knew that our parents would skin us alive if we weren't home directly. So we decided to take a short cut through the old Crossing House. It was dark and spooky inside and not too pleasant smelling as we tiptoed our way through.

Imagine our shock when from the back room, we heard suspicious moanings and groanings and thumpings.

'It's ghosts! It's ghosts!' I cried, and began to run.

She said she didn't think so, but joined me anyway. We hightailed it up Somenos as fast as our chubby, pre-adolescent legs could take us. We were so freaked by the experience that, when we got to my place, my elderly father took pity on Flora and gave her a ride home to Bell McKinnon. A few months or so later I learned (probably from my brother) that the goings on after dark in the old Crossing House were not the evil doings of ghosts. They were the nocturnal sounds of the local teenage boys and girls getting together. Rumor had it that a local girl became pregnant as a result of those nocturnal visits to the old Crossing House!

Years later, when I had completed college, I came home for a visit and to my chagrin noted that the old, red Crossing House on Somenos Road had disappeared. I don't know when or why it was removed. It had ceased to function as an ore delivery system years ago. I suspect that the nocturnal usage of the place was a factor. Also, the improvements on the New Highway rendered it obsolete. Fewer people were using the train for passenger service. Perhaps once the rail authorities realized what was going on in the House at night, they decided to shut it down.

I wish the locals had fought for Heritage designation and kept the Crossing House. I have a friend, also of Scottish heritage, who has cabins on Cameron Lake. She has given them intriguing names such as Kendrick, Bridak Lakeside, and Cameron Green Glades. One day, shortly after I had purchased my property up-island, my brother was visiting from Victoria. He decided that my new property should have a name. You guessed it. At Christmas, my brother arrived at my place with a large, hand-painted sign which now hangs prominently on my rustic garden shed. It says, simply, 'Stratford's Crossing':

So, the Crossing House at Stratfords was definitely the scariest building in the area, but it wasn't the only scary experience we had....

Hallowe'en

The crème de la crème experience in the Fall, of course, was Halloween. We'd stew for weeks over 'what costume to make this year'. Usually a pirate, a farmer or a cowgirl. Witches and ghosts were popular. The costume had to be manufactured from the materials at hand. A bed sheet (or part thereof) made a convenient ghost. Dad's work coveralls could double as farmer or logger. The kids at school would vie to see who could make the most imaginative creation.

I don't remember what year it was, but I distinctly remember the circumstances. A Hallowe'en party was held at the old school on Herd Road. We attended and they had a costume parade. Nearly everyone there, kids and adults alike, were wearing costumes. That night, I saw, bar none, the most humorous and effective costume I have ever seen. As he toddled along in the line-up of people, the ladies, particularly, laughed uproariously.

He was middle-aged, hairy chested and fat. Bald as a playground ball. He had a baby bottle stuck in his mouth, a ribbon bonnet on his head, and was wearing only one simple garment-a diaper. (His wife must have custom made it to fit his adult–and not-very-small bum.) As he toddled along, unsteadily, he made the appropriate gooing and 'ga-ga' noises. He won the costume contest.

'Trick or treating' at Halloween time was the highlight of our Fall festivities. As soon as the slightest hint of dark appeared, we kids would head out. Of course, when we were really small, my Dad would accompany us. After age eight or nine we'd hook up with a few of the neighborhood kids on the road. Then the delights began.

We'd usually go to the 'far away' neighbors first. My Dad always told us how far away we could range and approximately when he expected us back. Generally, my Dad never gave us a curfew. But I remember that, on Hallowe'en night, we had to be back in by nine o'clock or so. Otherwise, he would come looking for us. Mother would further admonish us:

'Do not go near the gravel pit at the big corner-especially you, dear' (meaning me). Bad things can happen in there.'

We never knew exactly what the bad things were, but by high school, suspected. I never went into that gravel pit except once, in the company of my brother to 'check it out'. It didn't look too scary to me except that it had a rounded, but fairly flat, bottom, and bowl-shaped sides. I guess that anyone who got trapped in there could not easily get out.

Usually, as it was growing dark, we'd start at our house and proceed south. When we got to Myrtle's we'd have to be on our toes. She'd open her door with her elderly husband behind her, silhouetted, and usually with a big grin on his face. They'd demand a 'trick' in exchange for the treat. Usually, we'd sing a song or recite a poem. Old 'Cougar' was adamant that no kid would get a treat unless a feat was performed.

Onward down the road to the two other Smythe families and the teacher's house. All made a point of being home so that they could treat the kids. When finally we got to the Crossing House we'd start quaking in our shoes. It was time to face the:

Scary Apple Witch

She lived on a small access road that jutted onto Somenos just behind the Crossing House. To us little kids, she was REAL SCARY. We never knew if the outfit she wore was a costume or if she just always dressed in dark, flowing garments. She had a long driveway that was black as pits. We'd try to take turns each year deciding whose turn it was to run up her steps and rap on the door. Usually, the kid who did the rapping stood well back as she opened up. Weird wails and noises emanated from within. We never knew what caused them but oft fantasized that they were the moans of tortured kids.

I can't remember exactly what she looked like, but it seems to me that she was short, bent and supremely ugly. May have been wearing a witch's hat. However, the 'reward' was worth the scare because she always had the best, most luscious treat of all the neighbors. Homemade caramel apples. I'll bet the apples came off her own tree; they were deliciously crisp and coated in rich, golden caramel. We'd snatch our treat, yet thank her politely, then make a run for it. The caramel delights were so yummy that we'd have them eaten before they made it to our bags.

One year we screwed up enough courage to hike up the long, muddy trail to hermit McGonagal's. He, of course, was not expecting children. He hemmed and hawed and expressed his confusion when we appeared at his door. Then, suddenly, he had an idea. He asked us to wait a minute and climbed up into his woodsy loft. He came down with a handful of chunks of what looked like tiny bricks. We smelled them. Maple sugar! What a treat! We stuffed some in our mouths and some in our bags on the way out. His modest cottage was on our list of 'favorites' for next year. I can't remember if we ever went to Nestor Nelson's tiny cottage or not. Since I don't recall, we probably never did or else the door was never opened to us.

When we were older, we'd venture further down Somenos and past the garbage dump. The trees along the huge curve in the road were dark and scary. I remember running like blazes as we hurried past the forbidden site. Soon we'd reach the haven of Mrs. P's. If we were pooped out by then, she'd phone Dad and he'd come to get us. By now we would have ranged almost two miles from home. However, those scary forays for goodies on Hallowe'en nights taught us lessons in imagination, in courage, and in generosity.

WINTER

Skating on the Flats

There were actually two areas that we kids called 'The Flats'. One comprised several acres and lay behind Captain Grove's huge mansion. The other (now known as Somenos Flats) was about three miles south of our place on the Island Highway. It has now been turned into kind of a nature preserve/bird habitat.

My favorite was the one behind the mansion. It was more secluded, within a long walk of our place and not as crowded. Only the neighborhood kids skated there. The downside was that it was much easier to drown. Nearly every time that we'd spend a day at the flats, we'd have to haul one or more water-soaked kids out of the 'deep part'.

The Flats were, of course, the Captain's cow pasture. It would flood in mid-winter and afford us good skating for a couple of months before the Spring thaw. I was never much of a skater, just 'dabbled' on the ice. However, my brother and his friends who were, had to be mindful of the reedy grasses which still protruded in spots and the only partially sunken fence posts. From time to time someone would trip and sprain an ankle. But invariably the kid would be back for more punishment next week.

I'll always remember the beautiful vista from the top of the rise at the Mansion proper. Blue skies, flat fields, crisp clear air and the sight of my warmly dressed pals, usually in old or borrowed skates, gliding along, their multi-colored wool scarves (if they had any) flailing in the ever-present wind.

Somenos Flats, as we called it, was an entirely different story. To access it, we either had to beg a ride with Dad, a neighbor, or hitchhike. Dad took a dim view of us hitch hiking at any time although, in those days, it was a common practice, especially amongst the boys. It was not generally thought of as illegal, as it is today. We didn't know what the Department of Motor Vehicles officially thought of the practice, and we didn't care. After all, this was the pre-seatbelt days. People then would have down-right hooted at the idea of air bags!

And another comment on 'traffic safety' (or lack thereof) in the Sixties: I distinctly remember my first year at U.Vic (1965) racing with a boyfriend up Fort Street on his big, black Harley. I was wearing a pair of high-heeled 'ankle strap' shoes and a mini-skirt. I am sure we were speeding. No helmet, no protective leathers. I remember him dropping me off, late, at the college dorm, relatively unscathed. Except for a noticeable burn on my bare leg from the bike's exhaust. I had been having so much fun that I didn't even notice it! (Somehow, we kids survived…..)

So we'd arrive at Somenos Flats. We were usually greeted by a long line-up of cars (probably illegally) parked on the road allowance. All manner of people would be there. Elderly, local natives and other ethnic groups, teenagers and younger kids-anyone who either wanted to skate or watch the skaters. Or anyone who just wanted a day out in the crisp, cold air.

These flats were a lot more crowded than Groves', but with fewer opportunities for wet pant legs or drownings. I, however, have always abhorred crowds of any kind and preferred the Captain's. But-it WAS much deeper and therefore, riskier. The Somenos ones have now been designated a protected area. I doubt that anything was protected in the mid-Fifties. It was probably just part of Farmer W's acreage. He had a big white house with red barn up on the hill. He was the farmer I eventually worked for, mostly berry-picking in Summers.

As he did with the little Kinsmen pool we swam in as young children, Dad would drop us off for the day. We usually had a bagged lunch and our old, hand-me-down skates slung over our shoulders. He'd pick us up towards evening if we hadn't managed to hitch a ride home with a trusted neighbor. I seem to remember we did not often choose Somenos Flats and did a lot more of our skating at Captain Grenfell's.

Captain Grenfell's Mansion

Did I describe to you Captain Grenfell's Mansion? Perhaps now would be a good time to do so:

Just south of Westholme on a rise overlooking thirty or so acres of pasture land, stood an enormous, pink-colored manse. A partly obscured, winding driveway about one quarter mile in length led to the imposing entranceway. I never quite figured out what gave it the pinkish tinge, but I think it was finished in a kind of stucco. It had huge chocolate-colored beamlike structures that provided trim. The numerous and enormous windows were leaded with Old English style cross-hatching. As an adult, I realized it was English Tudor in style.

It had been purchased from the Captain (or after his demise) by a family whose dad worked in the logging or fishing industry. I don't know if the new owner owned his own company, but he obviously had money (or his wife did). I recall him as a tall, well-built mid-Forties chap who always treated us kids well. Rumor had it that the property had been purchased for the enormous sum of thirty thousand dollars. It comprised twelve rooms (or was that twelve bedrooms?) and a tennis court on the lower level. I think I also observed the empty remains of a large swimming pool and it may have had stables and a riding ring. On the Golds property just down the road, there was a stable and a ring on the upper level.

I remember Mrs. Burns taking us for a tour when I was about ten years old. She was an impeccably groomed, petite blonde lady with a cultured English accent. My mother very much liked her and would go over to visit her from time to time. I don't ever remember her coming to our place.

On walking up the imposing front steps covered with an immense open porch, you entered a large foyer. I remember that the main floor seemed fairly dark because its walls were covered with rich-looking and highly polished ebony-colored wood. Whitewashed ceilings with dark oak beams were carried throughout. To the right, the main floor comprised an enormous carpeted living room about the size of the main floor of our entire house. Various other smaller rooms carried along to the left and ended with a huge kitchen area. The entire upstairs comprised numerous bedrooms and, probably several bathrooms. There was also one or two bathrooms on the main floor.

But the enormous kitchen took my breath away. It had high beamed ceilings (over fifteen feet to my recollection), a cookstove as big as my father's furnace, and an imposing walk-in pantry. A huge food preparation area covered with butcher block took up much of the center of the room. I think that the lady of the house must have had at least 'kitchen help' to manage all that. I also remember that whenever my little brother and I came to visit, we were hospitably treated and often introduced to 'fancy' foods we would never enjoy at home.

The best time of the year for visiting the manse was Christmas. The entire house, inside and out, would be covered with rich decorations, not the cheap popcorn strings and construction paper chains of our house. Real poinsettias in brilliant reds, wall wreaths of cedar and fir boughs, with silver and gold accents, and other costly décor adorned the walls.

But the best, of course, was the beautifully decorated tree in the living room. It, too, was probably close to fifteen feet high and stood in stately glory in the corner across from the immense fireplace. It was tastefully decorated, caked in rich adornments of every description. Glass-beaded creations, ceramic angels, softly colored lights, and enormous silver and gold garlands created a fairyland on the tree. We loved standing in the living room doorway and marveling at the sight.

Invariably, if we showed up around Christmas time, we would be treated to rich chocolates and home baked delicacies enough to rival a king. Sometimes, Mrs. B. would even have a Christmas gift for us, beautifully wrapped. Many of the neighbors knew that my mother was an invalid and, I think, treated us especially nicely because of it. Yes, I remember with great fondness our rare visits to Captain Grenfell's Mansion and the warm hospitality of the Burns'. I hope that the phrase 'all things are magnified in the eyes of a small child' did not hold true here. However, I did notice on the several times I revisited Stratfords Crossing, many things were much smaller than I remembered them as a child.

Christmas at Stratfords

Christmas at Stratfords was a magical time. For us kids, the excited anticipation would start just after Thanksgiving. My brother would start scoping out suitable trees in the forest. I would be thinking of what goodies we could choose to bake this year. And presents, of course. We'd start saving our meagre allowance to buy a small gift for our parents and sibling.

In early December, we'd haul out the old box of decorations from the basement. We'd check to see what we could afford to buy this year. Every year we tried to add one decoration and usually had to replace tinsel and other perishables. By mid-December, we'd usually have gifts purchased and be hounding Dad to let us get the tree. He believed in waiting to decorate till Xmas Eve. But we'd usually hound and cajole and be able to at least put it in place before then.

Christmas Eve saw the usual rituals-hanging the stockings, decorating the tree and putting the presents underneath. However, I don't remember him letting us open one ahead of time as many kids do today. Nor did we put out tidbits for the reindeer. (I'm not sure if that custom had been invented yet!) We did, when we were little, put out cookies and milk for Santa. Of course, it had all disappeared by the next morning.

That night was usually designated our annual Carol sing, our favorites being: Dad's (White Christmas, Bing Crosby version); Mom's: O Holy Night; Gary's: Rudolph the Red-Nosed Reindeer (Gene Autry version) and mine: Frosty the Snowman (my own version!) We were all good singers and those Christmas Eve Carol fests were only one of many occasions at which we practiced. When were young teens, we'd grab a few neighbourhood kids and carry candles down Somenos Road (weather permitting of course, or else our candles would blow out). We'd stand outside neighbours' houses and sing 'requests'.

Christmas Day saw us out of our beds by 6 a.m. Then we were allowed to dump out our stockings, but no touching the presents until my parents arose. Then, we had to wait till Dad had had his breakfast even if we had eaten goodies in our stockings and weren't hungry!

Our stockings invariably contained the requisite 'Jap orange' in its toe, a new pair of socks for school, usually a school item such as pencil or eraser, one or two other small gifts and, stuck in the top, a large striped candy cane. Sometimes a carefully wrapped chunk of mother's coconut fudge.

After breakfast, we opened our presents and prepared to help stuff the turkey. The four of us sat in a circle on our respective chairs and either my bro or I was delegated to play helpful elf. This prevented us kids from grabbing presents willy-nilly and throwing wrappings about. Particularly nice wrappings were carefully removed and folded to be saved in the Christmas box for next year's reuse.

If it was a particularly good Xmas, we'd have presents from the aunts in Vancouver. If we had received the usual and anxiously awaited Christmas Cheer Basket there would be a turkey and extra candy, sometimes a much-coveted box of chocolates. If no turkey arrived, we'd butcher one of Dad's fattest hens. We would have saved old bread crusts in our freezer for a month or two. If we'd remembered to thaw them the night before, it was usually my job to tear them into small pieces in our biggest mixing bowl, adding onion, melted margarine (we couldn't afford 'real' butter) and spices. Dad usually stuffed the bird. He'd set it to bake in the woodstove oven just before noon.

We'd have a late breakfast, or if full of candy and oranges, no breakfast. About three o'clock, Dad would declare the bird ready even though our noses had already registered the yummy smells emanating from our smallish oven. The Christmas dinner menu never varied. It usually consisted of stuffed, roast turkey with cranberry sauce, baked yams (the only time of year we ever had them) and whatever vegetables- usually carrots or beets- were in our root cellar. We usually had two desserts-pie and our annual treat-Mom's carrot pudding with caramel sauce. Pie was invariably home-baked, usually apple or pumpkin. If we didn't have whipping cream to put on it, Mom or I would whip up a sweet egg meringue for topping. I can't ever remember us inviting any relatives or guests (as we often do today.) I also never remember saying grace, even at the Xmas table. My old agnostic father would have scoffed at such foolishness!

By nightfall, we little kids would be so stuffed full and exhausted from the Christmas excitement, we'd either fall asleep on the couch or crawl off to our beds. When older, we'd all join in to do a jigsaw puzzle on a card table set up at the front of the living room beside the couch. Sometimes, we'd have a game of cards, even poker, with our parents. There would be no T.V. watching that special night as-for many years- we didn't have one!

Hiking in Snowland/The Trip to the Train *

I hated going to Stratfords Crossing in the snow except when on family adventures with my parents. My one and only pair of black rubber boots would fill up every time. How, you say, did we cope with owning only one pair of boots year-round? Well, if it was late Spring or early Fall, we wore light socks underneath. If the dead of Winter and heavy snow we doubled up on the socks or borrowed a pair of Dad's heavy work socks. If, in spite of all, our boots became water-logged, we'd stuff them with newspapers and leave them overnight in front of the oil stove or over the makeshift furnace registers. If it had recently snowed heavily, the narrow, winding road into town was often impassible, especially for my father's latest puddle-jumper.

However, the walk down to Stratfords was gorgeous. A mile or so of marshmallow-covered fields, their surfaces unmarked. Trees and bushes hugged the narrow, sparkling roadway, their branches hanging with spidery diamonds of frost. And always in the background, Prevost. That gorgeous, solid mountain that for over twelve years rose like a sentinel in my bedroom window which was on the back of our house. In the Winter, its twin snow-capped peaks glistened in stolid majesty beside us as we made our way South. That majestic, twin-peaked, Prevost was my Big Friend for many years.

*see p. 126 re stories from this section

When we were little and mother was yet well enough to accompany us, the trip to Duncan was a great family outing. Down the road our little group would march, singing, my baby brother thrown over my father's great shoulder. I would be holding my mother's hand as we trotted merrily down to 'meet the train to Cowichan' (or waded, up to our knees, if the snow plough had not come). When I was about ten, and my mother more infirm, the trips by train became less frequent. But then my Dad accompanied us, one of us on each side of him, holding hands.

It was a cold walk, but we were always warmly dressed, me in my tartan skirt and brown leggings or a dress with slacks under. That was the only time, except for the Wintery walks to school, when girls were allowed to wear pants.) We were always well-booted even if only in the black rubber gum boots with red-banded top that all the poor kids wore in those days. I write in Chapter IX, 'Stories of Somenos School' of the horrible smell that often emanated from the overheated cloak room of our local elementary school on 'rubber boot days'. And I always remember us merrily trotting down the road in high spirits, but returning in late afternoon, exhausted and grumpy. However, my remembrances of those Wintery sojourns to Duncan are among the highlights.

My memory of the train journey itself is foggy. I only remember that it was noisy and wobbly. In the late Eighties, I took the E&N, unfortunately in mid-Spring, from Duncan to Courtenay. I partly hoped to see if I could regenerate any of those fond memories. Not so. The trip was a night-mare. The noisy clackety-clack of the train tracks was anything but pleasant. The train was so crowded that my new husband and I could not find an unoccupied seat. We had to stand in a kind of unheated anteroom between the cars. We could see the tracks flashing by below us. I had had major spinal surgery by then and the prolonged standing and constant jarring of my back was no fun. Eventually, when we reached Nanaimo, enough people got off that we were able to get two adjoining seats. But by then disillusionment had set in. I never rode on a train again.

Another favorite pastime was sledding. When we were older, we had a well-used, but still serviceable, wooden sled. As kids, a piece of carpet or big chunk of cardboard would suffice. Initially, for a moderate-sized hill, all we had to do was walk out onto Somenos Road. Few cars ever passed, the snow plough wouldn't show up for days, and we could sled to our hearts content. For a bigger challenge, or when we were older, we'd sled down our back slope to the creek. Or we'd hit the high pasture land in Mickey's Field.

I wasn't keen on train travel as an adult, but as a young child seeking adventure, I thought the train trip enchanting. But even more enchanting the Christmasy sights when we got to town. By early December, many of the shops were decorated in tinsel finery and the slushy streets were a perfect backdrop. The entire downtown area looked like 'a jolly li'l bit of ol' England'. Quaint whitewashed buildings with leaded windows were covered in snowy scenes. Every shop window was a young child's delight. Each year we'd eagerly anticipate the new decorations and Christmasy themes. As we strolled along in this snowy Wonderland, we would see on each side of the street, quaintly decorated shops such as Westwell's, the 'five and dime' store and Charlie Onn's. But my favorite sight was the old Eaton's store:

Eaton's at Christmas*

A few years ago, I met an elderly lady, a little older than I, working in Tim Horton's in Ladysmith. Her name was Bev. I told her I was writing my early memoir and working on a section depicting the old Eaton's store* in Duncan. She told me she had a 'punkinhead' doll, now over sixty years old. It still had an Eaton's story booklet affixed to its neck. Inside, the booklet told the story of a little boy who was excited because he had received a special gift from his granny at Christmas-a handknitted sweater. Punkinhead was outfitted in the sweater! I wonder what a boy's reaction would be today to be given only a sweater for his Christmas present?

I had a nice chat with the store employee and it turned out that we had lived in Duncan at about the same time. She offered to bring the doll to work one day so that I could photograph it. Here is the photo:

    The old Eaton store, a solid two-storey brick structure, sat on the corner of Station and Craig Streets. For years it was a fixture. I remember my heightening excitement at we walked with Dad from the train station at the end of the street. As we approached the store's Wintery facade, my heart nearly burst with the curious anticipation of snowy delights. They decorated three windows, I believe. The two large ones facing Station St. and one on the side street. There may have been another one on the back of the store as well.

    I remember running joyously from window to window absorbing as much as I could of the festive displays. Manger scenes and Christmas angels. Santa Claus, Santa sleighs, elves, all in bright colors in windows often dark, but outlined in wonderful borders of fake snow. Ice skating and snow-sledding dioramas calling up delightful fantasies in the mind of an imaginative child. The displays seemed to change from year to year. One year I would be soaring high over rooftops delivering toys with Santa and other year I would imagine myself at Santa's workshop at the North Pole. Those snowy windows may have inspired a little poem I wrote years ago when a young child at Somenos School:

Santa

Every year, Christmas night
Santa Claus begins his flight
Over rooftops, over spires
Over trees and telephone wires.

In his sleigh a pack of toys
For all good little girls and boys.
He fills the stockings right up tight
And then departs through the night.
                              - Joy G. c. 1955?

Perhaps it was inspired by those annual sojourns to Eaton's. I don't think my little poem ever won any prizes, but at the time, I thought my rhyming of 'spires' and 'wires' inspired! It is hard to describe in words the excited glow that those beautifully decorated windows brought to my chest every year that I stood, spellbound, in front. However, the store had further delights to offer. Each department was similarly decorated in Christmas and Winter themes. But the 'creme de la crème' yet awaited us. As we walked through the front entrance and approached the open staircase, my heart would begin to pound.

For I knew that on the landing between floors stood the most wondrous sight of all. The Christmas tree! With real store-bought decorations! Not just construction paper chains and popcorn such as comprised our tree at school and most of the tree at home. I have a recollection of expensive (and breakable) glitter balls, some with scenes inside, red cardinals and other birds made of what looked like real feathers, mistletoe, angels, and other delights we never saw on trees at home. I think the tree was sprayed with snow yet it looked almost as real as the ones we passed on the way to the train. And it was always perfect, its branches thick and regular. It wasn't spindly in some spots like the one my brother often picked out when he went, axe in hand, into the woods with my father.

To me the tree seemed enormous, reaching up to the very top of the high ceiling. Layer upon layer of tinsel and ribbon and gorgeous fuzzy wreaths encircled it, resembling the tiers of a beautifully iced wedding cake. It might actually have been an artificial one, but it looked real enough to me. Of course, we were always admonished to, 'not touch' so the final glory of the trip to Eaton's remained forever from our grasp.

The presents! Under the tree were layers and layers of expensively wrapped gifts. Their metallic papers and enormous bows beckoned enticingly to itchy little fingers. But we knew we were in for it if we ever touched one of those gifts. And we were easy to convince that each contained a real present for the well-to-do children of the store managers and clerks, not for us. Probably a story my Dad made up to keep us from grabbing the gifts- 'Don't you touch those presents; they belong to somebody else.' (the packages were probably just 'fakes.') We never dared to imagine what riches those presents held.

But-I remember one year when I thought I received riches beyond measure:

No Gift for Christmas*

I was born December 31, only a week after Christmas. Often my birthday and Christmas presents were combined or my birthday gift was understandably modest. My mother had just died in September. As you know my father was, by then, an Old Age Pensioner. I didn't realize till later that his income had also been reduced. Because of her death, he had lost the necessary sum of one hundred dollars monthly (my mom's 'cripples' pension). Thus, my dad was broke and still heavily grieving his loss. I was sixteen and anticipated nothing for my birthday.

For Christmas, I may have received a small item that was often included in the Christmas hamper a local charity (or was it the City of Duncan?) dropped off at our door. But I had, as yet, received nothing from the family. However, with the optimism of youth, I waited hopefully all day. By nightfall I despaired of receiving a single gift. Imagine my joy when my elderly dad came to me, late New Year's Eve, with a small package hidden behind his back. My brother stood next to him, grinning. The box Dad held had no wrapping but was tied with a simple ribbon. Inside was sitting, on a plain cotton batting liner, the most beautiful piece of jewelry I had ever seen. It was a pearl necklace, five-and-dime store variety.

My seventy-two-year old dad had driven all the way into town that day to search for something his modest pensioner's income could procure. He told me that, just that day, in time for me, they had marked down all the pearl necklaces at the Five-and-Dime. That necklace had cost him the princely sum of sixty-five cents. Elizabeth Taylor could not have been more thrilled when Richard Burton gave her that obscenely huge diamond. I remember wearing the cheap pearls proudly on my back-turned black cardigan to my Grade Twelve classes that year.

Another feature of our wonderful Winters at Stratfords were the annual concerts at both the Sunday and elementary schools. For many years I attended the Brae Road Gospel Chapel in town. I enjoyed their Sunday school and often won the prize for 'most Bible verses memorized'. Each year we would have a concert of sorts, some as simple as a short depiction of Jesus in the manger, some more elaborate 'morality' plays. We did a lot of singing at both venues which I thoroughly enjoyed and sung in choirs and operettas all through my school years. The group singing I participated in as a child and teen gave me the confidence and background training to rejoin choir groups in my fifties.

In Chapter X, I talk about my School Days, both elementary and secondary. (I dubbed it School Daze, emphasizing the humorous side. I'll talk about the wonderful Christmas and other productions we performed in at both schools in that chapter.

  *Amended and enhanced versions of all three of the above stories were published in local newspapers in 2018 and 2019:

December 21 2018 Cowichan Valley Citizen 'No Gift for Xmas: A Cowichan Valley Story'

December 26 2018 Cowichan Valley Citizen 'Christmas at the Old Eatons Store was Magic'

December 22/2019 Province Newspaper Travel Section Dave Pottinger Ed. Winter Train Trip

CHAPTER VII   OUR NEIGHBOURS

(AND FRIENDS AND ENEMIES?)

'812L1'

Yep, for many years, that was our phone number. I think it was in the Seventies sometime that it became a 746 number. (746-7604 to be exact). At the time it was a five-digit number; we had a 'party line'. Often, we'd pick up the old and cumbersome black receiver only to hear Myrtle or Mrs. Mc's voice gossiping away. If it was an 'emergency' or the call urgent, one of us would politely ask if they could give up the line. They always did.

So- because of that party line, we perhaps knew all of our immediate neighbors better than most people do today. I often think the absence of television was a factor, too. We didn't get our second-hand Westinghouse in its chipped wood cabinet till I was eleven or twelve and in Grade Seven. Then, we only got two channels- 12 and 6. And Channel 12 was always a bit 'snowy'. However, it was clear enough for us to watch The Ed Sullivan Show and Bonanza on Sunday nights (when we were old enough for Dad to allow us to stay up that late.)

We also enjoyed the old oaters and 'cowboy' weeklies such as Roy Rogers and Dale Evans, Cheyenne and Have Gun Will Travel. Up until then, we used to hike it down to the Martineau's every Thursday after school to enjoy their T.V. But, in retrospect, I think all those years without the Boob Tube was good for us. We learned to tell stories, memorize verses, and play outside-pursuits much healthier for our brains and bodies!

Soon after we got the T.V., I can remember my bro huddling under the covers on the couch. If the Outer Limits or a 'spooker' movie (like The Invisible Man or The Mummy) were on, he'd often cry buckets; I wouldn't. I'd wonder what ailed him and sometimes put my arm around him to offer him comfort. However, if the movie was particularly romantic and the two leads were kissing, he'd cry out 'Aw, mush!' and pull a face. Or pull the blanket up over his face so he didn't have to witness the mushy kiss.

I think the fact that we didn't have television for all those years gave us the time and the wherewithal to visit the neighbors. We got to know and to trust those fine, local people, especially our neighborhood 'elders' in a way that kids today may not. We, in fact, regarded the local dads and moms of the neighborhood as pseudo aunties and uncles.

Our 'Poor' Neighbours- The McAvoys

I'll tell you about our neighbors in the order they lived from our place- from North to South. When we first moved to Stratfords in '52, our only neighbors to the immediate Northeast were the McAvoys. They were a disabled husband and 'stay at home' wife with seven kids. About ten years later, an elderly single man, Mr. A, bought a property nearer the highway to the North of us. When I was in high school, to our disgust, we had immediate neighbors. My Dad enjoyed his privacy and was disappointed that they built their house that close. But, they turned out to be nice people and we played with their boys and their goats. Eventually, they grew a large privacy hedge which, to our minds, spoiled the country ambiance. Soon, too, another house was built between the goat owners and Mr. A's. Although we lost some of our privacy, we gained some good friends. All four of those neighbors' children went to school with and played with us.

But, in '52, for about half a mile, there were no neighbors on either side of us. The property immediately across the road was Mr. Smythe's large pastureland. It comprised about thirty acres or more. Eventually, we had an immediate neighbor to the south-another Smythe. Further south and directly across from the Horton's house was Myrtle Smythe's. The two Smythes who owned the neighboring properties were brother and cousins of her husband, Nick's. Most of the neighbors had large acreages; ours was actually one of the smallest.

A Bit of Hair Pulling

Right across the road from us lived what, even for those days, would be considered a large family. However, they were not nearly as large as another town family of our acquaintance – eighteen! I'll talk more about that huge family later on in this chapter.

The McAvoys were a nice family although 'dirt poor' (as my father described them). Their family comprised six children. The parents had a lot of mouths to feed on the, I assume small, disability pension the husband received. He had a leg off, for whatever reason, and sometimes used a wheelchair. It was rumored that he drank, but I never saw any direct evidence of that the times I visited at their house.

The wife was a tall and buxom lady-a motherly type who, like most wives in those days could do just about anything. She could bake bread, split wood, scrub floors, milk the cow and make butter to feed her large brood, and even put in and maintain a huge garden. We never saw the invalid husband do much work around the place. I think he died soon after I left for college in '65.

I remember that for years I envied those girls at the bus stop their lean figures. Years later, I ran into the oldest McAvoy girl at a store in town. I told her how much I had envied her slimness. Her reply:

'Joy, much of the time we just didn't have enough to eat!'

Most of the kids would join us at the school bus stop my Dad had set up in front of our large garage. Two of the Smythe children would walk up from Mick's pastureland. So, on any given day we had about ten kids waiting at the bus stop. Thus, we became good friends. Except for the biggest McAvoy boy.

Well, he wasn't exactly an enemy. Who knows, he might even have been a little sweet on me because he tried to bully me on one or two occasions. I think in those days, a boy 'getting physical' with a girl was his perverse way of trying to show her he liked her. It didn't work with me.

For whatever reason, I was visiting at the McAvoy's one day. I was about ten or eleven years old. I think I had been playing in the barn with one or both of the boys. I can't remember whether my bro was there or not. I don't know how it happened but, suddenly, I was thrown on my back on the lawn. Eddie, the oldest boy and I were fighting. He being thirteen or fourteen and tall for his age was, I'm sure nearing six feet. I was probably still four-foot-nothing, but hefty and feisty.

I remember we were wrestling on the lawn, he screaming his guts out. At one point, I had rolled over on top of him, grabbed a handful of his longish hair and was, quite literally, pulling it out by the roots. I don't know exactly what he'd said or done to me (probably called me 'Fattie, Fattie, Two-by-Four' again), but I totally lost it.

I was on him like a banshee, smacking and pulling, smacking and pulling. He was screaming blue murder and calling for his 'ma'. Out she came. That buxom farm woman said she had a heck of a time pulling me off him. Finally, I desisted and, somehow all was resolved. I don't remember bearing the kid any ill-will and believe we remained friends. I guess in those days we didn't consider 'bullying' to be such a big deal as it is today.

However, I had previously had another incident of serious bullying by a big boy on the school bus. I was only in Grade Four and he was about Grade nine. I fixed him! And I'll tell you the details of that incident in the section entitled 'Stories of Somenos School'.

Sadly, we did have a family who were every bit as poor as the McAvoys and just as numerous. I shall call them the Taylors. The mentally and physically challenged parents also had six or seven children. They lived high on a hill just South of Stratfords. I think, for a time at least, their kids attended Somenos School. The family with sixteen or eighteen kids were cousins of theirs. It was rumored that Tansor School, West of town, had to maintain a 'special class' just for these numerous 'mentally challenged' kids. Although, 'learning disabled or 'challenged' are the terms that would be used today-in those Bad Ol' Days we considered the kids just plain 'dumb'. Sadly, they would have been dubbed 'stupid' or 'retarded'. I think that poverty and malnutrition were factors.

However, they were all nice children, although some of them 'talked funny'. My brother and I spent many happy days playing with these girls and their near-in-age brothers-four or five of them at least. The big drawing card was that they had goats. The buxom, hard working mother made her own cheese and even if there wasn't much store-bought food, they usually had plenty of milk.

They had a large house, unfinished, untidy-at times downright filthy, and always a 'work in progress'. The physically as well as intellectually-disabled dad never worked and may have had a drinking problem-I don't know for sure. He was missing either and arm and a leg or one eye, or both. Seems he had made a stupid mistake when working at a local sawmill. There were no decent disability pensions then, but he bragged to us that he received 'a lot of Welfare' for all those kids. Someone had even quoted numbers to us at one time. When mom was alive, my Dad got about three hundred dollars pension to live on. After mother died, about two hundred. These parents bragged to us that, even in that day, they were getting over seven hundred. Even twenty dollars bought a lot of groceries in those days!

Huge families seemed to be their family's trait. Several times my mom took us out to visit old lady Hawkins who lived West of Duncan. She was either Mrs. Wilkins' mother or aunt. Grossly obese and unkempt, she had even more children than her prolific niece. She was probably at least twenty years older than her niece and probably had had sixteen or eighteen children. I don't think they were all living. For, even in those days birth rates weren't as secure as they are today. It was quite common for mothers with such large families to lose one or two of them before they reached adulthood-either through miscarriage, birth traumas or accident.

In spite of that, the kids were poorly dressed and skinny. They all struggled in school and most quit without graduating. What they did after that, I don't know. I did however, run into one of the Taylor girls years later and she had a reasonable government job. Told me she had been married but was now a single parent –of two girls, I think. Seems like she did not intend to follow in her mother's (or aunt's) shoes and produce a whole brood. So, I, with only one brother, good food, reasonable clothing and plenty of freedom, felt myself pretty lucky by comparison.

But, I remember with fondness, our trips to the Taylor's rustic, undeveloped property. Heidi-like, we'd run on the grassy slopes with the goats and chase the odd assortment of other animals roaming free on the property. We had little supervision and not just because the parents were too infirm or obese to venture out. In those days, kids were not guarded and mollycoddled as they are today. In later years, the ironic thing to us was that these extremely poor dads were too infirm to work but not too disabled to produce more children!

Cougar and Myrtle Smythe

Our immediate neighbors to the south were the Smythes. An older 'farm' couple- they had, I think, nine children. Several were grown and most were in high school by the time my mother made good friends with Myrtle and we'd go down to visit. The elderly Dad's name was Nick, but most of us kids in the neighbourhood called him 'Cougar'. I have heard there was also another fellow dubbed 'cougar' living more towards Nanaimo. I believe he was a hunter as well.

Cougar Smythe, as the story goes, and one or two other local hunters had been contracted to eradicate most, if not all, of the cougars on the nearby mountains. I wonder if that is why we seem to be overrun with deer in this part of the Island today? Cougar and his oldest boy owned Big Jake, the huge hunting dog my brother was always warned to stay away from.

However, old Nick and his big son were good about keeping the vicious

136

animal penned. And Nick, like most of the dads in the neighborhood, was a good guy. Not only had he saved us that day from the huge bull, but we always knew that if we were out and about and got into trouble we could always go to Myrtles' house for help. If she happened to not be home, we could count on old Nick to bail us out of whatever scrape we had gotten ourselves into this time.

But, the most intriguing, heroic character of the neighborhood, I thought, was his long-suffering wife and my mother's best friend-Myrtle Smythe.

'Hillbilly' wasn't quite the word to describe Myrtle, but it was close. A practical, down-to-earth sort, she was a hard worker and toiled daily to feed her old husband and nine children. She was my mother's best friend. Almost every afternoon, when we were really little, Mom would toddle down to Myrtle's for 'afternoon tea'. Myrtle, for some reason, never came to our house. In the thirteen years I lived at Stratfords, I don't remember her (or her husband, for that matter) ever walking in the door. She probably didn't have the time!

Myrtle, as I mentioned, had nine kids-five boys and four girls. She lived in seemingly poor conditions on a large acreage which fronted the creek about a half mile from our place. And how that woman worked! Myrtle, probably about fifty or so, was tall (or at least tall compared to my diminutive mother) and lanky. Although she appeared slim, when she rolled up the sleeves of her old (invariably) grey housedress she revealed massive forearms. Probably developed from years of hauling buckets of water from the 'crik' and 'schuckin' corn. Her old farm smock was far from becoming but probably practical for the work she did, especially in the hot weather. Women rarely wore slacks in those days. I don't think my mother even owned a pair! However, most of Mother's dresses were shorter and stylish; Myrtle's baggy 'house dresses' hung almost to her ankles.

Her, to me, unpleasant' chores included hauling numerous buckets of water from the 'crik' behind her small farm house, tending the numerous chickens which clucked, roaming freely, around her yard, and yelling at Big Jake penned at the back of the house. 'Shaddap, ther Jake, you quiet down!' Although laconic in her speech she was clever in her own way. In those days, most of the locals believed in saying only what was necessary or 'speaking only when spoken to'. That definitely applied to kids as witness mother's favourite mantra: 'children should be seen, but not heard'. (Good luck with that one today.)

I remember my shock at first watching Myrtle peel potatoes. Sitting on her dilapidated wood porch, she would pour a small amount of water from the nearby bucket into a large basin. Then she'd dump in a dozen or so fresh-dug potatoes. Soon the water, the peels and the spuds took on an unpleasant grey color. At first, I thought her kids would be eating mud for supper. However, in time I realized that she would be boiling them in fresh water, anyway.

Reminds me of the first time I met Kurt-Christmas of '99. He served me 'grey' potatoes for Xmas dinner. 'Gross', I thought, as I surreptitiously pushed them around my plate. I surmised that he, too, hadn't washed them properly. It was weeks before I questioned his mother, (who was also at the dinner) and she told me he cooked in cast iron pots. The 'cast' as they called it, would put a grayish tinge on anything light colored.

Invariably on the warm Spring or Summer days when my Mom showed up, kiddies in tow, Myrtle would be sitting on her front porch. She was usually 'shuckin' corn, peeling potatoes or shellin' peas. It took a lot of work in those days to feed a family of eleven. Still does. Today, most mothers would be overwhelmed, but in those days large families were not uncommon. Earlier I mentioned the other two families nearby who each had six or seven children. Then, the one closer to town that had at least sixteen! Most of those kids were underweight and learning challenged.

Not so Myrtle's kids. They were well brought up and all grew up to be productive, hard workers. One girl even attended college and became a prominent scientist. Myrtle and her whole family spoke a lingo I wish I could replicate here. My clever brother, Gary, could mimic them perfectly. Her husband, as well as tending the small farm, had a lucrative job as a commercial fisherman. He would remind us of the acronym for Vancouver Island's three main industries- Fi-Lo-Mi. (Fishing, Logging, and Mining). Her older husband, like my Dad, loved to talk and regaled us with stories of everything from 'cuttin' trees' to local politics.

But besides the intriguing lifestyle our neighbours lived, we had another reason for relishing the daily visit to Myrtle's. On her porch stood a huge chest freezer-the only one we ever saw. (We only had the little one in the top of our old Westinghouse refrigerator- which didn't hold much- and our basement root cellar.) We'd gaze with envy as Myrtle popped the massive lid. Popsicles, juice, and other frozen treats, huge cartons of ice cream and other delights. I had never seen so much food altogether in one place in my life!

But- in her cupboards-the best treats of all 'real' Freshie and an assortment of cake mixes. 'Freshie' was a powdered juice-type drink loaded with sugar and food dyes. It was usually sold in packets which you tore open, dumped into a pitcher and added water. And Myrtle's cakes always had thick gobs of icing! Contrary to mother's healthier molasses, spice, and matrimonial* cakes, Myrtle's cakes were light and 'melt in your mouth' fluffy. She made them in an assortment of flavors from chocolate to lemon. Sometimes the cakes were pink tinged or had brightly colored icings. We thought these a great treat even though the food dyes in them were probably not good for us. Ditto the colored liquids that passed for 'juice'

Yet, the 'Freshie'. That was pure delight. We didn't often get fruit juice (unless it was from the blackberries, lemons and plums we squeezed ourselves.) However, we were always offered 'Freshie' at Myrtles. Freshie however, came in an exciting array of colors and flavors-from hot pink to dark purple. Mom could not convince us that the homemade drinks were 'healthier'. I can remember many hours of labor over Mom's old glass lemon squeezer and marveled that Myrtle only had to open a package, dump a little bit of the powder into a pitcher of water and stir it up! I guess with all the farm work and food prep she had to do, Freshie and cake mixes made her life a little easier.

I can remember my brother and I debating as we walked:

'What flavor of Freshie will she have for us today?' We also wondered if she'd have a fresh-baked cake dripping with frosting. Or perhaps she'd open one of her huge and ever-present ice cream tubs?'

In addition to hauling water, cooking, cleaning, and laundering, Myrtle tended a huge garden and semi-wild fruit orchard (as did we). However, my Dad always sprayed our fruit trees and kept the tent caterpillars at bay. One infestation of tents could spoil a whole year's fruit crop. Thus, we could use the fruit to bake homemade pies and cobblers of every type- apple, plum, cherry, even pear. I guess that, for Myrtle, home baking from 'scratch' was too time consuming for her as would be the upkeep of the trees.

Her kids all seemed to have better clothes than we did. Her youngest daughter played her record player (a treasured toy amongst young girls then) when I was still dreaming of having one. The boys were always kept well-stocked with huntin' rifles and fishin' poles. I guess because Cougar, although nearly my Dad's age, was still actively working, he brought in much better money than my 'pensioned off' father did.

I don't remember Myrtle ever visiting out place. As far as I know, she, like many women of the time, did not drive. Nor did she go out much. Perhaps occasionally, she and Nick would hop into their old pre-Fifties Ford truck. It sat in an open garage near the road for as long as I can remember. In later years, it was pretty rusted-out, but still ran. I don't think they worried about anyone stealing it as it probably wasn't worth much. And times were different then. In the thirteen years I lived at Stratfords, I can't ever remember a police car cruising the area. Nor do I remember reports of any thefts. The world was a different place in the Fifties.

Myrtle had a rather ancient and colorful mother-her name was Granny Harte. 'Granny' (as we all called her), also drove an old Ford truck. Bright lemon yellow and Forties vintage. Story goes, she was speeding down Bell McKinnon one hot Summer day and was stopped by a local cop. She was racing along, considerably over the speed limit (which, by the way, was miles-per-hour in those days). I know the limit on the highway (now properly called the Trans-Canada Highway) was 60 mph. I don't know what the limit was on the side roads, but I know she was considerably over it. We had occasionally noticed a blur whizzing by our door on Somenos. It was Granny. To her disgust, the young cop gave her a ticket, not seeing her obvious age as an excuse. Story has it, she was ninety-three!

Mutt Smythe

Just up the road from Myrtle lived another scion of the Smythe family-Mutt Smythe. The dairy farmer whose creamery made a good 'prison' for my rambunctious little brother. I had totally forgotten that story until about ten years ago when Kurt and I went down to visit the old couple. I did phone him first, and, although he told me he was well up in his Eighties, he was sharp as a tack and remembered me immediately. He invited us to come for tea the next day.

We did and that's when he reminded me of the 'creamery' incident. It seems that when my brother was about eight or so, he went missing for a day. Dad looked all over our property and, by nightfall, both he and mom were pretty frantic. I don't know if he called the police or not. I don't think you called the cops in those days unless someone was dead or dying!

I guess he then went around to or phoned all the immediate neighbors. No sign of the kid. By midnight, Dad must have been a wreck. Then he received a strange phone call. Mutt, for some reason, had gone out to check the upper part of his property late that night. He heard suspicious cries and snuffles coming from his 'creamery'. A creamery in those days was sort of a wooden hut in which they kept milk and cream specially to keep it cold. It was sometimes cut into the cool earth of a hillside and/or filled with huge blocks of ice.

He unlocked the door and there found the kid. I doubt the little room had any electric light and may have contained the dreaded ice. It sounds like it was a pretty frigid and scared little guy that Mutt carried in his arms down to his house. His old wife got up and fed my little brother hot chocolate till Dad came to collect him. How he had ended up in a locked creamery, door and window shut and not able to get out, I don't know. However, I suspect he shinnied in the window and then, for some reason couldn't get back out. Perhaps he had tried to stand on a block of ice and kept slipping off. Or by the time he thought to use a block of ice, it had largely melted. Anyone else would have suffered from frostbite. My 'nine lives' brother, of course, was perfectly fine by the next day.

Just to the north of Old man McGonagal's place lived the Hortons. Although primarily a farmer, Mr. Horton was a local politician of sorts. His wife had been a nurse and they were both exceedingly bright people. Late in life, they had one equally bright son who excelled at the local schools. Many neighbourhood children, including me, were envious of that boy's excellent grades. As a child, I don't remember visiting their place a lot, but I remember that, whenever I did, Mrs. Horton would be baking in her kitchen. She was a lovely person and a real lady 'of the old school'. She'd always allow me to help her and I remember spending a few pleasant afternoons in her woodsy but serviceable kitchen baking cookies and other desserts.

Her son, of course, played ball with us when we were older. I remember him as a tall, lanky O.K.-looking kid and an exceptionally good pitcher. He later told me he pitched in a men's baseball league well into his sixties. However, there was no one in the neighborhood, regardless of stature, who could pitch and catch like my brother could! My active bro was an All Star in the Little League several years in a row.

The Reading Tree

Between the Horton's and McGonagall's cabin lay a hilly acreage, ill-tended and wild. The acreage was so huge that it spread clear over to the highway on the East side. And it produced the best apples I have ever tasted (except for the tree at my place right now, of course). We called it simply: Old Man Whitehead's Orchard. We kids spent many a Summer day picking the small and somewhat scabious green apples, eating a few, then filling our pockets to take home to mother for pie.

At night, and especially at Hallowe'en, the scraggly growths took on an eerie appearance. The never-pruned trees were ancient and mossy, the moss and blight crusts hanging down like ghostly tendrils. No one (well at least no one under the age of about fifteen) dared go near the place after dark, but most especially on Hallowe'en night. We were sure that all manner of ghoulies and spirits inhabited the trees. They were just lying in wait for unsuspecting children whom they could torture and terrify.

But the aging orchard had one feature we always looked forward to with relish, especially in the warm Summers. I called it: The Reading Tree. It was the giant of the lot and probably the oldest. Its leafy and spreading branches were dominated by one particularly large one which spread conveniently in a horizontal direction about five feet off the ground. A good shinnier could climb up and lie prone in less than a minute even with book in hand.

And, of course, that was the main purpose to which it was put-reading. I can remember hiking it the mile or so down the road, book in hand. I'd spend a pleasant afternoon, semi-reclined on my back in the welcoming splendor, enjoying such favorites as Heidi, Little Women, and Anne of Green Gables. Its leafy canopy was cool, moist and incredibly quiet, except for the occasional trill of a bird. I remember experiencing a sense of peace and contentment I've rarely (if ever) experienced since.

I vaguely remember meeting Old man Whitehead on one occasion. I don't know if my dad took us up to his big house on the hill, or if we kids ventured up there alone. I remember that he was quite hospitable to us and told us we could eat as many apples off the old orchard trees as we wanted. I guess you would have to categorize him as one of our 'rich neighbours':

Our Rich Neighbors

To my mind, we only had two others: (the Burns' of Captain Grenfell's Mansion-already mentioned- and the Golds). Although, when I was in Senior High, a well-to-do family moved into a large acreage across the highway. Everyone else, even the nearby Pickerings (who also lived on the Westholme side of the highway near the Golds) had to scramble for a living. The father of that family only occasionally seemed to have outside employment. The Pickerings' farmhouse was serviceable, but dilapidated' and I'm sure they were quite dependent on the chickens and cow's milk to feed their kids.

Not so, the Golds. To us, they were wealthy. The Golds were a lovely family and their daughter, Flora was close in age to me. She became my best friend. We met, crossing the highway, when we were about six and have been friends for over sixty years! They had a modern (for the times), large house on about forty acres complete with barn and riding ring. Most of the time they kept one or two riding horses.

However, the family was not pretentious. The kids did not grow up with a 'silver spoon' attitude. Those kids were made to work just as we were. Flora would often tell me that today it was her job to 'muck out the barn'. Both parents were 'Brits' and the kids picked up their expressions, if not their accents. The family were church goers and, for years, attended a prominent church in town. In later years, the dad dedicated an entire stained-glass window (or two?) to that elegant church.

The Ride on a Sultan

I could tell you a lot about Flora, her personality, habits, amusements and so on. Ditto her brother. But, suffice it to say, they were both decent, conscientious Christian kids with a good dose of the old values. Flora was a 'Denny Bum'. In other words, for her entire school career, she attended private school in Duncan. In those days, I believe it was called 'Queen Margaret's (Riding) Academy for Girls'. Later boys were added. For many years the school was overseen by an extremely elderly single lady named Miss Denny. Thus, many students bore the label 'Denny Bums'.

Of course, 'Denny' signified 'Miss Denny and 'bums' had an interesting origin. (If the rumor I had heard from Flora was true). In those days a school uniform consisted of a navy-blue jumper, white shirt, tie, knee stockings, and heavy oxford shoes. They were very costly. Thus, many of the parents would let the girls wear their old uniforms until they became very short-well above their knees. They were costly to replace, well-made and lasted for years. Therefore, after the hem had been let down as many times as possible, the senior girls often ended up with mini-skirts. I guess when they bent over, that part of their anatomy depicted in the nickname was pretty obvious.

Flora, for many years, had a large, golden-colored horse. He was a nice animal, a good riding steed but definitely required a firm hand on the reins. I was a non-rider. However, one day, after I had known Flora for a couple of years, she undertook to 'teach the kid from Stratfords how to ride'. Of course, she rode English saddle, not 'Western'. It was a relatively flat saddle with no pommel. Thus, if you 'lost your seat', there was nothing to hold onto and you simply fell. I had watched both her and her brother ride many times and it looked easy to me.

So, one day, she walked the horse (and me) out to that long gravel track called Richards Trail. Sultan was by now getting a little antsy and ready for his daily exercise. She held the huge beast by its reins and instructed me in climbing on. Which side to mount from, how to put your foot in the stirrup, etc. After some struggling, I was finally able to stride the animal, but remember feeling very uncomfortable with the height. I was still pretty small and short for my age.

Before, we actually took off, Flora first went into an explanation of the art of 'posting'. If the horse trotted, cantered, or galloped and you didn't wish to be tossed around like a sack of rice, you had to grip with your knees. Every time the animal's back rose up, you had to, too. This, I learned required considerable leg muscle strength. Muscle strength I either didn't have or had never developed! So, I guess I nodded agreeably and off we went.

The lesson was uneventful as long as the horse was walking. But as soon as she let him break into a trot—I Caramba! I was jolted about like a sack of peas on an old buckboard wagon. Every moment, I was in terror of losing my seat. I think she yelled at me to 'grip with my knees'! What knees? Within seconds (but it felt like hours) the horse started to gallop. We went racing down the rough dirt road, me screaming blue murder. It felt like my brains were being rattled out! Somehow, I either pulled on the reins or, on his own, Sultan slowed a bit. Suddenly, Flora appeared beside me and took them from me. Gently crying:

"Whoa, Sultan, whoa, there, boy"

 She got him calmed down to a trot. As soon as I could, I slid down from the dizzying height. I have rarely been so happy to have my feet placed back on terra firma!

Neighborhood Weirdos:

Old Man McGonagal (who blew himself up with dynamite)

Just a little bit South and across the road from Cougar Smythe's there lay a long and muddy trail into the forest. You could hardly call it a road yet, if you weren't too worried about the state your vehicle would be in, you could drive on it. That drive would take you to a rough clearing. On it stood a rather picturesque, if smallish, two-storey log cabin. It comprised an open main floor and a large upper loft. The cabin belonged to Old Man McGonagal, a frugal Scot and another of our 'neighborhood characters'.

The cabin and meager outbuildings had been constructed by the old man over several years from hand-hewn logs dragged up from the neighboring forest. Often, on the rare occasions when we kids came to visit, the old man would be standing, framed in the large doorway, waiting for us. We stood a little in awe of the old man; I don't know exactly why. Perhaps it was that, like Nestor Nelson, he was described to us as a hermit. And the concept of 'hermit', to us, held a spectre of mystery and danger we didn't wish to risk running afoul of.

However, I can remember on one occasion when we were about eight and nine, my father had been hired by the old man to do some work for him. Glory! We were going to be allowed to accompany my dad and poke around the huge, undeveloped forest property. Not so. Dad said he was going to be doing some blasting and we would have to stay in the house.

It turned out that McGonagal, who was from the East and knew very little about clearing forest land, had had to hire my father. Dad was, as I said earlier, a 'jack of all trades', and a master of most of them. He knew the art of blasting stumps with dynamite sticks learned, I suppose, in his mining days back in the Twenties. So-for the day, we were restricted to the rather large cabin and the company of old McGonagal.

Although a confirmed bachelor and not much of a talker, he treated us well. His cabin was made of split and peeled logs and gave off a 'woodsy' odor. It was delightfully friendly, cluttered and messy. After poking around the shelves and cupboards on the lower floor, we were allowed to climb the makeshift ladder to the loft. Or perhaps he just sent us up there to get us out of his hair. We discovered the delights of the upper loft.

The loft had a pointy ceiling and a small window with a forest view. It held his single bed over in the corner, some simple shelving loaded with 'treasures' and glory of glories- stack after stack of newspapers lying helter-skelter about the floor. We spent about an hour poring over those old 20's papers and I think many were from Toronto as well as Vancouver. We read while the Old man went out to help Dad and maybe learn about the art of blasting from him.

At some point my Dad had told us that Mr. McG had a nice chunk of 'bottom' land, marshy and excellent for farming. I'm not sure why he wanted to clear more, but surmised that he either wanted to put in a bigger garden or run animals, perhaps cattle or goats.

So-we spent an intriguing afternoon after being treated to a good dose of venison stew. At one point, he said he was sorry that he didn't have any candy for us. But, later, an idea came to him. He told us to climb up into the loft and look for a certain box. The box had been sent to him all the way from Ontario. It contained a treat that we had never seen before. Golden chunks of dried maple sugar. Yum! Yum! He gave each of us a generous piece and I guess that kept us quiet for another half hour or so.

Guess where, every year after that, we chose to go to 'trick or treat'? Even though the neighborhood children were 'too chicken' to hike the daunting forest track and face up to the Old Man, we weren't. Most years, we were duly rewarded with the maple treat.

Unfortunately, the story of Old Man McGonagall had a sad ending. When my brother and I were in high school, my father received bad news. I guess the Old man at some point had decided that he knew enough about blasting and had no further need to hire my father. The news filtered up from the neighbours South. The Horton boy, then a young teen, had been ranging the forest one afternoon. He came upon the old man lying next to a huge, blackened stump. He was dead. He had blown his leg off and bled to death. That poor teenager was the one to discover him.

He told me, years later, that it was a horrible shock and he had nightmares for a long time afterwards. I spoke with an old blaster and he told me that the biggest mistake the men made when blasting with sticks was that they didn't know how much to use. He said that, in some cases, even for a large stump, one half stick was enough. I guess the old man had used too much, with tragic results.

The experienced blaster also told me it was important to know when not to blast. Witness my friends up-island who own an old farmhouse with cracked living room windows. They found out, by crawling under that the old house, that it doesn't even have a proper foundation. It sits basically on bare dirt and the remains of a huge old stump that was never properly blasted and removed. Over time, the stump started to regrow and send out tendrils. It was this growth that was somehow lifting the non-existent foundation, cracking walls and windows.

My friends' husband called in a blaster. He said 'absolutely not'-too dangerous. So-Blake, crawled under the house and removed as much of the old stump as he could by sawing it out and hauling away the chunks. 'Discretion is the better part of valor,' he had decided. Thirty years later, the couple, now nearing eighty, are still living in the old farmhouse.

Had McGonagal called in a good blaster or again had my dad do the work for him, his tragic accident may have never occurred.

I already mentioned the 'old witch' who lived just across the Stratfords Crossing tracks. I don't know if you could actually characterize her as 'weird', but she was sure scary come October 31st!

Nestor* Nelson

Most people have in the back of their minds the image of one particular childhood personality who stood apart from all the rest. Deceptively simple, yet somehow aloof and surrounded by mystery-in short, the neighborhood oddball. Ours took the form of a man, tall, silent and muscular, of indeterminate age. No one knew his real first name or where he came from. In the neighborhood, he was known by both kids and adults alike as Nestor Nelson.

Nestor was a hermit. About a mile down the road from our place stood his tidy homestead, neatly fenced with hand split rails. In the Spring and early summer, when riding by on our bikes or the school bus, we'd spot him-stripped to the waist. He'd be hand-spading his immense garden or splitting and stacking stove wood in neat piles against the side of the house. This was so it would 'season' by Winter as 'green' wood emitted a nasty smoke and didn't burn as well.

At night and throughout the Winter, his curtains were always drawn. Not a single ray of light escaped to show the way for prying eyes. Many people passed his little whitewashed shack, staring into his yard. But I never heard him volunteer a pleasant word to man or child.

In the Winter he'd remain secluded for weeks at a time-then, one day we'd spy him, knapsack on his strong back, cycling into town for his meager supply of staples. Or else he'd pass us on one of his innumerable walks, hips swaying and arms churning like an Olympic champion. However, we never got a chance to speak because he was always headed straight across the road and into the forest. Once, when Gary and I were laboring up an almost vertical mountain trail, Nelson charged past us, puffing like an engine, but never once slackening his pace. The big kids said that he hiked to the top of Mount Prevost and back through dense bush every morning before breakfast. We were skeptical of that story, because the distance represented a good day-long hike for even the hardiest among us.

Once we heard that the Nestor's brother had been a famous boxer; this, in itself, had been enough to fill our childish minds with awe. I remember how my brother's mouth hung open the next time Nelson passed us on the road. If it hadn't been for the inborn fear of the unknown we all share, we might have asked him for his brother's autograph. Perhaps his brother's prowess in the ring provided an explanation for this weird fellow's athletic ability. However, I can remember wondering why his brother never seemed to come to visit him.

Some said he and his brother had fought over a woman and had a falling out. Another rumor circulated that he had once killed a man in the United States and fled to Canada to escape his fate. And yet, it was because of a woman that we came to know him better. We had more contact with him than any other children in the neighborhood did.

My mother was an outgoing person. 'Flamboyant' and 'a bit eccentric' was the way some described her. To her, good friends were all-important She possessed a few persistent qualities which eventually won over the old nestor to some kind of a tolerant acquaintance. Though small and plump like a banty hen, she was the nerviest person I ever knew. She never took 'no' for an answer.

When we were very young, and before my mother's illness prevented, she took us for daily walks down our narrow, picturesque country road. Most often we'd stop in at Myrtles for tea, or visit the farmer's wife. It was there, one fateful day, she learned that a real, live hermit existed under her very nose just a few hundred yards up the road. So-she took it upon herself to investigate. She resolved to try to change Nelson into a model of civilized culture as she felt she had done with all her other friends. (However, not so my ever-resistant pater!) Little did she know that most people accepted her meddling ministrations with a large grain of salt.

So, one Summer, when I was about eight, her plot began. Her tactics ran thusly: Step 1 was the nodding and smiling stage. For about a month she did every time we walked by Mr. Nelson's. Soon she began calling cheery greetings over the low fence. She was sometimes rewarded with an unintelligible grunt in reply.

Step 2 of her tactics required gaining access to the front yard. It was effectively barred by a massive wooden gate. Hence, one afternoon, she called to the hermit over the fence and asked to use his bathroom. Now what man, no matter how reclusive, could be so ungallant as to refuse a lady's so distressful plea? The gate was soon opened and mother was able to use his little outhouse beside the shed.

Step 3: When Fall came, Mother took an empty cardboard box on one of her solo sojourns. To our surprise, she returned with a gift of a half-box of his homegrown apples. Luckily, we children were still too young to be embarrassed by all this; we were only filled with a sense of awe at being the only kids in the area who had visited The Hermit.

Step 4: Now that she was on speaking terms with him, it didn't take long for her to gain access to his house. One day, when averting her nose from the bachelor dust, she spied a collection of musty symphonic records near a neglected-looking phonograph. Here was the expedient she had been looking for. She and the nestor struck up quite a conversation about music that day. We were invited to stay for a glass of goat's milk and homemade bannock bread. It was arranged for us to return the next week so that Mom could share with him this unusual love of classical music.

My brother and I were in a high pitch of excitement when the appointed day arrived. Imagine, at last, our golden chance to snoop at our leisure through all the intriguing bachelor possessions we imagined lay within the tiny house. We had had a quick glimpse of a bookshelf one day when the door was open and wondered what treasures it contained. Perhaps, in these, we'd find a key to the man's odd character.

Finally, the appointed afternoon arrived. It found our little trio standing impatiently on the homemade door stoop. Mother knocked loudly. When, after a time, no reply was heard, she boldly thrust open the weathered door. Imagine our consternation to discover old Nelson sitting stark naked in a small washtub. He was in the middle of the kitchen floor taking his weekly bath! However, no social blunder ever phased my indomitable mother. With a polite, 'Excuse me, Mr. Nelson', she discreetly closed the door halfway. She called sweetly through the opening that she would return again another day. And she did.

CHAPTER VIII   OUR RELATIVES

I guess no matter how perfect you think your family life is or how idyllic your childhood, we all have some difficult relatives we have to deal with. Mine were a mixture of sane and questionable...

Dad's:

My father had five brothers and sisters, my mother two. Both would be considered 'large' families today. Nada compared to previous generations. My father's dad, Grandfather Carruthers, came from a family of fourteen children, his father (back in Scotland in the 1800's) a family of twenty! I don't know how many siblings my maternal grandmother had, but my Mom always bragged that her granny had had perfect twins at the age of fifty-two! I know that for a fact because my grandmother was one of them.

In toto, I had four uncles. Three of them were nice guys. The eldest, was a kindly, gentle prairie farmer I tell you more about him later. Uncle Eb, my brother's youngest brother was also a somewhat quiet, but pleasant chap. (He had to be to stomach wicked Aunt Elvira all those years!) His third brother was 'questionable'.

Uncle Gunther, The Pervert

This uncle was not very savory. He was tall, loud and possessed suspiciously 'beady' eyes of a watery grey hue. We kids mistrusted him on sight. We didn't see him often, but were subjected to 'duty' visits every year or two.

He lived a rather solitary life, on a houseboat in the middle of a harbor somewhere further south of us. He was a fisherman and a pretty good one, so the family said. I remember on one occasion driving some distance with Dad to visit his bro.

The little house, made of rough-hewn lumber was actually more of a shack. It was messy, in fact, downright dirty. Although he had had a wife long ago and four children, he lived a bachelor life. Rumor had it that, for some reason, probably 'the drink', he was unable to care for his kids. That lot fell to my Aunt Letitia in Vancouver. She did a creditable job of it, too.

We kids were enthralled with the houseboat, but I remember being leery of 'falling in the drink.' Dad helped me navigate the narrow board that served as entrance to his 'house.' My uncle invited us to stay for supper and cooked a 'bachelor's meal' of meat and potatoes. I can't remember if there were any vegetables. My brother and I held back, thinking, 'if he can cook a good meal from scratch, he must have prepared a really good dessert.' I remember we purposely ate lightly so we could have a big portion of the pie or cake we were sure he would serve. We waited and waited. Everyone had finished eating, the plates had been cleared and, no dessert. My Dad acted as if he was preparing to leave. I guess we kids had tears in our eyes because Dad asked us if something was wrong. One of us blurted:

'We didn't eat very much because we were saving up for dessert!'

The Unc, somewhat taken aback, produced a box of somewhat stale chocolates. Left over from Christmas a month or more before, I imagine. We ate them anyway.

Uncle G. was also a bit of a perv. (Or is that like being a 'little bit' pregnant?) Are there degrees of perversion or is any unwanted act indicative of 'pervert' status? I dunno. All I know is that the guy almost made my flesh crawl.

As far as I know, back in the Fifties, the word 'pedophile' had not yet been coined. But as stats show today, the likelihood is that a child will be molested by a near relative rather than a stranger.

It was when The Unc was visiting our farmhouse at Stratfords that the incident happened. I think he had just come in, picked my brother up and flung him about, making rude noises and insulting comments (which I suspect my brother also hated). I think he also made a rude comment to me about my weight. He then proceeded to give me a big, fat wet slobbery kiss and, horror of horrors, stuck his tongue in my mouth!

I was both flabbergasted and horrified. But, being a feisty little kid of about ten and having infinite faith in the wisdom of my elderly father, I went running right to him:

'Dad, Uncle Gunther kissed me and-and-he stuck his tongue down my throat!' (I think I was probably sobbing by this time.)

My elderly father, never phased by any calamity, thought for a minute, then leaned over and whispered in my ear:

'You go tell him that if he ever tries to do that to you again, you'll bite his tongue off'.

Totally trusting in my father's judgment, I ran back to uncle G. and in a loud, bossy voice, proclaimed just that:

'Uncle Gunther, my Daddy says if you ever stick your tongue down my throat again, I'm to bite it off!'

As far as I recall, Uncle G. just blinked. However, a few minutes later we kids had our radar out. The Unc had come in and was speaking with my Dad in the living room. Or rather, Dad was speaking with him. My father, although a bit shorter, than the Unc's six foot two, had Uncle G. by the shirt front. His face was almost up against his nose. He threatened words to the effect that:

'If you ever so much as touch my little girl again, not only will you never see me or any of my family, but I'll break every bone in your body.'

That did it. I think the Unc almost burst into tears and cried that he would never touch me again. He never did.

Too bad, today, we don't have a little more of the 'frontier justice' that worked to protect kids, especially girls, from those power-hungry (or just plain horny'?) males who would prey upon them.

In contrast-

My Wonderful Old Aunts

I had three nice and, to a kid's mind, elderly aunties and one nasty one. I have already told you about the vicious aunt and the pulp mill fart. She wasn't a 'real' aunt anyway, but an aunt by marriage. My Uncle Eb's wife. I think she was a devout Jehovah's Witness or Seventh Day Adventist and, probably for that reason, appeared stern and critical. I won't depress you by telling you very much about her. Except to tell you that she was tall, willowy and slim. Had a long beak for a nose and coarse, kinky black hair unattractively shot with grey. Looked a lot like the green-faced witch in The Wizard of Oz who dissolved when Dorothy inadvertently threw the water on her. There were times I wished I could have helped my nasty old Aunt Elvira meet the same fate!

However, my other three aunts were lovely. Very supportive, especially after my mother died. Two, my Aunties Vi and Lottie (Leticia), were my Dad's sisters. The other, my Aunt Edith, my mother's. Aunt Edith, unfortunately, was severely mentally ill. Of course, we kids didn't figure that out till we were well into adulthood. In those days, anyone who was mentally disturbed was usually referred to as 'eccentric'. However, her untreated (or under treated) mental illness caused serious consequences for her family as you will see later. However, she, like my other aunts, to the best of her ability was very supportive of me. Especially so after the premature death of my mother in 1964.

Auntie Vi

Hair, hair, everywhere! That was my Auntie Vi. Used to wear garter stockings like my mom. Only somewhat opaque. She affected the milky beige, unattractively thick kind. Only problem-she never shaved her legs. That long, black leg hair looked pretty gross mashed under those skin-tight nylons. Ugh! It gave the long black strings of hair under her stockings an even uglier hue than if her legs had just been left bare.

The facial hair was equally thick and noticeable. She probably would have had a full man-size beard if left alone. However, she battled her facial hair by shaving. We usually made a quick check to see the status of her most recent shave before subjecting ourselves to the mandatory 'Auntie Kiss'. If the coast was clear, we'd allow her to kiss us wherever. If she was looking decidedly stubbly, we'd try to move so as only to receive a glancing blow. Not only did the stubble feel eerily prickly to a little kid, it sometimes left a red mark on our faces! We all, in secret, sympathized with her condition. Except for my little brother; he didn't sympathize with anything! I can even remember my mother and I speaking about it

Aunt Vi was short in stature and shaped exactly like a barrel. Looked a lot like the chubby fairy Godmother in the old (1930's) Walt Disney version of Cinderella. Just as jolly and feisty, too. In Vancouver she almost single-handedly ran a 'rooming house', raised two kids and semi-supported her husband, so we were told. She also helped my crippled mother with the two of us as much as she could.

She was very creative; played the piano well. She wrote over one hundred songs; even set them to music. I don't know if she ever published any of them, though. As a little kid I, of course, never heard them. However, much later, probably in my thirties and after her death, my cousin showed me copies and I read them. They were very good. Not as syrupy as I had expected. Quite acceptable for the time although they'd probably bring finger-gagging expressions of nausea today.

I think my loving auntie was also a frustrated singer and musician. She spent years scrubbing floors in that large house so that my rather tall and tomboyish cousin, Geri, could study voice, piano and tap dance. I don't think my cousin, although slim and attractive enough, was much interested in being on the stage. To my aunt's eventual chagrin, she became an auto mechanic and later an army sergeant. I had remembered my overworked and exhausted aunt, in her late forties or even early fifties sitting up late nights. She'd be sewing a fancy party dress or some kind of lavish, if makeshift, costume for my cousin to wear. The young girl sang in events such as the Kitsilano Showboat (Vancouver.) I don't know whether she performed willingly or not!

Later, I was amused to see her marching in the Scottish pipe band playing the bag pipes and wearing definitely masculine-looking regalia. The fuzzy sporran and extra-thick wool socks, turned down roughly below decidedly hairy knees. She at one time showed me, giggling, that she only shaved the part that showed above her socks. I guess she had inherited her mother's tendency to being hirsute. Eventually, Geri married a man twenty years her senior and joined him in running a night-time security business. I'm not sure if she wore a gun on her hip, but if she did, I would not have been surprised!

We heard that, after Uncle J passed on, Auntie Vi remarried. She was well into her sixties by this time and marrying a well-to-do oldster of eighty. To prepare for the wedding, she spent over a thousand dollars for electrolysis treatments, a small fortune in those days. She went on a binge diet and lost about forty pounds. I still have a copy of her wedding photo, in color by then, wearing a rather tight-fitting short dress and a little pillbox hat with short net veil. She was, obviously, stuffed into a girdle and looked like a fat sausage in lace. The forty pounds helped, but she had needed to lose more like sixty or seventy! So, if I've had to battle the pounds over the years, I guess I inherited the familial tendency.

My Aunt Lottie was similarly rotund but not downright obese. My Auntie E (on Mother's side) had a real problem I think related to her obvious bouts of depression. Plus the fact that in those days 'mothers' didn't exercise. If they weren't squatting to milk cows and hauling buckets of water on the farm, they ran to fat. There was no such thing as women jogging or working out in gyms as we do today. I'll bet neither Vi nor Leticia had been fat when working the farm back in Manitoba. As a matter of fact, I have pictures of them both as young girls and they looked slim. However, a few years in Vancouver changed that. And for 'older' mothers in the Forties, Weight Watchers and Curves were not options. Women didn't 'work out'; it would have been seen as 'unladylike'. I think the word has gone out of our vocabulary, now. In the Bad ol' Days, it was considered that the women got enough exercise hauling babies around and doing the laundry. Unfortunately, nobody considered what they put into their mouths, either.

One of the reasons women didn't exercise was they never wore pants. And many wore high heels. I never recall any of my aunts wearing pants, or 'slacks' as they were called then. They always wore dresses. Slacks would have meant they were 'coarse' or 'unrefined'. Thanks, in part to the Feminists (of which, I confess, I was one), that attitude changed.

I was one of the first female teachers, if not THE first, in Victoria to wear a pant suit. It was early Seventies. I blush to admit that I did 'run it through' the principal in his office before deigning to be so bold. I didn't exactly ask him if I could wear my conservatively cut outfit. But I told him ahead of time that I intended to do so. I assured him that it was a soft-green blazer-slacks combo, the jacket matching the slacks. I wore a white, long-sleeved buttoned blouse under it.

When he asked me why-I replied that wearing dresses and stockings were not practical for a P.E. teacher. He, luckily, had no objection. I guess the Union, in those days still called the B.C.T.F. (B.C. Teachers' Federation), had alerted school administrators that a change was coming. I may have even specified that I was sick of putting my knee through my stockings and they were costing me a fortune. Also, after showering and racing to class with wet legs, it was Hell to try and wrestle into tight hose.

The Sixties principals would have had a fit of apoplexy had they seen future hordes of female P.E. teachers. I've seen them teaching an academic class wearing short shorts and sweat tops either prior to or just after an active P.E. class. A sprightly but not-too-young teacher at an elementary school I taught at (mid-Eighties) looked exactly like a 'biker chick'. She'd show up on her motorcycle wearing black leathers, or at least the jacket. All day she wore heavy jeans and biker boots. She taught Kindergarten. How the times-and the dress code -has changed!

It was not only the lack of heavy exercise that did my aunts in. Desserts were big in our family. It made the women big, too. I remember that once, on a visit to Vancouver, after my mother had died, my Aunt Vi confided to me that she had diabetes. She then proceeded to haul a huge, overly-sweet, home-baked pie out of the fridge and slather it with ice cream. She served the huge portion to her new' and elderly husband taking an only slightly smaller one for herself. With the admonition:

'Oh, I know I'm not really supposed to have this, but one little slice won't hurt.'`

Oh, yeaaahhh!

Mom's Relatives:

Uncle Milton

My Uncle Milt (on my mother's side) was a lovely guy, according to Mom. He was brilliant, well-educated and probably, sadly, a drug addict. Did I later infer that or had I heard rumors growing up as a child? Brilliant Uncle Milt wrote mother an extraordinary letter in 1952 from jail. Why he was there, I have no idea.

Luckily, Mom retained the copy as it is the only memento (other than a photo or two) that I have of my tortured Uncle Milton. I still have it, and enjoy reading it again from time to time. Its almost poetic, studious language is penned in a well-practiced hand. It is sadly, stamped Provincial Gaol, Province of Alberta. Another stamp on it states: 'prisoners allowed no parcels except clothing and reading matter.' I include a copy of the original below: (The top of the letter has been cropped to maintain privacy.)

Provincial Gaol Province of Alberta Aug 6 1952   My Dear M______

Immediately recognizing the inimitable inscriptions of your letter, it was opened and perused with considerable trepidations. But, however, it was not as censorious as I anticipated considering that I labour under such a feeling of defeatism at the moment. It is like a nightmare-this sense of frustration that keeps on returning to torment me with insidious, implacable regularity "like a deep-toned grief that stirs in me somehow by some inexplicable sense of my soul's strangeness and its part in the dark march of human destiny."*

However, it was indeed pleasant to receive a letter from somebody since it is the first personal letter that I have received since I left Squamish, B.C. for the Peace River Country in 1948. Since then I have been wading bravely through the mud, but without the courage (or is it patience, forbearance and humility) necessary to scale the heights. And, as a consequence, I have acquired nothing economically or socially-no money and no friends.

So before the arrival of your letter I felt as though I had been deserted by God, Man, and the Devil. Also, it is not improbable that, when I am released on Oct 4th, 52, that I shall find the country in which I hoped to accomplish so much and yet have done so little, will also have been taken away from me by the D.P.'s * the only country in history that stands to be conquered without a shot being fired. I am happy to note the descriptions of your children (names omitted) and you can tell them that as soon as possible, I shall try to see them and then shall buy them the biggest lollypop and ice cream cone available.

You can rest assured that this time I am going to make a determined effort to change my pattern of determinate behaviour. "in all acts of apparent choice, we are merely the mechanical expression of our heredity and part

environment." (I am not sure the source of this quote, or perhaps my uncle made this up himself.) Yours for the better, Milton (written on side of page)
   This letter's language shows my uncle was obviously well-read:

the inimitable inscription of your letter, it was opened & perused with considerable trepidation — but, however, it was not as censorious as I anticipated considering that I do look under such a feeling of dejection at the moment. It is like a nightmare — this sense of frustration that keeps returning to torment me with inexorable implacable regularity. "Like a deep-troubled gulf that stares me somehow by some inexplicable sort a sense of my soul's strangeness and its part in the dark march of human destiny."

However, it was indeed pleasant to receive a letter from somebody, since it is the first personal letter that I have received since I left Squamish, B.C. for the Peace River Country in 1948. Since then I have been wading slowly through the mud, but without the courage (or is it patience, forbearance & humility) necessary to scale the heights. And, as a consequence, I have acquired

In it, my, obviously loving, uncle addresses my mother as 'My Dear' and talks of his joy in hearing of the birth of his niece and nephews. He promises to come visit us in Vancouver as soon as he can and buy us each an enormous lollipop. He, tragically, it was rumored, died of an overdose less than a year later. Perhaps in that same prison. I suspect that he, too, bore the family scourge of mental illness. I have no idea how old he was at the time, but since he was the middle child of three (my mother being the youngest) and, my mother having been born in 1908, I assume he was only in his late forties.

Aunt Edith subsequently spent a lot of time in Crease Clinic, a part of Essondale Institution, I believe. It is shocking how inheritable mental illness is. As far as I know, the only ones in my immediate family who did not suffer mental illnesses were my father, me, and a few cousins. ADHD has now proven to be highly inheritable on my father's side; major illnesses such as Bipolar disorder and schizophrenia, on my mother's.

Shockingly, my lovely aunt weighed over three hundred pounds when I last met her. She was semi-reclined in an enormous easy chair. Her huge, flabby abdomen moved in an involuntary rolling motion as she sat. Sort of like the waves of the ocean. Bizarre. A result of bad psyche meds or depression, or both?

Aunt E, the eldest, was also well-educated, gentle and kindly. She was a brilliant woman. Had trained at the Alberta Conservatory as a concert pianist. She used to play for us occasionally in the boarding house when we visited her and her plumber husband in Vancouver. She was very well-spoken and well-bred. I always liked her. She sent me small, but thoughtful presents every Christmas. We were shocked that she'd married a plumber who spoke in a high-pitched voice as if he were a bit simple. Or lacked testosterone, or something. He was a nice man, though.

She had a severely crippled daughter and an O.K. son. Babs looked like a dark, shriveled-up little monkey. 'Spastic' they called it in those days. My Dad insisted there had been nothing wrong with her when she was born. He insisted it was my aunt's neglect, resulting in rickets and other severe problems that ruined Babs. My uncle would not let his daughter be institutionalized. My aunt saw his refusal as a punishment, I was told. I think the onerous care of the seriously handicapped child was too much for my aunt. Her house was a pig-sty. Absolutely filthy compared to the clean and well-kept (if old) farmhouse we had back on The Island.

Like my mom, she had a weight problem. It blossomed into severe obesity by the time she was in her fifties. Her problem was so out-of-control that I guestimate, the last time I saw her in the Seventies, she weighed three hundred pounds. And she wasn`t much taller than my five-foot-three stature. The causes of her overweight were probably many and complex-her obvious mental illness, her difficult marriage and home situation and the obvious stresses of raising a severely handicapped child whom I shall call:

Poor, Tortured Babsie

I almost hate to tell you the story of my troubled aunt's unfortunate child. It is a sad one. But a story which was all too common in the days before the Ministry of Children and Families and social workers. Well, there may have been a few social workers in the Vancouver area in the early Forties, but, seemingly, they didn't help Babsie.

My dear Aunt Edna was severely mentally ill. This, of course, didn't become evident to us kids till years later. In those days mental illness was never talked about. Sufferers were termed 'eccentric', or maybe 'different'. But the terms Schizophrenia, Bipolar Disorder, Depression and the like were never used. They may not have been invented yet. It turned out later on that mental illness was rife on my mother's side of the family.

When I first met my aunt, we were still living in Vancouver and I was very young. I don't remember much about her at that time. I have vague memories of visiting in a huge, dark, multi-storied house. It seemed about three times the size of ours. And ours was not small. It turned out that it was a large house my aunt and her mother (my mother's mother whom I never met) had purchased. Years previously, they had used it as a rooming house. I guess that was a few years after my grandfather was killed in the Winnipeg General Strike of 1919.

I suspect that my grandmother had 'coping problems' as well. Rumor had it that my grandfather had left his family a small fortune-a large, palatial house in Winnipeg and about thirty thousand dollars in cash. Supposedly, my grandmother gave away a goodly portion of it to the Catholic Church even though she had three small children to raise. However, she must have retained enough of the wealth to subsequently move out to Vancouver with her daughter and buy the rooming house.

At some point, 'later in life', my aunt married a plumber and had two children. The boy, subsequently, seemed to be all right; the poor girl was a sad case. My Uncle Jack, the plumber was a unique man. He was relatively short and chubby, yet had the build of a hard worker. He also had the highest pitched 'giggly' voice I have ever heard on a man. At first I thought that he was a bit 'simple'. Maybe so, but I remember that he was always friendly and kind to us kids. How much he loved kids was soon evident to us. It was reflected in the way he treated his severely disabled daughter.

It was also reflected in the way he treated me. While we lived at Stratfords we made several forays over to Van-perhaps twice a year. We were usually in the company of my mother. However, a trip we made when I was twelve or thirteen also included my dad. I guess, by then, my mother was getting so infirm that she couldn't travel alone. It was getting close to Christmas time or just after. I remember that, for years, I had wished to have a doll. The only soft toy I can ever remember having was a little lamb only about six inches long. For years I had longed for a real, chubby 'baby doll' with blonde, 'saran hair*'.

Somehow, one day when we were visiting at my aunt's, my dad and uncle got talking. My father, asked him where he could finally get a nice doll for me in

Vancouver. Uncle Jack told him, and offered to share the cost as a Christmas present. How joyful I was when they both took me on the street car to pick out the coveted gift. And I found the perfect one. A plump, smiling rubbery baby in a fluffy pink dress with bonnet and blue satin bows. She had combable hair. What joy! And even more exciting, she lay in her own sateen-lined bed in a sturdy cardboard box with a cellophane window. Thus, I could leave her, well-protected (especially from my brother!) in her box on my shelf and still see her face.

I remember gleefully showing her to all the members of my pop Bottle Club and then putting her away. I had named her Betsy. Perhaps once or twice over the next year or so I took her out to comb her hair. I never did get or make any other dresses for her. I guess she had been so late in coming that I soon 'outgrew' her. However, I treasured that doll and remember enjoying seeing her perched on the shelf in my bedroom for several years. She was, of course, particularly special because she was the only gift I had ever received from my uncle.

However, my wonderful aunt usually sent us something for Christmas every year. The long-awaited box from Aunt E would be opened with rapt anticipation. One year, a small 'sailor' doll (only about five inches high) complete with little navy blue suit and hat. The suit was authentically trimmed and the matching pillbox hat even had a black ribbon hanging down. Another year a uniquely hand-knitted and 'rolled' pin cushion. The last year an off-white ceramic plate with gold leaf trim and colorful leaves painted on it. I still have the latter two items and treasure them. The ceramic plate has been the 'small junk collector' above my fridge for nearly fifty years! I don't know what ever happened to the little sailor, but a lot of precious things went missing from the old farmhouse after my stepmother hove in sight.

About five years after I left college, my father moved into W.S.'s house in town. I went there to look for my stuff, especially the doll. The elderly couple had by then taken in W.S.'s somewhat mentally challenged son and his illegitimate baby daughter.

Seems when Boris had been in Vancouver in his thirties, he had hooked up with an older prostitute. She had become pregnant and agreed to come to the island with him and live with his mother and my father. NOT! I could have told her that that would never work out because my stepmother was far too controlling. Had my father, at the time, not been so elderly (eighties) and dependent, I think he would have split with her. Or never got hooked up with her in the first place! He later told my brother and I that he married her because he 'didn't want to be a burden to us kids' in his old age.

Callie, Boris' 'girlfriend', was obese and most unattractive (as was Boris) but she successfully delivered the child. Then to hear her tell it, the fur started to fly. My stepmother set up a number of 'rules' which she was to follow. Although Callie was not the brightest, she refused to knuckle under to W.S.'s tyranny. Instead, to everyone's shock, she left the baby in the crib when it was six months old and the household was out shopping. She went back to the mainland. The story I later heard was that this (also mentally challenged) older mother had left eleven other babes in various parts of the province for the Ministry to raise! According to W.S., she phoned once about six months later. I guess it was to see if the child was all right. Then they never heard from her again.

However, that child was only two years older than my son and was about seven or eight when I went back to W.S's house to claim my doll. Lily had been playing with it. To her credit, she had taken good care of it. The doll was still in its lovely box, although the box was definitely showing signs of wear. I don't know where I was living at the time, but probably had my young son in tow. I had no really good place to store the doll. So, soft-hearted old me, I told her she could play with it until I had a good place to keep it. I asked my stepmother to keep an eye on the doll and I'd take it back in a year or two. You guessed it, by then the doll, the box, and nearly every other precious piece of my mother's, had disappeared.

Like I said, the real tragedy was that it was particularly precious to me because it was the only gift I had ever received from my dear uncle. But in giving the gift his love for me was evident as it was for his own precious child. And his own child, Babsie, was so disabled that she could probably not have enjoyed playing with a doll. Although she became a severe burden, he refused to give her up. I don't know whether he did her a kindness or not. But, my nasty Aunt Elvira, the religious fanatic, said he refused to put Babs in a home in order to punish Aunt E for having such a severely disabled child. I think that idea was bunk.

But, according to my father, the child was born perfectly normal. My aunt was by then fortyish, but that didn't seem to account for the child's subsequent tragic disabilities. In fact, two or three years later, Aunt Edith produced a normal son. My father believed that the infant had starved. My severely depressed aunt was too incapacitated to get out of her bed to feed the baby regularly. Infant starvation or 'failure to thrive' as it is still euphemistically labelled is a tragedy. The brain damage that can result is horrific as evidenced by my cousin Barbara's severe disabilities. We later had a similar tragedy almost happen again in our family in the early 2000's which I will tell about in my next book.

When we first saw poor little Babs, we were horrified. She was about ten years old but looked about five or six. She was monkey-like in both appearance and stature. I was told that she was two years older than me, but she was several inches shorter and many pounds lighter. Pitifully thin and incontinent, she wore diapers. My aunt fed her baby food. I don't know if the doctor has ordered that for stomach problems or if it was my equally tortured aunt's idea. Perhaps to make her life easier? I don't know it that was appropriate or not. The poor child probably still didn't get enough calories.

She could not speak, but babbled a kind of moaning sound. She drooled constantly. She could walk, after a fashion, but her gait was uneven and slow. She couldn't run and had serious balance problems. I guess in those days there was no Ministry of Children and Families to rescue or assist this child. They lived tortured lives and often died prematurely and tragically.

I think that, so did my aunt. The guilt of what she, in her severely depressed state had done to her child, must have been huge. When last I saw her, it was in Vancouver in, perhaps, the early Seventies. Babsie was long dead. I had heard nothing about a funeral; there probably wasn't one.

All I can remember is that my aunt was sitting in a large easy chair in a different house in the Vancouver suburbs. It was a bungalow, much smaller than the big 'rooming house' they had owned. Perhaps my uncle, being elderly, wasn't doing so well at his carpentry business. I don't think that either my uncle or cousin were there. Perhaps out working as my aunt told me that my cousin (who also always appeared to be 'a bit simple') was assisting his dad in the business.

Aunt Edith now weighed over three hundred pounds-grossly obese. She never moved out of her chair the whole time I was there. She was probably in her late sixties by then. My aunt spoke to me in a friendly way and quite coherently, although she had, by now, developed several nervous tics. (Nasty consequences of the old Fifties psyche meds?) The most horrible was a kind of peristaltic action of her abdomen. The huge mounds of fat would roll and roil like ocean waves as she spoke. I have never seen anything like it before or since. Most disconcerting! I don't remember questioning her about it; one didn't in those days. I assume she died soon after although I heard nothing more of her or the rest of her family. Although my brother and I have tried, we have never been able to locate her son (my cousin) in Vancouver.

I can hardly write this next paragraph as the memory of it is so horrible. I will have to muster every iota of 'guts' I possess to tell you this. (As I will have to muster all my strength to tell you, in the next book, the tragic story of my grandchildren.) We kids mistreated her. We were cruel to the poor, suffering little thing. I send a prayer up to heaven that she will forgive us. I guess the only thing I can say in defense of small children's meanness is that we were confused and overwhelmed. We didn't know what to make of this tragic child. And we certainly didn't know how to care for her. We resented the 'burden' of having to look after the annoying creature. We wanted to run and play, not nursemaid a handicapped child. To us, she was so 'gross' that we didn't even want to have to touch her.

Little Babs was so severely brain damaged that we even had to 'shadow' her when she walked on our lawn. My dad had placed wooden two-by-fours around the edges to mark the start of a bordering path. There was a slight slope down. Although I think that the child could see, she would walk right over the wooden object, trip, fall, and we would have to pick her up and set her back on her feet. I don't remember us ever doing anything overtly mean to her-like hitting her or anything-but I do remember we sometimes just let her fall instead of helping her. Or let her stumble around.

And I don't remember our aunt or uncle ever 'having a talk with us' about little Babsie or how to handle her. My dad did try to tell us a few things when we were older. Perhaps if my aunt and uncle had had a talk with us it might have helped. I remember feeling very burdened with the care of Babs and not knowing how to do so. However, I realize now that the hour or two of 'respite' my aunt got when my brother and I were with Babsie was probably the only break she got from the misery of the care giving. Especially after she had her little boy, three or four years younger.

Later, my Dad (or one of his sisters) also told me that it had been suggested that my aunt put little Babsie in a care home. Supposedly, my uncle refused to let her go. Largely it was because, in his own way, he truly loved the child. I wonder if it really was to suitably 'punish' my tormented aunt for having unintentionally starved the child. I don't remember ever seeing my uncle share in the caregiving. All the work seemed to be left to my, obviously stressed, and obese aunt. Or it could simply be that, in those days, institutionalizing a child probably cost a lot of money. Money which the struggling blue collar family probably didn't have.

My dad said that, years ago, when still living in Vancouver, he occasionally went over to visit my mom's sister. She had just had the baby. The child was totally normal as far as he could see. As my aunt's mental condition deteriorated, however, so did the baby's. My dad said he'd often feel and clean up the poor infant when he found it lying for hours (if not days at a time) in its own feces and urine in its crib. I suspect my mother was not mentally stable enough most times to help, either. The 'rescue' role fell to my father.

Whether or not he ever contacted any 'authorities' to report the neglected child (or spoke with her, possibly also mentally-challenged) husband, I don't know. Tragically, mental illness was simply not recognized or talked about back in the forties-at least not in our neck of the woods. Their unfortunate progeny suffered without help because of their parents' inability to parent.

I now have a different perspective on euthanasia. Perhaps the poor, tortured child would have been better off if a loving parent had, (as we would have done with a horse or a cow that was this sick) 'put her down'. I sympathize tremendously with Robert Latimer, the, in my opinion, loving and courageous Saskatchewan father who put his beloved child out of her misery. I don't know if his daughter's condition caused her as much misery as poor Babsie suffered, but suspect that it did. I heard he did ten years for his 'crime'. And probably glad to do it, too because it saved his child from years of misery. It saved his child from the 'life sentence' of torment and pain that my poor little cousin endured for sixteen years. Of course, I don't know every detail of the case, but I don't think he should have done ten minutes of jail time! If I were in little Babsie's shoes or in the tragic circumstances of Mr. Latimer's child, I think I would have wanted my misery to end.

I doubt it was the truth that little Babsie died at the age of sixteen 'because she couldn't have her period' (as I was told). I suspect she perished (and probably horribly) from the years of ongoing neglect, possibly ongoing starvation, by these severely dysfunctional parents. Ironically, though, the younger brother, the few times that I saw him, seemed normal. As normal, I guess, as one can be when having to live with and assist with the caregiving of such a tragic child.

At the time though, I don't think my brother and I were in any way traumatized by our contact with Babsie or any of our other dysfunctional relatives, for that matter. We had little contact with Babs, Uncle Gunther, or Aunt E. and just took these incidents as a matter of course. 'Our relatives' were our relatives and that was all there was to that.....

It has only been in recent years I've heard from my youngest cousin that I, too, was neglected as an infant. Shortly after I was born, my Aunt Vi, my Dad's sister, who also lived in Vancouver, would go over to check on me. Sometimes my Dad probably reported to her that my mom was not doing well. My father, at the time although nearly sixty, was working long, hard hours for the city of Vancouver. I have a couple of tiny 'Brownie' camera photos showing my big, harried father, hard hat and work clothes still on, hanging a basket of diapers out on an outside clothes line. We infants were lying on a blanket on the grass while he worked. Where my mother was at the time I don't know. As far as I know my mom was never hospitalized for mental illness, although she probably should have been.

Vi, on the rare occasions that she could come over, would find the same thing as my father found when he visited my mother's sister—me wet, poopy and reeking, lying in my crib. It was said that I did not walk till I was over two. Perhaps my mother kept me in the crib because I was too much for her to handle if I was toddling around. I was also told that I broke my left collar bone when I was about two. Supposedly, I fell off my mother's obese belly when she fell asleep on the bed holding me. It must have been true because I have a heck of a lump on it to this day.

And I seem to have had, in childhood, dark memories of a hospital experience. I remember a long, dim hallway, me in a wheelchair. I am screaming. Probably more from the terror of being taken away from my parents by strangers (probably nurses), than from the pain of my injury. But you know how, over time, actual memories get comingled with stories we are told of 'what actually happened'. Perhaps this memory was a combination of both.

My Dad also told me what I believe to be the origins of my childhood obesity. He said that when he was away at work, my mother was feeding me inappropriate amounts of sweetened milk and sugar foods. Up to two tablespoons (not teaspoons- tablespoons!) of Karo corn syrup in each of my bottles. So-what, to this day, do you think my favorite comfort food is? Think ice cold sweetened milk/cream. You guessed it ice cream! Sweetened milk/cream, but frozen, n'est-ce-pas? Again, when I was about two, my father said he came home from work one day to find her stuffing chocolates into my mouth. Said she had this fantasy to have the 'chubbiest' (to her, healthiest-looking) baby on the block. We now know that obese infants are not healthy and fat does not mean 'well-tended'. I was so overweight during my elementary years that I started actively dieting at the age of seven in Grade Two!

But, somehow I survived and eventually lost most of my baby weight. I actually became quite healthy and fit for my years (although, of course, never slim). I later read in health books that once those fat cells are produced they are there for life. One can never completely get rid of them, only shrink them down. The little suckers are there beckoning at the chocolate box with their chubby fingers. Just begging their unwitting owners to overindulge and plump the cells up again!

I quit eating anything chocolate several years ago. I eat sugar-free Jello as my main dessert item now and it's very low in calories.

A friend once said: "All that aspartame is gonna kill ya!" My reply: "Well, at least I'll die slim!"

I avoid high-sugar fruits and eat nothing containing white sugar. I limit breads and baked goods, including pancakes. At my age, I also have to limit portion size-darn! I have also fairly recently discovered sugar-free ice cream-but even that I have to limit. Drinking plenty of plain water helps, too.

During my elementary years I thrived in spite of ongoing 'chubbiness'. In high school I got into sports in a minor way and learned more about 'healthy eating'. By Grade Twelve, I was an acceptable one hundred fifty pounds or so on a fairly muscular (if short) frame.

I excelled as a student and achieved exemplary grades. But, as I continued on into High School, I realized one important fact; I was poor. This idea had been introduced to me by two teachers standing in the hallway of Somenos School when I was in about Grade five. They made a comment something like:

`There go those unfortunate children. Their father is so elderly and their mother so ill. That family is so poor.'

Up until that time, I just thought that everybody pinched pennies the way we did. Their rather shocking revelation was a primary motivator for me to achieve good grades and try for university. Whether or not I would go on to follow my dream was, at this point, uncertain. However, for all of my years growing up at Stratfords I knew that, for me, there was but one road out of poverty. That road was Education……

……And here I include a subset of stories I wrote for the Somenos School 50th Reunion in 2002.

Stories Of Somenos School
Dedication

To all the past teachers of Somenos School: I now know how difficult their jobs were........

Statement: I am no historian. The following stories are merely the recollections of a young child and should not be taken as fact. To the best of my recollection, I attended Somenos School in the years 1952-58. I had very little contact with the school after that except for attending their 50th Reunion and one or two open houses and fun fairs.

I also wrote a letter to The Board in 2004 when they were thinking of closing the school. It was all about the benefits of a small, country school education (which certainly stood me in good stead in later years). I would like to think that my letter was influential in keeping the school open for another few years.

Unfortunately, I have not had the time to extensively research school records, museum documents and the like. I did, however, go through old copies of the Cowichan Leader newspapers for those years and gleaned some information regarding school events and teachers. Please forgive me for any inaccuracies in the dates, and facts, and substitute your own recollections if they are more accurate or honest than mine. Most names have been altered.

Tamara Scarlet*

My middle names are Tamara Scarlet. My first name had three syllables in it, so it was shortened. An interesting story about my middle names goes something like this. My mother was a brilliant, finishing- school educated lady (often considered a creative, if not an outright eccentric). She had a barren, seventeen-year marriage to my father who was, ironically, seventeen years older than she. Imagine her shock to find that at the age of forty, she was expecting me. Thus, I think she threw every name in her repertoire at me (and, later, did the same with my brother; he ended up with Gary Carruthers Ellis Duncan). I ended up with Skylark Tamara Scarlet. Perhaps my mother had just recently finished reading a copy of 'Gone with the Wind' when she named me.

Mr. David McKinley*, who had taught at the high school for some years, made a remark to me about ten years ago. He had once had occasion to register the class that I was in. He later taught my brother for a couple of years. He was somewhat taken aback when he saw my name(s) presented in the class register. It was over twenty years later that I remet him at a town meeting. He remembered me not by my first name, but by my rather unusual middle names!

*A pseudonym

I also have an unusual birthdate- four o'clock pm., December 31, (year, censored). Here is the story that my dad told about that:

My mother was an invalid and quite crippled up with Parkinson's Disease. For her difficult pregnancy, she was under the care of an obstetrician in Vancouver. She was scheduled for a Caesarian section in early January. Yup, you guessed it. Dad got the phone call late on December 30:

'Mr. McLeod, I've been invited out to a big party for New Years Eve and I'm not sure I'll be in any shape to do your wife's surgery on January 2. Could you bring her in tomorrow and I'll do it then?'

So-because of a 'tipsy' surgeon, I was born at four p.m. on the last day of the year. I quip that if I had been born one day later, I'd be a whole year younger!

School Day Mornings

Shuffle, slap! Shuffle slap! I will always remember the distinctive sound Dad's slippers made as they echoed down the short hallway when he came to wake us up. Seven a.m. precisely. It never wavered. We had to catch the bus on the road in front of our house at exactly eight am. They were typical Old Guy slippers- brown leather with white fur trim, the fur by now grungy from years of use. Flat leather soles. It was the hard leather that made the flapping sound.

Pip-puhlop! Pip-puhlop! The sounds of the slippers were always accompanied by the sounds and smells of the coffee brewing. The regular pip-pip-pip of the pot, pot, pot. It was the dark liquid hopping in the little glass globe on the top of the pot. And the aroma. To almost quote Dickens-oh, the aroma! NO coffee today can come close to the rich, aromatic smell of that old Nabob coffee.

I was usually awakened with a kiss and a hug and then Dad toddled off to the onerous task of waking my brother. When I was little, my mother was well enough to help me dress. Wrestling myself into the tight opaque stockings I wore under my 'shortie' kilt was the worst! As the years progressed and so did my mother's illness, I became the dresser.

In the hour or so I had before the school bus came, I not only had to dress myself, but also to assist my ailing mom. She was partly Alberta Cree-Grande Prairie area. She had long, straight black hair with few streaks of grey. Mine, (like my Dad's had been before he went bald), was shorter, brunette and curly. I remember the challenging task of brushing out and braiding Mom's long hair nearly every morning before I had to run to the bus. Thankfully, as I mentioned before, the bus stop was right in front of our house. My mother invariably wore the braids pinned up on top of her head, Scandinavian style. I also remember, not too fondly, wrestling with those numerous 'bobbie' pins every morning.

Then, I'd eat the breakfast my dad had usually prepared, grab my school bag and lunch, and head out the door. I often was at the stop in time to visit with the eight or so other children before the bus arrived. Then I'd board last so that I could yell at my brother who usually struggled to get out the door. Here he'd finally come, bare-chested, shirt half off and flying in the wind his running created. Dad would have shoved a piece of toast and jam in his mouth which he'd finish on the bus.

With a 'Hi, Ernie, let's go!' we'd be off on the lengthy four or five mile drive to school.

Clap Your Hands

Old school children's song circa 1900:

(Sung to us by my dad as we went off on our first forays to elementary school. It doesn't seem to be anywhere on the Internet. Did he write it?)

'Clap your hands, stamp your feet, twirling around in merry glee
Snap your fingers, tap the desk, happy children we.

Now we raise the right hand up, now the left you see
Waving them we gladly cry, happy children we!

Clap your hands, stamp your feet, twirling around in merry glee,
Snap your fingers, tap the desk, happy children we!'

For five stimulating years, I attended two schools at Somenos: Old Somenos in '52 and New Somenos from 1953-58. I achieved a good basic education, was considered one of the 'top' students, and had a lot of fun.

The hours were nine to three, five days per week. There were no ProD (Professional Development) Days or teacher prep time. The attitude then was that the teachers should be happy to have such short hours. Most workers, especially farmers, toiled much later than that and felt that teachers 'had it pretty easy' by comparison. I remember my Dad telling me when I was yet a little kid- 'With your gift of the gab, daughter, you should become a teacher. It's a reasonably paid job and you don't have to get your hands dirty'.

I think, years later, I went home to Stratfords and showed him the chalk dust all over both the front and back of my jacket. In the years before WHMIS (Workplace Safety Standards) organization which came in in the early 80's or so, there were quite a few 'workplace hazards'. The inhalation of chalk dust was found to cause a host of problems. Combined with the need to speak loudly to nearly forty children or yell in a gymnasium of up to sixty, accounted for many teachers having 'throat trouble'. Allergies, too. We later found out that the 'overhead pens' (inks that we used for the overhead projector) were mildly toxic. But, in those days, workplace hazards were not really thought about or discussed.

Attacks by students were not as rampant (or as fatal) as they are now, but DID occasionally happen. In 1967, while trying to ref a girls' softball practice, we were 'menaced' by a big native boy. He continually stole our ball, sassed me, and just generally disrupted our game. I was only nineteen and new to the school. I felt I had to prove myself as well as gain respect. I hit him across the face with a lightweight notebook. He stopped bugging us and disrupting our game. Ironically, he and I became 'buddies' after that as he knew I was a person who 'wouldn't put up with any crap'. Although, the incident happened after school hours, today I'd have probably been severely reprimanded. Or, in fact, I might have lost my teaching license.

In the early Nineties, I was a teacher new to the school district. In the school yard, just after school was out, I was threatened with attack by a group of troubled, mostly native, girls. To my chagrin, I had had to be rescued by a male teacher. For details, read my memoirs as this book is meant to cover only the years of my childhood. Its intent is to point out the mostly happy times and show the contrast between things as they were then and today.

According to my father, in the Fifties we had substantially shorter school hours than he had at the turn of the Twentieth Century. However, the farm boys didn't attend as long-only three or four months. They had to stay home in the late Summer to help with the harvest and in late Spring to plant.

Classes in the one-room farming community schoolhouse my dad attended comprised up to eighty students. Because of that, both the strap and the cane were liberally used. He said that he had had his left hand repeatedly 'caned' by the teacher when he had the audacity to use it to write. Until his death, his chicken scratchings with his crippled right hand (crippled from when the wagon ran over him at the age of eight) were nearly illegible. In addition, he, like me and most family members, was a 'natural leftie.' However, left-handedness was not permitted in the 'bad ol' days'. Luckily, by then, my south paw was not 'corrected'.

However, my father also iterated that his country school house (combined with the small, local church) was the hub of social activity for the district. School picnics, dances, concerts, and Spring teas, formed the basis for a pretty active community social life. As did our little three-room country school.

Ready for School

My younger brother and I were rural kids, many of whom were the sons and daughters of local loggers and fishermen. We lived a relatively active, healthy lifestyle (when measured by today's standards) on our little truck farm at Somenos. We were lucky to have our own, if small, local schools to attend.

I attended 'Old' Somenos (which is now the little community centre on Herd) road in 1952/53. The other we dubbed 'New' Somenos which was opened in 1953. Most of the town kids-sons and daughters of local merchants and professionals, attended Duncan Elementary. It was, to us, a huge ivory-covered brick castle.

The 'rich' kids attended several prestigious and costly "private schools in the Valley. The girls could attend Queen Margaret's School for Girls) in Duncan (at the bottom of the new hospital hill). The boys had a choice of a private school in Mill Bay or Shawnigan Lake Boys' school. Thank God, the controversial Prince of Wales Farm School at Fairbridge for uprooted British children had closed in '51 just before I started school.

At Queen Maggie's, as it was affectionately dubbed, my good friend Flora G. and others endured the ministrations of a supposedly ancient crone named Miss Denny. Rumor had it she was ninety and still teaching. Thus, the girls were mischievously labelled, 'Denny Bums'. How I was told the 'Denny Bum' moniker attached was as follows: Most school uniforms were expensive to buy. The girls grew rapidly but their parents did not want to replace the uniforms any more often than absolutely necessary. Many sported navy blue or dark green 'tunics' well above their knees. When they bent over….well, you can guess why they were nicknamed Denny 'bums'. (There might have been a less naughty explanation, but that's the one I was given!)

I, being more than a year older than my brother, attended the Old Somenos in '52 just before New Somenos was completed. However, because of when his birthday fell, he was placed two years behind me. I attended Somenos School until the end of grade five (which was as high as the three-room school could take us in those days). I did my Grade Six year at the brick, architect-designed pile of Duncan Elementary. Half of grade seven was at Cowichan High School until the 'junior high', Mt. Prevost School was completed.

Background to Stories of Somenos School:

Recently, I went to the Cowichan Valley Museum Archives at the train station in Duncan. I read through old Cowichan Leader* copies on microfiche and did some minor research. I gleaned a few interesting facts about the area in 1952 which you may find interesting:

-The Cowichan Leader (for many years our only newspaper) at that time cost seven cents per copy. It has now become the Cowichan Valley Citizen which has published several of my short stories.

-A three pound box of Quaker Oats cost thirty-four cents.

-Major world events: Korean War, King George VI dies, the Old age Pension was established,

-Dignitaries and officials were: U.S. President -Harry Truman; Prime Minister of Canada- Louis St. Laurent   B.C. Minister of Education-W.T. Straith

-Local dignitaries: Duncan Elementary School principal-Mr. Bill Allester; Reeve of North Cowichan-Mr. Beasley; Mayor of Duncan-J.C. Wragg; M.L.A.- A. Whisker

-Major local topics of interest: Chinchilla Breeders' Association; civil defense, sewing circles, raffles (no bingo allowed), 'stork' showers, lockjaw victims, milk controls, cougar bounties, deer and cougar control, St. Catherine's Indian Day School

Other events:

G.P. McMillan (lumbering magnate?) retires; March, '52-Third Annual Cowichan Music Festival; mobile library from Nanaimo to Mill Bay established; P.M. St. Laurent raises eyebrows at age seventy by saying that he WILL accept the newly established (twenty-nine dollar) Old Age Pension; (Eighty-year-olds and singles on Welfare got forty dollars per month), Feb. 14-Banner Headline: Don Morton, 'Good Citizen of the Year,' receives Prize Cow as Gift,

1952-53 Educational Background to Stories of Somenos School

-W Straith, Minister of Education, is called upon to resolve Board election deadlock between George Whitaker and J.H. Moore to fill School Trustee vacancy

-March '52- Mr. Allester, who tested me, speaks at Somenos PTA meeting. (I later attended high school with his niece.) Mr. A. announces a five and a half year plan for new schools- $22,000 to be spent initially building Somenos, then, Duncan townsite, Cowichan Lake Road, and Koksilah schools: 'the present Somenos School is most in need as water has to be carried from the janitor's home every day'.

-1951-52: School buses cost $27,500 and carried fifty-five students.

-The teacher salary budget was $265,000.

-Elementary basic annual salary: $1680; raised to $2000

-Secondary teachers' annual salary: $2100; raised to $2500.

(interesting to note that, at that time, most elementary teachers were female and most high school teachers male!)

-Janitor's pay increase: to $45.00 from $29 per month for cleaning a one-room school

June '52-trustees purchase fourteen acres situated one quarter mile from Herd Road on the Island Highway for $1500.00 for New Somenos School site

The firm of A and B Construction, Nanaimo, is hired to build Somenos School at a cost of $29,450.

January, 1953-Somenos School opens; the principal is B. Severson; teachers are Miss C. Joughin and Miss M. Lowe

And, a special note, the import of which will become clear:

-Duncan Elementary School pupils, under Mr. W. Allester's principalship raise $75.00 for Greek school children

*note: Since, unfortunately, many of the copies of the Leader from the early Fifties were missing or misfiled, I was not able to get accurate dates in all cases. For some dates, we will have to rely on elders' memories, including the school opening day. I could find no record of a school opening ceremony.

However, in honor of the school's 50th Reunion in June of 2003, I wrote stories of my earliest remembrances of the schools at Somenos. I took them to the Reunion and several former neighbours and teachers told me they read them. I later expanded them into the following:

I Shock the District Principal

In Late '51 or so, I was driven by my elderly and long-suffering father in our little 'puddle-jumper' Austin to the huge old brick pile of Duncan Elementary. This was so that I could be assessed by the District Principal, Mr. Allester. Too young to be terrified, or even worried, I bore all the optimistic self-confidence of most five-year-olds who had not yet been tainted by worldly realism. Boldly, I marched up the lengthy stairs hand-in-hand with my father.

We were ushered into the office of a grandfatherly and kindly man. As the story goes, I proceeded to regale him with a great deal more information than he required for the basic 'school readiness testing' I assumed most five-year-olds had to undergo. (My birthday as I mentioned, fell rather inconveniently, for registration purposes, on Dec. 31.) It was not generally known that, at that time, children did not have to attend school until age seven. I think several boys (who tend to mature later than girls) were advised 'not to register just yet'.

As the story goes, I did extremely well on the half hour or so of pre-primer readiness tests. Finished them in about half the time normally allotted. (Unless that was just my elderly parents' bragging about their precocious five-year-old!) Then, much to Mr. A's amusement, I proceeded to regale the school board official with some highly advanced poetry, possibly even some Shakespearean verses my mother had taught me and probably a few lengthy verses from my favorite English long poem, 'Horatius', by Lord Macaulay. That was a poem which to this day causes Grade Eight students to sweat uncomfortably.

I think that the lines I recited by Lord Macaulay went something like this:

'Lars Porsena of Clusium by the Nine Gods he swore
That the great house of Tarquin should suffer wrong no more.
By the Nine Gods he swore it and named a trysting day
And bade his messengers ride forth,
  East and West and South and North
To summon his array.'

Or I may have recited my favorite:

'From where sweet Clannis wanders, through corns and vines and flowers
From where Curtona lifts to heaven her diadem of towers….'
Horatius at the Bridge Lord Macaulay 1842

This poem continued on for more than sixty colorful, but incredibly boring verses all of which I knew by heart. Little did Mr. Allester know that I had memorized only by rote and understood nary a word of the complex verse I was reciting! (Or, being the experienced teacher he was, he probably guessed!)

I had no idea who 'sweet Clannis' was or what a 'diadem of towers' was. I didn't care; I simply loved the sound of the flowery language and was able to mimic it perfectly. However, my elderly father, age 61 at that time, insists that

Mr. Allester was appropriately impressed, if not overwhelmed, by my verbal precociousness. He gave his stamp of approval to my entering Grade One at Old Somenos the following September at the age of five. There were, as far as I know, no kindergarten classes in the District at that time.

My father insists that on my way out I further shocked the 'District Superintendent.' (as he would be called today). I regaled him with one of my mother's old drinking songs from her youthful days in Paris (circa 1927). She had been a cabaret dancer and tambourine player for a couple of years. One of her favorites was called: 'Roll 'em, Girls, Roll, 'em.' Before you read the words, you need 'to know to what 'roll 'em girls' actually referred.

The Twenties were the pre-garter belt and panty hose days. The only way girls could hold up their stockings were to wear actual garters above their knees, usually half-way up their thighs. In the older days, the garters were tied with ribbons, later elastics were used. I can remember my mother's chubby lower thighs being permanently indented from wearing those tight garters.

I also once read in a medical book that the early surgeons, when operating on old ladies, would often note that their livers, rib cages, etc. were similarly indented from wearing tightly-laced stays.

Roll 'Em Girls   (Old 20's Cabaret Song)

Roll 'em girls, roll 'em
Go ahead and roll 'em
Roll 'em down and show
Your pretty knees.
(Referring to the long silk stockings and garters)

Don't let people tell you
That it's shocking.
Paint your sweetie's picture
On your stocking.

Laugh at Ma, laugh at Pa
Give them all the Ha! Ha! Ha!

Roll 'em down and show
Your pretty knees!

Several times when I was quite small, my mom took me with her on a trip to Vancouver to visit her sister. For travel money she took only a single hundred dollar bill which she rolled up in the garter of one of her stockings!

OLD SOMENOS '52

The old school or 'Old Somenos' as we called it, was, indeed, a country schoolhouse. Barn-like, although small, it comprised a single classroom in a strange storey-and-a-half. It has a partially open basement underneath. This 'basement' has since been closed in, I believe. The old building still stands in a small meadow near the corner of Herd and Somenos Roads. It has been repainted (the last time I checked) sort of a creamy yellow although my childhood recollection of it is an imposing dark brown, and now serves as the Somenos Community Hall, a flea market venue.

Old Somenos School, now a Community Center c. 2019

(I suspect the front section was added later as I remember the school as having only one large room with a small anteroom as entrance.)

I was shocked to discover how small it seemed and how much less expansive the land around it, compared to my childhood memories of the place. I guess all things are magnified by the eyes of a small child. I also remember it as having a rather steep hill at the back which I did not detect on my revisit in 1994. I remember, being unusually small and rotund for my age, having to shinny down it in order to use the smelly and wobbly outhouse at the back. Recently, however, no trace of the old outhouse could be found.

Thank goodness for Augie T., whose important job it was to keep the toilet(s) well-limed for sanitary reasons. That job always went to the 'biggest' boy and in those days of 'strap 'em and fail 'em', there were many. I think Augie was at least seven, possibly eight. He came from one of the biggest and most underprivileged families in the area. I think he had been 'held back' at least once, possibly twice.

I believe it was also his job (or one of the bigger boy's) to tend the potbellied stove. It stood in the school's anteroom and had to be well-stoked for heat in the Winter. On rainy days it dried the assortment of soggy children's garments draped over it or on the bench in front. I remember it as being rather large and imposing, a monster of cast-iron with a simple wooden bench in front. It also served as the discipline area for detentioned students. (Again, the eyes of a small child?)

The little school was situated on (what seemed to us at the time) a vast expanse of meadowland hopping with rabbits, birds, and butterflies. It grew the best wild strawberries I have ever tasted and was perfect territory for the annual school Easter egg hunt.

First Day Jitters

I'll never forget the day I first arrived at the school. Although only five, I was the eldest of two children in a farm family with elderly parents. One's first day of school, especially to older parents like mine, was a major event. So- needless to say, when the Big Day finally arrived, my parents were as excited as I was.

I remember my dad waking me up bright and early. Since my mother was an invalid it was he who hustled me out to the school bus stop, lunch kit in hand. My father had graveled a patch of dirt in front of our large garage which fronted on Somenos Road. It became a major bus stop servicing several families in the area- the two of us, the seven McAvoy children, the two Smythe children, and later two new neighbor girls. I think that the Horton boy and the other Smythe kids, Glory, particularly, had their own stop about a quarter of a mile down Somenos. Ours was the nearest stop to what was then called The Cloverleaf (where Somenos Road crossed the Highway on the way out to Westholme).

Later, in high school, two or three teens from the other side of the Cloverleaf joined us. We had to be at the stop by no later than eight a.m. as school hours in those days were a sensible nine-to-three. However, it still meant getting up by 6:30 or seven, a challenge for a small child. In later years, my younger brother was invariably tardy, racing bare-chested to the stop with his shirt over one shoulder and a hastily-snatched piece of toast in his mouth. Our long-suffering bus driver, Dick, and later, a kindly chap named Ernie, would wait patiently, not wanting one of their precious charges to miss one minute of school.

I recall that, in high school, Ernie won our hearts by rigging up an old radio and rudimentary sound system in the bus so that we could listen to Elvis, Orbison, (later The Beatles) and other rock idols. We lived about three miles from Somenos School and four or five miles from Cowichan High. Somenos Road was, and still is, narrow and winding. So- the bus trip, with frequent stops and starts took a good forty-five minutes or more. However, we used the time wisely, making new friends or working on homework or 'library book reading.' Some of the kids took it as an opportunity to be bullies.

Denny Bums and Puddle Jumpers

My brother and I were rural kids, many of us the sons and daughters of local farmers, loggers, and fishermen. We lived a healthy and active outdoor lifestyle on our little 'truck farm' at Somenos. We enjoyed attending our small, local three-room school. At the age of five, I first attended 'Old' Somenos School on Herd Road. The next year I attended New Somenos on Hall Road. The two schools were approximately a mile-and-a-half apart and about three to four miles from our house.

Most of the 'town' kids, sons and daughters of local merchants and professional people, attended Duncan Elementary. It was, to us, a huge, brick ivy-covered castle located right in town near the old Kings' Daughters Hospital. As I mentioned earlier, the girls from 'wealthy' families attended the prestigious and costly 'Queen Maggies' (Queen Margaret's School for Girls) in Duncan .

My best chum from Westholme, Flora G., attended that school. When I again commented to her about the shortness of the skirts on her school uniforms she commented:

'These uniforms are so expensive that my parents will only buy me new ones every three or four years. In the meantime I grow!'

I did end up attending Duncan Elementary in Grade Six because Somenos only went up to Grade Five. At that time, the High School (later Cowichan Sr. Secondary) started at Grade Seven until, in the early-60's Mount Prevost Jr. Secondary was built.

As I detailed earlier, I had whizzed through the half-hour or so of 'school readiness' testing. I think the readiness tests may have come about because, although most parents didn't know, for years one did not have to enroll one's child in elementary school till he/she reached the age of seven. Although only five years old, I was reading at a grade two or three level, thanks to my elderly, well-lettered parents. My father, although always professing to be an atheist, was a Biblical scholar. He let slip years later that his mother had always dragged him to church on Sundays and he in fact had sung an excellent tenor in the church choir. My mother of course had been 'well-lettered' at a prestigious finishing school in Winnipeg. She was multi-lingual and a Classics scholar. She knew Latin.

Later in school, I memorized such old saws as 'Pirate Don Durk of Dowdee', 'The Yak', 'Sea Fever' written by John Masefield and snippets of other poets such as Robert Frost. The 'Pirate' begins......

> 'Ho, for the pirate, Don Durk of Dowdee
> For he was as wicked as wicked could be
> But, oh, he was perfectly gorgeous to see,
> The pirate, Don Durk, of Dowdee.'
> The Pirate Don Durk of Dowdee   poem, M.P. Meigs 1923

In High School, I memorized everything from Ogden Nash's 'Old Dog' to lengthy segments of Shakespeare. Perhaps that is why I, and many of my former school mates continue to have good memories. (Or is it because I watch 'Jeopardy, 'Wheel of Fortune,' and constantly work crossword and jigsaw puzzles?)

I still believe Nash' two-line poem to be the most concisely expressive piece ever written:

> 'The old dog barks backward without getting up
> I can remember when he was a pup.'
> The Old Dog Barks...   Ogden Nash 1972

Now that I am a senior, I can definitely relate to that poem in a way I never could before!

I think it is indeed a shame that the 'art of memorization' seems to have left the public school system.

The old school or 'Old Somenos' as we called it, was a country schoolhouse. Nevertheless, my father helped me get all dressed up in my best outfit to make a good impression the first day of school. Short brown kilt-type skirt, proper white 'leggings' and brown oxfords. I pranced out to the kitchen wearing my new finery, non-existent chest puffed out with pride. Once my 'coatie' was on, my Dad took me by the hand and walked me up the lawn to the waiting school bus.

But as soon as I saw that monstrous yellow bus and those even–more-monstrous kids, I balked. Dad coaxed. I was having none of it. The driver coaxed. I wouldn't budge. All I could see were scores of huge, 'smartie' faces leering at me from above. The teenagers were particularly daunting. The partially enclosed stairwell I had to mount looked like the maw of a huge monster. The stairs were the teeth. I set up quite a howl. Finally, my compassionate father picked me up in his arms and said:

'It's O.K., it's her very first day and she's only five. I'll drive her.' My deliverance was at hand!

So-Dad took me back to the house, washed my teary face, and set off with me in our '46 Austin puddle jumper. It was some distance to the old school-two or three miles along Somenos Road and then a quarter mile or so along Herd to the Old School site.

Imagine my inflated sense of importance when my 'chauffered limo' arrived at the school and was greeted by a melee of grinning, squawking six-year-olds. They leapt and climbed on the hood of our car. They pulled their lower eyelids down with chubby fingers in grotesque, mask-like gestures. My father feared I'd be terrified. But, 'au contraire', I took these cheeky actions as a sign of welcome- 'Welcome to Somenos School.' Thus, as a recipient of such personal encouragement, I pranced joyously into the yard, similarly pulling down my eyelids! I was relieved that, at last, I had found a passel of new friends who understood me.

It is a real tribute to Mrs. B. and her encouraging introduction to my Grade One studies that I awoke the next day eager to return to school. I tremulously boarded the school bus, braving the icy stares of the Big Kids, knowing that it was worth enduring the frightening and lengthy ride. I now knew that my humorous pals at Somenos School would be gleefully waiting for me at the end of my weary trip.

Mrs. B's Class

There has been some controversy over whether I started at Old Somenos in '52 or '53. I have a class photo of me at Duncan Elementary (for Grade Six) dated 1958 in pencil on the back. It is likely that my four years at Somenos comprised 1952-57. The schools had the same photographer, Old Mr. Gibson, for years. I suspect that he, and later his son, took care of every school on the Island. He, seemingly, didn't label the slate with a split year eg. 1952-53 until after 1964. Thus, it was hard to know what the September starting date had been.

Mrs. B had a real mixed bag of students in her class. She not only had students spanning three or four years in both age and ability levels, but the physical conditions of the school would have been considered primitive by today's standards. She had students, like me, as young as five, because there was no kindergarten. Although only five and a half, chubby, and small for my age, I could recite several advanced poems fluently, read at about a grade three level, and had a large repertoire of songs.

On the other hand, Mrs. B. had to deal with much older students who had been 'flunked' two or three times. I think there was a big boy of about eight (possibly nine) in the class. Some parents didn't register their kids till they were the mandatory seven. Many students read at the pre-primer level; many could not recite the alphabet.

Mrs. B. and later, Miss J at the new school, had their own ways of dealing with the 'bright' students in the days when there was no such thing as enrichment education. Later in the year, after I turned six, I was given the low reading group. It was my job to read to them and hear them read. I taught them basic phonics or 'sounding out' words (as soon as I learned it, myself!)

My parents had taught me some phonics, but I believe I largely learned to read by 'sight'. I read visualizing the word pictures, rather than sounding out syllables and blends. Although we would have been considered poor by today's standards, for a time, my parents subscribed to a newspaper- I believe the Vancouver Sun. had accomplished this by, nearly every night, holding me on his knee and getting me to read the 'funny papers' to him. He told us that when we could read all the easy comics to him he would give us a quarter. When we could read them all, fluently, he gave us a dollar.

Thus, I loved teaching reading to the slow group; it gave me a sense of importance and broke up the boredom factor of a regular classroom. My mother insisted that, initially, I would complete about one reading workbook per week. When I was finished one, Mrs. B. simply gave me another one. Mom said that I had finished doing (and I assume, 'redoing') twenty-six workbooks before the teacher got the idea of me teaching reading to the other students. Or maybe I had just started helping the slower ones on my own. I don't know where she ever got all those workbooks from. Perhaps she had three or four different ones and simply rotated them!

Although easily bored, I was a cooperative student. I worshipped my teacher and would do anything she asked without complaint. I remained that way through most of my school years. However, I did become more outspoken and opinionated in Senior High and university.

My mother said it was also suggested that I skip a grade. But she put her foot down and would not allow it for two reasons:

1. I was small for my age and

2. She didn't want me to be in a Grade 2 class of much bigger children at the age of six! I was also the smallest kid on the school bus which included, to me, HUGE kids up to age 18 or 19 (grade twelve).

Also, 'New Somenos' may have been in the construction stage and, if so, I would have had to go to the huge Duncan Elementary in town. A long trip and a huge, frightening environment for a six-year-old to have to deal with. So, we opted for Mrs. B.'s brand of 'enrichment'. My teaching of the beginning readers was probably a large factor in my later career choice (which for now, I shall let remain a secret) Or maybe I can credit the large bookshelf of children's novels in the Grade 4 classroom at 'New' Somenos, most of which I had devoured by Easter. After I entered New Somenos, I WAS skipped (temporarily, so it turned out) from Grade Three to Grade Five. The consequences were somewhat disastrous largely due to the draconian tactics of the male teacher. Read on for that story.

So, although I mostly enjoyed teaching the slow group of readers, the task could be challenging at times. Our early reading groups had cheerful bird names such as the Robins and the Bluejays, but I often thought my group should have been called the Buzzards!

Hubba-Hubba , Ding-Ding!

The old school, to my fragile recollection, had a strange sort of half-storey on the upper floor which left, underneath, an open basement. I believe its floor was dirt. (It's no longer visible in the preceding photo as it has been largely boxed in.) Within its dark and murky lair the boys would huddle, hatching plots of nefarious evil and stories so despicable that we girls were terrified to approach the place. Although other school mates I have met swear there was no adult-imposed segregation of boys and girls at the time, we, in effect, segregated ourselves. We girls knew never to venture under the basement overhang without being prepared to fight for our rights and our dignity, perhaps even our lives! Although the boys would sit huddled in semi-darkness taunting us with everything from deceptively friendly gestures to taunts of 'scaredy-cat' and 'I double-dog dare ya,' I never gave in. I had a fear of dark, enclosed spaces which somewhat remains with me today.

'Run out quickly and close the garage door, Joy!'

I blame that fear of the dark on the almost nightly runs my father made me do at home. At his urging, I would sprint across our large lawn, terrified, to the forbidding spectre of our half-open garage door near the road. I can still picture my father, waiting, silhouetted eerily in the lighted doorway of our house. I, terrified, sprinted back to him as fast as my chubby legs would carry me.

This brings to mind another unnerving task that my mother had me do. It added to my fears. Even as a small child, it was my job to change the light bulb above the kitchen table. I can still picture the scary spectacle of the light socket far above me. How I dreaded hearing the fateful words: 'the light bulb is out again.' The climb from floor to kitchen table wasn't too bad, as my mother usually assisted me. However, terror set in when I had to stand erect on the table.

Maintaining perfect balance, I had to reach up on tippy-toe to screw in the bulb. Horror of horrors, my mother would often try to assist me by holding the leg of the foot I was trying to balance on. I guess she was afraid I'd slip and fall off the table. Because her hands shook, I was more terrified that she'd PULL ME OFF the table! As I mentioned earlier, my mother suffered from Parkinson's disease, otherwise known in those days as the 'shaking palsy'.

You guessed it- as soon as she grabbed my leg, it would be shaken by her unsteady hand. Imagine my fright at trying to stretch up on tiptoe, balance on one leg in order to reach, and try to make adjustments in my balance for my mother's hand shaking. And all that without crushing or dropping the fragile glass globe in my little hand. I don't think I ever did tell her how freaked out I was by the whole experience. However, on the bright, side it may have accounted for the fact that I have always had excellent balance. Because of it, I even taught Yoga for a time! But then, I didn't trust the dark, or wobbly objects- or boys. In retrospect, this distrust of boys stood me in good stead in my college days during the 'Sexy Sixties'. No early pregnancies for this 'pre-pill' girlie!

Other things I remember about that little school were the fact that it was woodstove heated. The grotesque iron monster stood in a small anteroom at the classroom entrance. Around it was a low ledge or shelf on which we placed wet clothing on rainy days. What a stench!

It is also my unfortunate duty to report that it had no indoor washroom. We used an old outhouse outside. It was usually the duty of the oldest (and dumbest?) big boy to lime the toilet daily to keep the smell (and other problems?) in check. I don't remember being too bothered by having to use an outhouse. I guess we kids just thought it was another common aspect of country living. However, it could have been another factor in the Board's decision to make the immediate construction of the new Somenos School a priority!

Unfortunately, I can't remember any other stories about high jinx at Old Somenos, although I'm sure there were many. I mostly remember braving the basement taunts hurled at me and the other girls. The boys spent many hours trying to entice us into their lair and did not give up easily. I would love to be able to relate that I valiantly braved the taunts, and entered the boys' secret domain, knocking heads to left and right. I would like to relate that I confronted my deepest fears and their darkest secrets. But, alas, the self-preserving coward in me prevailed. After all, I was only small, naive and young; I wasn't stupid!

'NEW' SOMENOS   1953-58

'New' Somenos was situated at the end of a long, skinny dirt and gravel road called Hall Road. (I still have some scars on my oft-skinned knees to prove it!). It came off the larger, and paved, Herd Road which connected with Somenos Road. Like 'Old Somenos', it may have originally been painted brown. My best recollection is of a flat-roofed, stark white, rather imposing building situated on a little rise above the trans-Canada highway. It was a little above and behind what are now the District of North Cowichan municipal buildings. At that time, there was no connecting road from the school to the highway and the municipal buildings did not exist.

When I started at New Somenos, (Grade Two in 1953), initially, it had only three school rooms. It had a grade two class, a grade three class and a split grade 4-5 class, I believe. My grade two class was taught by a young female teacher who, I heard, later married and moved to the Mainland. Initially, Mr. M. taught the four-five split. But I think he moved after only a year or two and was replaced by Mr. Mc, nicknamed 'Scottie' by some of the cheekier kids. In those days, we wouldn't have dared to address a teacher by his or her first name. In fact, I did not know any of their first names until years later. I still don't know some of them!

However, Scottie was an interesting and well-liked man with a noticeable Scottish accent. He may have originally been one of the many teachers brought out from Great Britain in those days to teach the British children at Fairbridge Farm School. His lovely wife, Mrs. Mc, taught at the high school (Cowichan Senior Secondary), and was my homeroom teacher in Grade Seven (before we were transferred to the new Mount Prevost Jr. Secondary in '58 or '59.

I don't remember much about my four years at new Somenos except that, with one exception, I enjoyed them immensely. I remember that, for grade two I had a young, beginning female teacher, Miss J. I enjoyed her class. Mrs. L., a 'music specialist' supervised the Christmas concerts and any dramas and was my excellent teacher for Grade Three. She was an older lady, and very experienced. Her daughter also, for a time, attended and, I think later became a teacher. Mrs. L., gave me roles in at least two plays; in one I played the lead.

Another teacher, also a Miss J, came to the school about that time. I believe she taught my brother and remained at the school for over forty years! That is not so common now.) In my Fourth Grade year, I was skipped ahead (from Grade Three to Grade Five) to Mr. M's class. Having started Grade One at the age of five, I was only eight and small for my age. I was in a four/five split class, a rather large one. Some of the Grade Fives were eleven or twelve. The teacher ruled with an iron hand. I was not used to this.

'You- come up here!' (It was obvious to whom he was pointing!) What is that horrible noise you have made?'

It was about one o'clock, just after lunch. The older, male teacher, a rigid disciplinarian, had been reading orally part of a long chapter in a complicated book. 'Moby Dick' or some similar lengthy Classic of that ilk. He had been reading for over half an hour, a long time for an eight-year-old to sit without moving.

I guess I had reached into my desk to find something to fiddle with and bumped my wooden pencil case. It crashed to the floor. Shaking badly, I toddled up to the front of the large class of older students. All eyes were upon me. I was too terrified to speak.

What a clamor I had made! I knew I was 'in for it' now, but I didn't realize how badly. Many years have passed so I don't remember the teacher's next words, but am sure they were shouted at me. I think at that point I tried to slink back to my desk. Determined to make an example of me (the smallest and youngest kid in the class), he grabbed me by the arm.

He started to shake me. Although he was not a tall man, he was very fat- probably weighed two hundred pounds to my sixty or so. I felt like my brains were rattling. So-I set my feet. I distinctly remember I was standing with one foot in front of the other so that he couldn't shake me further. I don't think I said anything. That incensed him.

He muttered something nasty, then flung me completely around. I flew through space. As I fell, I landed painfully on the sharp corner of the first desk in the row. It nailed me right in the middle of my spine. Hurt like the devil. I crippled on back to my seat, contrite. I made no attempt to pick up my things from the floor as I feared that if I generated more noise, he might kill me.

The teacher continued to read the advanced, complicated story with the class now fearfully silent. I remember that my back was sore for the rest of the day. I often wonder if that episode either started or contributed to my later, ongoing back trouble.

That night, I told my father what the cruel teacher had done. Dad was absolutely against physical violence of any kind and was outraged. He rushed down to the school with us kids in tow. My mother was probably again 'indisposed.' I remember we hung around outside the school and peeked in at the large window to see what was going on. To my utter amazement and glee, my elderly father was speaking very firmly to the teacher. The teacher was shaking his head in denial and my dad suddenly got much louder.

"My daughter will NOT remain in your class another day. Tomorrow morning her desk will be moved back into the Grade Four classroom."

But, the fatso sputtered, "Miss So and So' already has too many students."

"Well as of tomorrow, she will have one more! My daughter is a bright, cooperative child, but she has been unhappy ever since coming in to your classroom. She will not give her new teacher any trouble. And I will not let her be subjected to any more of your bullying." (or words to that effect)

The fat, red-faced, educator stood about five-foot-six to my Dad's six feet. My Dad now had him by the collar of his suit and was holding him up off the ground, toe-tips just barely touching the floor. My father's face was right in his and I guess he knew he was in for it if he defied my, by now irate, old dad. My brother and I stood outside the low school windows spying and hopping up and down with glee.

Dad had known for some time that this teacher was making my life a misery. I would be coming home from school, loaded with homework and shaking. I wasn't sleeping well at night for the worry of trying to keep up my grades and putting up with the 'miseries' this so-called teacher heaped upon me. Although I had achieved reasonable grades by Christmas, they were mostly C's and B's. I was used to receiving mostl A's and found the Mathematics extremely difficut. Another disappointing thing I remember is that Mr. M. still made us write with the old quill ink pens for part of our writing class. Of course, I was a leftie and the 'writing compendiums' were set up for 'right-handers. My hand would drag in the ink. That caused unsightly blotches on nearly every page.

Guess what the old beast would do? Rip out the entire page and make me recopy it. By Christmas, I was a nervous wreck. I was also used to getting top marks with little effort. For that reason and others which I cannot delineate here, my father went in to the school and demanded that I be put back into the regular Grade Four class. The next morning when I arrived at school, my desk was in the Grade Four classroom.

There, I met my all-time favorite teacher, Miss L. She was a breath of fresh air and my personal savior after the persecutions I had suffered in Mr. Horror's class. It may have been her first year of teaching because she was only about eighteen at the time and very energetic. I found her class to be much easier and the activities for me, more enriched. Glory of glories-she had an entire wall of low shelves under the windows on which were ranged a rich assortment of children's books. I think I had most of those books devoured by Easter. Official school libraries, in those days, were non-existent and if a public library did exist in Duncan, I had never been taken to it.

I achieved top student status that year. In 1958, I believe, my name was added to a rather attractive dark, rosewood-coloured plaque. It was shaped like a shield and displayed on a wall in the hallway. I believe it had been purchased by the P.T.A. and my name was engraved on a brass plate on the front of it. It was presented for top achievement in that year. I wish I had been able to retreive it before they closed the school.

The next year, Grade Five, Mr. Mc, an excellent English teacher and grammarian, came to teach at Somenos. I can still to this day remember his English skills charts ranged around the classroom above and below the chalkboards. Many comprised clever verses or sayings and were illustrated with colourful stick figures. Here's one (origin unknown):

> There is a little word named 'Got'
> That should be put into a great big pot
>
> And boiled, and boiled and boiled all day
> And then should be canned and put away.

It is a real testament in favor of Early Childhood Education that many of my early school (and pre-school) verses are still with me today, almost sixty years later. Now I just wish I could remember where I put my car keys!

Haywire

> 'Cuz you'll look sweet,
> Upon the seat of a bicycle…'
> Song: Daisy Bell   Harry Dacre   1892

There was no such thing as Kindergarten when I began school in 1952. Six-year-olds were enrolled directly into Grade One at 'Old Somenos' but, until Christmas, the school day ended for us at two p.m. (I think) instead of three. As you know, I, being a December baby, started school in Grade One at the age of five. Thus, the following year, when we began Grade Two at New Somenos, I was only six years old, chubby but small for my grade.

The school bus brought us only as far as the corner of Somenos and Herd Roads. It was up to each student to make his/her way along Herd, nearly a mile of badly paved road. Then it was another half mile or so into the school. So, each daily round trip probably comprised three miles of fairly tough biking. It was a long and intimidating twice-daily trek for such a young child. I 'ditched it' badly on more than one occasion. I have the scars on my knees and various other parts of my anatomy to prove it.

So- my elderly and understanding father (age sixty-two when I was six) made special arrangements for me. An East Indian gentleman had recently bought the 'old lady's store when she moved her business over to the highway. My dad was able to arrange with him for me to store my bike in his shed every night. I think he paid the fellow a small fee. Then I could ride it daily to and from the school upon alighting from the bus. That is how 'old haywire' came to be.

She was a dark blue and white 'two-wheeler' with foot pedal brakes–gearless, of course. The bike was not new but, for it, my dad had paid the princely sum of five dollars! I believe he repainted it himself. Then he created, joy of joys, a wire basket to transport my lunch kit and books. The basket he also obtained second hand and, unfortunately, it had a hole or two in the wire mesh. Luckily, my dad was chicken farming at the time so had plenty of spare wire lying around. He simply wired up the holes. Hence, my small and eventually battered (but much loved) bicycle was dubbed 'Haywire'!

Being chubby, but fit and well-coordinated, I learned to ride it easily. I was soon whizzing down the paved Herd Road with the older kids. Their long legs walking took them at almost the same pace my bike took me. Hall Road, however, was a different story. Not only was it merely hard-packed dirt with a skim of gravel, it had a couple of nasty hills. And big ditches, in those days on both sides. Several times that Fall, I picked myself up from the ditch, my knees embedded with gravel, after roaring down a steep hill.

One particular time, I applied the brakes without pumping them and skidded sideways along the gravel. The bike ended up in the deep ditch with me under it. I don't know if that was the origin of the particularly long scar on my right knee. However, I remember on one occasion riding into the school, blood streaming down my leg. I don't remember the teacher even giving me a band aid, although she may have. I was certainly never taken in for stitches. I think after that, my dad got permission for me to wear pants under my school dresses. I, of course, had to take them off in the furnace room once I got to school!

In spite of tribulations, however, I rode daily to school, proud of my old bike-being one of the few kids in our neighborhood who owned one.

I've often been accused of having a 'big mouth'. But, there was at least one time when being 'overly talkative' served me well. It was about Grade Five and I was playing alary* ball or skipping on the cement in a covered overhang attached to the back of the school. Suddenly, I noticed something different happening. Actually, it was 'some ones'. Two awkward-looking students, both girls. I had never seen them before. They were wearing rather long, tacky, dresses. Both had sensible oxfords instead of the penny-loafers and saddle shoes the well-to-do girls affected. They were kind of slinking along the school wall in an embarrassed manner.

According to a couple of witnesses who later reported, I bounced up to them in my usual jaunty manner. I stuck out my hand and blurted out the following:

"Hi, my name's Joy. I'm nine years old and in Grade Four. Who are you? Do you want to be friends?"

Those shy, awkward little girls just beamed. They told me their names and I invited them to join in one of our games-probably alarey ball or skipping. On questioning them, as all inquisitive nine-year-olds would do, I found out that they were recent transplants from Scotland. Seemingly, they had had an arduous journey and were feeling totally new and strange in this scary place called Canada. I soon cured that.

It was years later, probably in high school, that the older girl confided to me that she had been terrified. She praised me for rescuing her from embarrassment in front of all those strange children. By then, we had become fast friends and I regret that we lost track of each other after spending a couple of years at college together. She had said it was one of the nicest things anyone had ever done for her. To me, however, it was just 'all in the day's work of bein' a kid!'

Yes, for five wonderful years I enjoyed my studies and playtimes at the two little schools at Somenos. We played outdoor sports such as basketball and baseball. The school had no gym. 'Red Rover', skipping and alarey ball were just part of the repertoire of games. I acted in plays and performed in concerts. We had parent teas and other community events, especially at the old school.

My studies were, for the most part interesting and character building, especially the competitive Spelling Bees. I read all the books in the classroom library in short order and my teacher was challenged (so she said) to keep me in new ones. I excelled as a student, thrilled at the end of my Grade Four year to receive mostly silver stars on my attractive, cardboard report card. My lovely young teacher (only about ten years older than I), stated that I had been 'a boon to the class.') Ironically, I didn't know what 'boon' meant, but my Dad soon elucidated!

'Southpaws' 'n Inkwells

Unfortunately, for me:
'The moving finger writes
And, having writ, moves on
Nor all thy piety nor wit
Shall lure it back
To cancel half a line……'
The Rubaiyat   Omar Khayyam 1859

Writing class was, for me, a nightmare. I can not-so-fondly remember struggling valiantly with the old steel-nibbed pens. The school issue were longer than today's ballpoints-bright red in color. They had a flat, ridged area near the nib, supposedly for uncoordinated, chubby fingers to grip more easily. The nib itself was an ugly arrowhead of metal with a slit up the middle. To me, it resembled the head of a cobra. Its ugly round 'eye' seemed to stare at me accusingly whenever I exerted too much pressure. This forced the nib apart with disastrous results. Nasty blobs of ink spread all over-everywhere but where I wanted the ink, that is! I bear a noticeable callous today on the third finger of my left hand as proof of the difficulty of controlling those pens.

Being a leftie or 'southpaw' as we were called in those days, I soon learned that the writing compendiums were set up strictly for 'right-handers.' Margins seemed reversed. With each stroke of my wobbly, dripping pen, my wee fingers dragged miserably through the lines previously written. The difficulties of transferring the ink cleanly from inkwell to pen nib were beyond me. The result was often a series of unsightly streaks and blotches from dragging my 'baby finger'.

We 'lefties' tried arching our wrists above the lines or actually lifting our hands entirely off the paper (as in 'air writing') with only the nib connecting. But the miserable blotches still magically appeared on nearly every page. And there were no such things as ink erasers or correction fluid just yet. If there had been, I doubt we would have been allowed to use them. Each compendium page was expected to be letter-perfect and virgin of blotches. Hence, the only remedy-rip out the offending page and laboriously start again. A remedy which, unfortunately my first male Grade Five teacher liberally used before I was rescued and sent back 'down' to Miss L's room.

Imagine my feelings of relief and almost 'divine' deliverance when later, in Junior High, we were permitted to use ball points. Hallelujah, they did not have to be dipped in ink wells! To this day, just hearing the word 'compendium' would be akin to the smells in a dentist's office-sending icy fingers of fear floating up my spine.

One eventful, blustery day in Miss L's class, the boy sitting behind me decided to do a little 'pigtail dipping'. (Pigtails were the long, tight braids often worn by the girls since long hair hanging in one's face was a no-no in those days.) The lucky girls with attentive mothers had French braids artfully woven from the scalp. Those of us who had to braid our own could only start at the back of the head, achieving 'plain piggies' which did not have that artful, woven look. However, they did the trick in keeping our long hair tamed.

Unfortunately for me, just as the boy decided to dip one of my pigtails, ribbons and all, in his inkwell, I stood up. I upended almost his entire bottle of ink down the back of my light, printed cotton dress. It was a difficult 'back-buttoner', of course, and Miss L. had to rush me to the girls' washroom. She had quite a time extricating her teary student from the dripping garment. She had to wash both it and most of my back in the small basin. Luckily there was plenty of cheap liquid soap available, but I don't think she got a lot of the ink out of the dress. That stuff was pretty indelible. Nevertheless, she decided she couldn't send me home to my mother covered in ink stains.

It was a day in late Spring. To my utter mortification, she hung the dress out the washroom window to dry. I don't remember what, if anything, she was able to give me to wear till it dried-perhaps a coat? I have memories of an interminable afternoon spent huddling in the room near the toilet while the boys rampaged and teased outside.

'Fatty, fatty's wet her dress, what a big fat, dirty mess!'
(Or words to that effect.)

Miss L. had somehow managed to hang if from the flagpole and it crackled and flapped in the breeze as it dried. She probably gave me some art work to do, but I remember an afternoon of disheartening ostracism. It probably took only an hour or so for the light cloth to dry. To me it seemed like a life sentence as the dress dried excruciatingly slowly. I would have to wear it, damp or not, on the long ride home. That is one of the few nasty memories I have of my otherwise wonderful years at Somenos School.

The School Strap and the Big Brat

Luckily, I was never its recipient. My brother was, on many occasions. So was the unfortunate sod my son later dubbed 'Unca Ray'. They had both been strapped so many times that eventually the boys competed to see who could get the most strappings in one month. However, I had just once, the sad occasion to be on the delivery end.

I was a beginning teacher in Nanaimo in the mid-sixties. At the tender age of nineteen, I was told by the principal that he wanted me to strap a rebellious student from my class, partly to learn the routine. I was, of course, reluctant. It was subtly inferred to me that, if I did not learn strapping procedure, I would be seen as uncooperative and that could go 'on record'.

There was a definite legal procedure to be followed including: full legal name, date, reason for administration, number of blows administered, etc. The event had to be witnessed by one other colleague. The school secretary was often recruited for that unhappy task. It was usually up to the principal to decide how many blows were to be delivered-usually in increments of two. I have no idea how he decided who should get what.

The instrument was comprised of a quarter to half-inch thickness of (I assume) solid leather. It was coated with a whitish, burlap-type material. It was purposely made to withstand years of wear when slapping against the many palms it had to contact. The student was asked to stretch out his or her hand. Yes, girls could be strapped, too, although the strapping of females was far less common.

In my case, unfortunately, it WAS a native girl who was the recipient. She was a tall, buxom girl, technically in Grade six but working at about a Grade Three level. She had sworn at me in the hallway in the presence of student witnesses; therefore the vice principal insisted I must strap her 'or else'. I suspect the entire nasty procedure was harder on me than it was on her. Afterwards, the principal's one complaint: I didn't hit her hard enough.

The procedure was as follows: the student was asked to stretch out his/her hand. Most automatically took up a defensive posture and braced their feet so as not to be knocked over by the blow. The teacher then faced the student sideways and grasped him firmly by the wrist. This was partly for stability and partly, I assumed, to avoid breaking the student's wrist with the blow. It also prevented the student from tearing his hand away at the last minute as my father bragged that he had done.

According to dear ol' Dad, he also had a 'Mr. Mean' for a teacher. When that punitive personage attempted to strap Dad, Dad quickly pulled his hand away. The teacher dealt himself a nasty blow right on the shins! Luckily, in the number of 'strapping years' I attended and taught, I never heard of a broken wrist or other serious injury through strapping. Or else 'accidents' were just not talked about. I think we teachers were merely lucky.

I, an inexperienced beginning teacher, was ordered to perform the painful duty. I was only nineteen myself and she about twelve or thirteen and my size. It was physically painful for her but emotionally painful for me.

I was given the following instructions: Aim for the meaty part of her hand so as to avoid breaking or straining her fingers. (I also suspect the youngish vice-principal recruited me to strap the girl largely because he had no stomach for the task himself.) However, he stated that I needed the experience and the girl was registered in my class. She had sworn at me in the hallway (in front of student witnesses) so that merited a few smacks.

But I can assure you-I have no desire now or ever in the future to repeat the exercise. To me, a teacher's duty should not include 'beating' her students. I think that the principal soon realized the experience was more painful for me than for the sullen, seasoned student. After a few paltry licks and some 'correcting', I was permitted to desist.

I now realize that the child was terribly unhappy, probably suffering from culture shock as a 'reserve' child in a foreign-feeling, big city school. She probably also had a learning disability as she could not read well. The absolute last thing she needed was a beating by authority figures. However, even in the late Sixties there was little in the way of school psychologists or counselling available. Certainly nothing that even superficially addressed the natives' problems.

The girl, (I shall call her Doris) had a pal in the class. A rather pretty girl of twelve or thirteen who became pregnant by Easter. I heard that she subsequently ran away from Nanaimo to a relative's in Seattle. I remember having spent months after school trying to help both girls with (what we teachers perceived as) their retarded reading and writing skills. I had spent many a morning encouraging Shasta to write and she balked me constantly.

Sadly, after her departure, I was unloading her desk and discovered a series of letters she had written. They were poignantly emotional and written to her 'true love', an older boy who, I assume, had impregnated her at one of the potlatches. She had had an ongoing relationship with him and wrote simplistically, but eloquently, of her sadness at being parted from him. He was on a reserve on an island somewhere and she was captive in 'Whitieland'- (my description, not hers). It just goes to show that most people have it in them to be writers. It just behooves us as teachers to help them find the subject that they truly want to write about.

So-after administering four or five licks to Doris, I was allowed, by the principal, to desist. It was increasingly evident that I would burst into tears before the student did! Thank God for Eileen Daly, the NDP Minister of Education who, in the early Seventies removed the strap from all schools. I whole-heartedly agreed with her decision. I now fervently wish that the Powers that Be would do the same with the barbaric practice of Child Apprehension by the Ministry of Children and Families (but that's a story for my next book.)

My younger brother, Gary, tells a poignant story of how he revisited Somenos School. He had heard it was his former principal's final year of teaching. The administrator, after chatting with my brother in his office for a time, looked up the old records of discipline. Surprise, surprise, my brother had received the strap more times in his six or seven years of attendance than any other student in the history of the school. More than fifty occasions and I don't know how many hundred strokes!

I am now convinced that my brother, like many impulsive and risk-taking students, suffers from severe ADHD*. I am so thankful that now (in most jurisdictions) we give them medication, E.A.'s and counselling instead of beatings. In fact, I believe that the recipients of this archaic, barbaric form of punishment were invariably the 'disadvantaged' students. Most suffered from burgeoning, untreated mental illnesses or learning disabilities. I'm sure that the pain, both emotional and physical, of strappings negatively and permanently impacted their lives.

That very leather strap prominently emblazoned with the words 'Somenos School', now sits above my brother's fridge in his kitchen in Victoria. The principal asked him if he would like to have it to keep and he said 'yes'. I would not have believed his story had I not seen the strap on several occasions when visiting.

Again, at the time, my brother's repeated strappings were seen as a 'family joke,' even bragged about. And in fact, both he and 'Unca Ray' (his close school chum who was also from Somenos) had blustered and bragged about their numerous visits to the office. However, years later, my now fortyish bro confessed to me the ongoing mental anguish he had suffered because of it. I am sure it was a contributor to many battered students' subsequent alcohol and drug problems. Or, as in the case of 'Unca Ray', it exacerbated his, probably genetically inherited, major mental illness (bipolar disorder, I believe).

However, in spite of my brother's tribulations, he was an intelligent capable guy, if a little eccentric. He later went on the start a business in the Big City. As for me, I generally had positive, even uplifting experiences at Somenos School, had lots of good times, and made many friends. With one exception....

He was huge. Probably close to six feet. Grade 9 or so, so considerably older than I. He was about fourteen and also pudgy-a big guy. I distinctly remember I was only eight or 9 and in Grade Four when it happened:

This big guy had been tormenting me on the school bus for months. I had no idea why. I think he was also one of the 'baddies' that old Dick regularly kicked off the bus. If not, it was probably one of his brothers. I didn't know him well with me being in elementary school and him now at Cowichan High. I had no idea why he chose me to torment. Unless it WAS because I was chubby and small for my age.

This particular afternoon he was in fine form. Making nasty, rude, (pseudo-sexual) comments about me in a big loud voice. I was so young that I didn't really understand what some of them meant, but knew the innuendo wasn't good. I tried my usual method of avoiding trouble. I retreated to the big seat at the back of the bus even though we weren't supposed to change seats once the bus was moving. I was a proper little kid who always obeyed the rules. After graduation, I prided myself on the fact that, in a twelve-year school career, I never had the strap or even a detention. At the time of the incident, I was so mad that I believed this was one kid that deserved the strap!

Anyway, taking matters into my own hands (as we did in those days), I moved. Unfortunately, I forgot that the seat at the far back of the bus was a long bench-type. Plenty of room for my tormentor to follow me there and continue to torment me. I think he was now making filthy comments about my weight which I thought was bloody ironic because he was no 'light weight' himself! Finally, I could endure no longer. I grabbed my old, but trusty, metal lunch kit which was on the seat beside me.

Wham! I smacked him a good one-right up the side of the head. And yelled at him, for all the world to hear:

'If you don't leave me alone, I'm gonna tell Dick what you've been saying to me!'

Well, he moved to the far side of the seat like the sidewinder that he was, and I didn't hear another peep out of him. However, my father did. A couple of hours after I got home, the phone rang, It was the kid's distraught mother. I only heard my Dad's side of the conversation:

"No, I don't think he would have a concussion. She's a lot smaller than he is and it was only a small lunch kit'.

Well, look, maybe you'd better tell that big boy of yours to stop bullying my little girl. She's complained to me about your son's behavior before. And she's just a little girl- only in Grade Four, you know.

Well, you just tell him, he better leave my girl alone. Even if he is about a foot taller than she is, she's liable to kill him next time!

Well, that's too bad. No, I don't think it'll do any good to discuss it further. Just tell him to leave her alone.

Good evening, Mrs. ______." (I never had any trouble from the kid again).

I never did confess to my Dad that even though it was a smallish lunch kit, I'd forgotten that it still had my big metal thermos in it!

Ironically, I remet the boy years later in Ladysmith, B.C. and we had a pleasant chat. He didn't even remember the incident. He said they had been so poor and his family so violent that one whack from a little kid on the school bus would have been no big deal in those days! I experienced only one other incident of bullying that I can remember. That occurred in High School so I'll tell you about it in the next chapter. My brother took care of that one……

Handbells and Meat Paste

Bzz, bzz, bzz! Not! None of that horrible buzzer sound for our delicate ear drums. No, instead, we were summoned each morning by the clack, clack, clackety-clack of the school bell. About five or six inches in length, it comprised a brass bell-shaped end with a black wooden handle. Its clacker was 'formidable' as we would have said en Francais. That sucker could be heard not only throughout the school but also for a good distance into the school yard.

It was only slightly more pleasant to the eardrums than today's annoying modern buzzers. However, it performed its job of calling in the students. It was rung, usually by the principal, but sometimes a student or teacher.

Approximately five to nine on school mornings, then again around ten for recess. Lunch was at twelve and then it rang again to call us back in at 1 pm. precisely. The final ding-a-ling was heard at three p.m. for dismissal. The schools kept 'sensible' hours in those days. None of this 8:25 or 1:17 as they do today.

We all vied for the privilege of being permitted to ring the school bell. The only greater honor for an elementary student was the privilege of going outside a little early to bang the chalk board erasers and clean the 'shammy' (if the teacher even had one.)

The shammy's were made of chamois hide, a type of African goat or antelope, I believe. They were quite expensive. A teacher was lucky to get one and that one had to last her all year. I know we had them when I first started teaching in the late Sixties, but I'm not sure that Somenos had them. I do know however, that we had many of those dark-colored felt erasers with the wooden backs. On teacher's orders, we would take two or three of them outside after class and bang them up against the school wall to clean them. If we were lucky enough to have a shammy, we were very careful with it!

'Pease* porridge hot, pease porridge cold,
Pease porridge in the pot-nine days old!'
Wikipedia: O.E. spelling from John Newbury's Mother Goose Melody, c. 1760

This old nursery rhyme has brought to mind the matter of school lunches. Those were the days when a lunch hour was a lunch hour! School was in session from nine to twelve precisely with a full hour for lunch. Unfortunately, back in the 'bad ol' days' of teaching, most of us didn't get the lunch hour off, as we sat with our students for the first twenty minutes. After that, we often did yard duty as well.

Afternoon session was from one to three except for the Grade Ones who, I believe, were dismissed at two from September to January. All schools in the District opened and closed at the same times. Many students vied for the privilege of being dismissed five minutes early to ring the old metal hand bell at recess, noon and after school.

Our morning always began with a short Bible reading (usually read by the teacher, but sometimes by a privileged student.) Each teacher was given a list in September as set down by the Department of Education. It detailed which verses were to be read each day. It was followed by group recital of the Lord's Prayer. ('Our Father, which art in Heaven, etc.) We all had to recite the words, whether we understood them or not.

Ditto the dictum to listen politely to the complicated King James version texts even though most of it, to us, sounded like gobbled-gook. I guess that was meant to instill in us a respect for our Judeo-Christian culture, most prevalent at the time. Not so today. I guess a teacher would be 'drawn, hung and quartered' for having the students utilize the same morning routine now!

The dreaded hand and fingernail inspection usually followed. It was considered to be a black mark on one's character to be one of the children sent to the bathroom to 'rewash'. I often thought they should have done a 'foot inspection', too, for there is no smell on earth worse to my recollection than that of wet socks in soggy rubbers after a child has run around in them on a rainy day!

As I mentioned earlier, the 'furnace room' often reeked from the smelly rubbers drying out on benches. At lunchtime, the teachers sat with the students in their classrooms for the first half hour or so. The teacher was usually eating her own lunch, marking papers, or wrestling with the figures in an unbalanced Register of Students. (I had many a battle with the aforementioned in my teaching days before school secretaries- later computers, came in and saved us a lot of grief.)

Some teachers would not allow us out until the mandatory twenty minutes eating-time was up. I guess that was to give the 'duty' teacher time to get outside. If we scarfed our lunch too fast, we'd have to sit there-reading a book or participating in some similar quiet activity. Hence the presence of the teacher because many of the kids, particularly small boys, were disinclined to behave after a morning of arduous study.

Needless to say, I loved board games and usually hated my lunch unless it had home-made chocolate cake in it. I often rushed my lunch so that I could play a board game if it was a rainy day or before we had to go outside. That may have had something to do with why I am a fast eater to this day.

A typical school lunch is easy for me to describe. I ate virtually the same thing with very little variation for eight or ten years. Then we became teenagers and were usually too lazy to make our lunches. By then, my elderly Dad had abdicated that responsibility. We either starved and then woofed sandwiches, apples and cake when we got home or bought a fudgsicle and chips in the high school cafeteria.

My father packed the same thing in our substantial plastic or metal lunch boxes for us all through elementary school. One sandwich and one apple, sometimes a dessert if we had any left over from supper. In the Winter, a thermos full of Campbell's soup, usually vegetable beef, which Dad thought was the healthiest. Or some Freshie of varied flavors. I can't remember him ever buying 'real' fruit juice.

In late spring, with the garden in, the sandwich was invariably lettuce and tomato with mayonnaise. In the Winter the dreaded 'potted meat', a.k.a. meat paste. For real excitement, we'd have banana and peanut butter or just plain peanut butter. All usually on the cheapest bread Dad could buy, sometimes white, sometimes brown. He favored shopping at the Safeway store in Duncan and often used their 'bargain' Ovenjoy brand which I will not touch to this day (if it still exists!). While mother was still alive, she sometimes shopped at one of the better bakeries, bringing home a loaf of heavy-grained and unsliced bread for a healthier treat.

When my father raised chickens, we ate a lot of 'egg salad' sandwiches and often had a boiled egg on the side. Too often, however the sandwiches contained the dreaded meat paste. My father preferred to call it potted meat. To us it tasted like and had the texture of dog food and smelled even worse. I trust that it has now gone off the market. Just the thought of its gritty, greasy, overly salty flavor and pasty texture revolt me to this day. I often endeavored to trade it off to some unsuspecting (especially, if new) pupil. But eventually the kids were wise and I was stuck with the 'luncheonus horribilus.'

Once in a while we could trade all or part of our lunch for a rare treat- chocolate oreo cookies. It was our habit was to lick out the white, sweet filling before munching the dark brown wafers down. My mother, when she was not too ill, baked lovely, moist cookies. Date and Raisin or Peanut Butter. (No peanut allergies in the schools in those days!) Of course, we preferred the overly sweet and 'store bought' Oreos. Almost anything 'store bought' was a rare treat then. However, I always did, and still do, detest store bought white bread.

No ice packs or insulated lunch bags for us in those days. If we had a sturdy metal 'kit', our lunch didn't fare too badly, But, later in high school it was considered uncool to pack a kit. A simple brown paper bag was de rigueur. On a hot day, our otherwise appetizing lunch became a squished-up, soggy mess especially after being jostled around in our looseleafs* and on the school bus.

If it were Spring and the garden was in, the leaf lettuce on our sandwich added a layer of wilt to the sog. In the heat of the school room the egg sandwiches and greyish, rubbery overcooked eggs were an offense to the nostrils. We hated being identified as 'the kids who had smelly eggs in their lunches again'.

We felt duly deprived. There were never any Twinkies, potato chips, soda pop, gum or similar junk food. In those days, the term 'junk food' didn't exist. Food was food and most people were glad to have whatever they could get. The nearest corner store was three or four miles from our house. Few farm families could afford such luxuries as store-bought treats or desserts. I never tasted French fries or chips (except home-made ones) till I was a teen. Potato chips and pizza never passed my lips until I was an adult. When I am playing T.V. Jeopardy, I marvel at the junk foods that are popular in the U.S. Most I have never even heard of!

Our major store-bought treat was a brick of ice cream. We enjoyed this perhaps once a month in Summer. I believe the cost was forty cents, so each serving cost a dime. A pittance today, but 'real money' in those days. Today, for some families, ice cream is an everyday staple. For us, ice cream day was an occasion. Even the dishing-up of the ice cream was a treasured ritual. A small 'brick' was just big enough for our family of four to each have one serving. The pint was first carefully halved, then halved again to be shared equally. If the divider's hand should happen to err, we'd argue to see who could get the slightly larger slice. But any 'sneaky server' who was caught purposely adjusting the size was in deep doo-doo!

As further illustration of the cost of treats- our weekly allowance (while it lasted) was only thirty-five cents. The admission to the Odeon theatre matinee was exactly that so we usually had no treat money unless we earned it ourselves. However, if we had had a successful morning lugging the old grain sack along the highway, we could trade in the two cent beer bottles for pocket money. For only two cents apiece we could feast on licorice ropes or for five cents, I think, for the licorice Nibs. A pack of Wrigley's spearmint gum was ten cents. Penny candy of all types and colours abounded.

Later, as a young teen, and much as I hated the job, I did a lot of babysitting to get 'spending money'. However, by then, nearly every precious cent went towards my college fund.

Our Schoolyard Games

In the early Fifties at Somenos School, the school yard games were played in the surrounding fields or under the trees. There was also a half-covered cemented area at the side of the school. This cemented area was handy for bouncing balls or marking hopscotch boxes, especially on rainy days. For hopscotch, we used worn chalkboard tidbits we mooched from the teachers. The school yard games I most enjoyed were: Dutch rope skipping, hopscotch, alarey* ball, jacks, and, of course, baseball. In Grade Six at Duncan Elementary, I broke my foot while Double Dutch skipping in a rocky area.

We also held marble tourneys although the really 'hot' tournaments took place at Duncan El's mudholes a few years later. I was surprised to see recently, in an old edition of the Cowichan Leader, that the finals of these marble tour- neys were a community event. I noted that one year, the Reeve's son, a neighbor and school mate of ours, won the tournament. Accolades with his picture were printed.

And there was, of course, baseball. I think we would play scrub at lunch hours and the more official version during P.E. (Physical Education) classes and after school (for those of us who could stay). I broke two fingers during those early years catching 'burners' for my brother, a star Little League pitcher and back catcher. As I recall, Somenos had a small but 'official' backstop for baseball and, I think, real base bags and markers. You can imagine the excitement for rural kids who were used to using dried cow pies in the fields for bases!

Unorganized Games

Marbles

I don't remember all the rules of the somewhat complicated marble tourneys we held in the two schoolyards. Initially Somenos, but then Duncan Elementary for Grade Six. I remember that, at Somenos, we mostly played one-on-one with no teams or formal competitions. I guess that got us in practice for the brutal tourneys that occurred at the much bigger 'downtown' school a few years later.

The marbles were small round balls about the size of a large cherry and made of glass. Perhaps the glass was specially tempered, because in all the years I played, I don't remember one shattering. I do, however, remember playing with a chipped marble. The glass was imbedded with interesting shapes or patterns, possibly plastic. They came in a kaleidoscope of colors. I don't remember the cost, but they must have been dirt cheap (pardon the pun!) or my bro and I couldn't have afforded to buy any. But perhaps we 'scrounged' or traded. The beauty of living back in the 'stone ages' was that my brother and I could often procure goods (or 'goodies') with no money ever changing hands!

I do remember some of the terminology- 'kid-speak', as it were. Ordinary small marbles were 'cats eyes'. The big fat ones were 'bullfudgers'. The small ones were held on the forefinger and flicked with the thumb. As it rolled forward, it knocked the opponent's marble askew or blocked it from getting to its target. The target was often, but not always, a series of holes dug in the dirt. I must try to research the rules of the marble tourneys that took place in Duncan in the Fifties and early Sixties. Or-accost some old codger in one of the local coffee shops who remembers playing 'by the rules'.

I know that the Duncan El contests were often adult-led or at least monitored and adjudicated by adults. Actual prizes were awarded. I was considered a competent marble player, but not a 'champ.' My accident-prone and sometimes less-than-competent brother, however, excelled at all things physical. He won every marble tourney that I lost!

Alary Ball

I had no idea how to spell alary ball so I decided to look it up. At first I thought the spelling might be Allaire or Alarie. I had no idea what the word meant. I found no helpful references. So I decided to spell it phonetically (just the way it sounds) as follows: 'alary'.

Do you remember what an alary ball was or how to play? We girls at Somenos spent many a happy hour perfecting our alary skills at recess and lunch hour. Since my bro and I were bus students, I don't remember ever playing much after school.

A 1920's rhyme of my mother's was, basically gobbledegook:

Eerie, iry ory iry ickery Ann
Filsey folsey Nicholas John....

Our first old alarey rhyme was a counting one:

'One two three alarey
My first name is Mary.
If you think it necessary
Look it up in the dictionary'.

Of course, we kids didn't care whether we understood what we were reciting or not. Alary ball was great, especially for poor students. All you needed was an India rubber ball that bounced well, and a hard surface. The preferred ball was a hard one, usually white, but sometimes black and the size of a small child's fist. It had to be just the right size to hold while gripped tightly in the

194

palm. Those balls bounced easily so woe betide the poor child who leaned forward too far while bouncing-it delivered a hearty whack to the underside of the chin.

Mastering control of the ball took weeks to months of practice. Once the initial bouncing and catching was mastered, there were progressively more elaborate moves to master. One-handed bouncing was mandatory-catching with two hands was considered cheating. Then there was the correct sequencing of moves, beginning with the easier motions such as 'single leg over' and ending with more difficult maneuvers such as 'frog jump'.

Each 'stunt' with the ball had a name, many of which I have, unfortunately, forgotten. However, I remember that a 'pocket' a 'basket' and a 'skirtsey' were three of the easier moves. They all relied on use of a skirt, hence only the 'sissy' boys participated. The ball was either bounced through, under or over the piece of clothing. If the girl didn't happen to be wearing a skirt, a long shirt tail would do.

The more advanced moves were difficult to do because of the skirt! A 'British Columbia' and 'Around the World' were two of them. The first required a front jump (much like a 'leap frog') directly over the bouncing ball, the latter involved bouncing the ball entirely around one's body while standing still. Various refinements of those moves were invented and kept us girls busy and happy for many hours of free time at school.

But, back to Alary Ball: After the bouncing, hand and clothing maneuvers, came the 'leg over' and jumping. These involved either flinging one's leg over the ball as it bounced or somehow jumping over it. The difficult 'leap frog' move (a 'British Columbia'?) had the ball bounced expertly through the legs and behind the student. The girl had to turn quickly to meet it and it was deemed 'foul' if she missed catching the ball on the next bounce. As I said, I think the 'Around the World' maneuver was bounced around the body using either one or two hands.

Pig In the Middle

Another bouncing and throwing ball game still enjoyed today involved a much larger ball. A minimum of three kids were required. The game was played by having one student, the 'pig,' stand in between two others. The other players would attempt to throw the ball to each other; the 'pig' vying to see if he/she could catch it. If the pig was able to catch the ball, then the player who had thrown it became the next 'pig'.

Dodge Ball

A more sophisticated version of 'Pig' was Dodge Ball. I don't know if they still play this one or not. Probably not, as the 'powers that be' would be paranoid about the students suffering from ankle bruises (of which I had many and still survived). In later years, we played it in gym class, with the kids forming a large circle. At Somenos, we played outside as there was no gym.

A few 'pigs' stood in the middle of a large ring of other students. The children in the outside ring progressively took turns at hitting the pigs in the middle with the ball. A strict rule about 'hitting only below the waist' prevailed. Again, if a 'pig' was hit, he/she had to exchange places with the kicker. Other common sense' rules prevailed (as they did for most kids' games). 'No picking the ball up in your hands to throw the ball at somebody's head', and 'no hitting from behind'. One had to act in a sportsmanlike manner at all times or be ostracized from further play.

Rope Skipping

I must have been the most aerobically fit 'fat kid' who ever lived. Not only did I spend hours 'pumping' on a swing and riding my bike, I was the school skipper extraordinaire. I could probably skip 'pepper' for twenty minutes straight. I am sure I could skip a full hour at a moderate pace-or until I tripped on the rope-or until my little legs started to ache! In Grade Two and three, I became one of the best 'short rope' skippers in the school. Guess what part of my routine at my fitness gym still comprises now, even in my seventies? (Yep, you guessed it: pepper skipping!)

We would sometimes have informal contests to see who could skip the longest before 'pooping out.' Or who could go the fastest or longest for 'pip, pap, pepper' (turning the rope as fast as you can). A few 'trick maneuvers' included crossing arms while jumping, skipping only on one foot, and turning rope backwards. 'Skip once, turn rope twice' really took some coordination and time to master. I know a few kids, adults today, who never could do it. I could manage it most times. By about Grade Four, I had graduated to the team effort required for 'Double Dutch'.

Double Dutch Rope Skipping

'Double Dutch' involved at least three or four players-two to stand on each end of the rope to turn it and one or two to skip. Obviously an extra-long or 'double' rope was used. One turner held the two handles of the long rope, the other the curved end, but in two hands. Thus, they turned the rope almost as if it were two separate ropes.

As the ropes turned in an alternating sequence, there was an 'easy' side and a 'hard' side. The skipper would first have to decide which side to enter from. Then the object was to keep successfully jumping inside the doubled ropes without getting tangled up in or stomping on them. If one stepped on the rope, it became the next person's turn. A variation was to have two or more players jump in and skip in concert without 'fouling' the moving rope. I found it to be a lot more difficult than single rope skipping.

This type of skipping was a complicated skill and became a competitive sport in New York City in the 1970's. Its origin is unclear but it is thought that it could have come over with Dutch settlers or was invented in the first half of the 1900's. There are now even competitive DD teams as I understand. As far as I can remember, the skipping songs used were the same as for single rope skipping.

Swinging

'Let's go fly a kite, up to the highest heights'
Let's Go Fly... from Disney musical, Mary Poppins 1964

That song had not yet been written when I soared on one particular swing in the playground at the back of the school. And I know it was meant to describe kite-flying. It also describes the way I felt swinging 'to the highest heights' on the old board-and-rope swing. We had always been cautioned not to swing so high that we flipped around the long metal crossbar at the top. I never did, but I came close. There were, however, a couple of daredevil boys who would regularly 'flip'. I don't know how they avoided breaking their necks! In later years, the swing seats were made of plastic or rubber and were held with sturdy chains. Unfortunately, the chains were prone to rust and often creaked abominably.

There were no bucket-style baby swings as I recall. But what the installers did was build the sand up higher underneath for the littler kids. Over the months of school, the sand would be worn down by scores of landing feet and the sand would have to be built up again.

For most of those years, I had a rather unusual 'swingin' partner-a boy. Ironically, he was considerably bigger than I was and probably a bit older. A nice kid who had suffered from polio. He couldn't walk very well and wore a leg brace. I guess that's why he spent so much time swinging on the swings. I remember competing with him to see who could go the highest. I also remember that I could stand up on the swing to 'pump' myself higher. I don't remember if he could or not. But although, at the time, I was not overly fond of boys, I do remember spending many a pleasant hour swinging next to B.R. the 'little crippled boy' on the big kids' swing set at Somenos School.

Pitchin' Pop Balls 'n Poppin' Pitch Blisters

We also loved 'pitchin' pop balls' and poppin' 'pitch blisters.' Popballs were the fat, white berries that grew on local bushes along the roadsides in the Spring. The game was to throw them by handfuls onto the nearest available patch of concrete or strip of asphalt. (impossible to do on Hall road because, as I recall, it was, initially, unpaved.) The first person to pop the most by jumping on them was the winner.

Of course, hot arguments ensued because once the clods of mushy berries were reduced to a streaky pulp, it was pretty hard to count them and decide who had squished the most. Also, having a lot of kids play was a disadvantage as they would inadvertently stomp on too many of one's berries. So- we usually played this one only in pairs.

This was a game that was participated in almost equally by boys as well as girls. I guess that in those days, about half the games were co-ed. The boys usually chose the more active games. Baseball, dodgeball, marbles, Red Rover and the Poppin' games were O.K. for the boys. However, most 'real boys' would not be caught dead skipping or bouncing an alarey ball. I think it is sad that our segregated P.E. classes and restricted school yard games have done away with the easy comraderie that existed between boys and girls in those days.

In the late Spring, we would shinny up school yard poplar or birch trees. We'd pop the bulging blisters of pitch adhering to their trunks with our grimy fingernails. The kid that had the most 'goo' dripping down his or her fingers would be considered the best popper. There was no formal (or even informal) recognition for this feat, however. By afternoon, our fingers would be quite a mess. We prayed that the teacher would not be having afternoon writing class, the goo being virtually unwashable. I couldn't bear to face my old nemesis, writing compendium practice, after poppin' pitch blisters!

Organized Games

I call the next few games 'organized' because they required a level of cooperation and organization in order to succeed. I already told you about Double Dutch skipping and I include it again here because it required that two girls work in concert. If they didn't, the rope would became a limp and useless noodle lying on the ground. Or a tangled mess. We used a long, double-sized rope, usually with plastic or wooden handles and bent it in half. Then, with two expert 'turners', one at each end, we could begin. We preferred girls who generally had a better sense of timing and level of interest than most boys. However, if we were desperate, a boy would be allowed to turn the rope. (They usually made lousy skippers.)

To play, the turners had to alternate the ropes in a steady rhythm. The rope would be swung exceptionally high to allow the taller kids to jump in. Skipping the ropes required either jumping from the 'easy' side (when the rope was low or from the 'hard' side (when the rope was high). Good turners could turn the ropes so fast that many good skippers would soon be put out of the game.

'Double' skipping took considerably more skill for each girl (or occasional boy) than skipping the usual, single one. One had to watch the two ropes carefully and jump in just at the second that one was high and one low. Otherwise the skipper would either trip on the bottom rope or almost get 'hung' with the top one! Most boys in those days who joined us girls for skipping were considered 'sissies'.

'Red Rover, Red Rover, Send Somebody Over!'

If I had to name one childhood game that was my favorite-it would have to be Red Rover. We played it as a team sport. We were even allowed to play it in P.E. class or with the teacher at lunch hour. It could be played by virtually any group of students. For once, I was a popular player, because size and weight were a definite advantage. Being one of the fattest kids made me a popular player of the game. I was often one of the first to be chosen. Although bulky, I was a good runner and the combination of bulk and speed made me a 'natural'.

The game began by appointing two team captains. Sometimes a squabble ensued as to who would lead each team for they had the prestigious job of choosing team members. Usually it was done by the considered fair logic of 'you had your turn last time, now it's our turn'. Fair mindedness and 'taking turns' were essential for the success of our school yard games. Those principles were always in effect and rarely cheated upon. Any kid who 'cheated' was ostracized and often banned from play next time. (till he 'learned his lesson'). The object of the game was to run like Hell through a phalanx of peers and break through to the other side. If you broke through, you could choose a 'captive' to take back to your own team. If you couldn't break through for whatever reason, you became 'captive and had to immediately join the other team perhaps giving it even more power.

The bigger and more popular students usually were allowed to be captain, but for fairness, the 'little guys' were given their turn occasionally, too. The captains had the choice of naming their teams if they so wished-for instance the Red Fireballs vs the Jackrabbits. All kids chosen formed two long lines facing each other. The captain usually stood in the middle. Each player either held hands or locked and 'splinted' wrists with the player standing beside. We soon learned that simply holding hands didn't make for a very strong opposition to the bulky kids who were fast runners. However, the 'chicken' kids who didn't want to get their arm broken did that so that the opponent could easily break through. Or if it was a 'frail' girl or a favored pal, it was a way of letting the little person through.

However, to form a really effective barrier you 'splinted wrists.' This was done by grabbing the outside of the forearm of your partner. That, effectively, presented two forearms as a barrier instead of one.

'Red Rover, Red Rover, Send Somebody Over!' The challenge was called out by the captain and the game was on! The 'somebody' of course was a person you wanted to run. Refinements included specifying the name of the person who had to tackle your team. That would invariably be somebody we considered a 'weak' runner. The heavy-duty kids were held off till last, perhaps in hopes that something catastrophic would happen to them in the meantime. Teams were usually mixed, but sometimes we played 'girls against the boys'. Since, at that age, girls were pretty buxom and the boys still shrimpy, the girls had a 'fighting chance'.

The challenge for the runner was to identify the 'weak spot' in the phalanx so that he/she could break through. If the player was captured, he was added to the team. If he was able to break through, he could choose a 'captive' to take back to his team. However, the captive player was supposed to switch loyalties to the new team. That didn't always happen and thus the team now had a 'weak spot'. The team that had the most members when the school bell rang was usually declared the winner. However, if a team had the most pooped kids, or a lot of sore wrists, it could abdicate. 'Little kids' often simply wandered away, but that was frowned upon. In all the years I played Red Rover, I never heard of any child suffering a broken bone. Today, it would be considered a 'brutal' sport and probably banned!

After a lunch hour of active play, we would often go inside to prepare for our next school play or Christmas concert:

The 'Interrupted' Mandarin

There was one particular teacher who took a keen interest in the Fine Arts at Somenos School. Mrs. L. coordinated a Christmas Concert which was the highlight of the school year. As far as I know, each grade participated. Each class made its own contribution, quite different from the other. The concerts were sponsored in part by the PTA* who provided goodies afterwards. We kids would wait in high anticipation for the annual candy cane and mandarin orange provided at this event.

I remember having an important, if brief, role as early as Grade Two. Being still only six, I had only a vague idea of who, exactly, I was to portray in the presentation. It wasn't till much later that I became duly embarrassed.

All I knew at the time was that the morning of the important concert my mother dressed me in brown leggings, a brown, rather shapeless blouse and brown skirt. I even wore my brown leather oxfords which coordinated the whole outfit. I don't remember being particularly nervous although I knew I had an important line to say. I was determined to project it to the best of my ability.

All day you could feel the excitement build throughout the school. Finally, my mom and dad brought me back for the important event. I remember being behind a makeshift curtain. Someone put a cage-like affair around me constructed entirely of brown crepe paper. And, at the last minute, probably that same someone pinned a sprig of holly into my hair right on the top of my head. The curtain opened and I found myself sitting, with my chubby legs fully crossed, on a large table. I remember nothing of the 'play', if such it was, or the other players. However, I do remember delivering my one line clearly and flawlessly:

'Hurrah, for the plum pudding upon the table!'

Unfortunately, sometime later, I learned what a plum pudding was. I figured out the implied analogy. I feared that I had probably been chosen because I was the chubbiest little kid in the class. I was somewhat chagrined, and I actually started seriously dieting. I have pictures of me losing noticeable poundage that year. However, my temporary chagrin didn't seem to deter me from 'starring' in future productions. My performance, according to my family, had been spectacular. In fact, my mother related to her friends that: 'You could have heard her in Nanaimo!'

I also recall acting in a full-length play when I was still at Somenos. I have a vague recollection of starring as a doctor complete with white coat and stethoscope. However, I remember neither the title of the play nor the plot. I seem to remember, though, that it was about grade three or four and I had the starring role. In those days, I was very good at memorization and, to this day, can remember large chunks of many long poems I memorized both at Somenos and in Junior High at Mt. Prevost School. I think it's a real shame that kids don't seem to do memorizations of long poems any more in school.

I recently obtained a copy of my old Grade Eight poetry text entitled: 'Poems for Boys and Girls Book 3'.* It featured poems from such famous authors as Robt. Browning, Burns, Frost, Coleridge, De La Mare, Masefield, Scott, Kipling, Nash (my favourite), Shelley, Wordsworth- even The Bible! The little book was organized into sections with titles such as: Times and Seasons, The Roving Heart (containing 'Cargoes' and 'Sea Fever' by Masefield), ...Imagination, Birds and Animals, ...Contemplation, Light Verse (including three by Ogden Nash- to my mind, the all-time master of rhyme) and others. I think the students' learning today suffers from the supposedly innovative removal of textbooks from schools. The deemphasis on memorization, especially of long poems, was an important 'brain-building' tool that kids will now lack.

I don't remember details of the other two concerts I acted in during the four years I attended New Somenos. I only remember that Christmas was a magical time both at home and at school. My brother and I looked forward to the special foods and special events of the Christmas season with relish. After the Christmas concerts, I think we were all given a big candy cane to take home-an exquisite treat. Our excitement would build exponentially from Halloween to December.

I think it is indeed a shame that 'political correctness' dictates we use the euphemism 'holiday' instead of Christmas. To me, Christmas is Christmas is Christmas, darn it!

In Grade Seven, I played Ma Cratchit in 'A Christmas Carol.' By then I was at the High School. As I mentioned previously, I also sang in and acted in a couple of operettas in Grade Nine and Ten. I sung in Music Festival choirs several times and thoroughly enjoyed the experience. I think that contributed to my penchant for singing at local Open Mikes and jam sessions even today.

But the crème de la crème of all performances had to be my little brother's. He was only about ten or so and was playing the lead in a school performance of The Mikado. The troupe was entered in the Cowichan Music Festival. He, as I mentioned previously, was hyperactive, but brilliant. I believe he had a photographic memory for he could memorize huge sections of text and stated that he 'saw' all the words and page numbers in his mind the next day. In fact, in Grade Eleven, he aced the History exam by never taking a note, but instead memorizing the textbook the night before! He wrote 98% on the test.

In Grade 5 or 6, he was cast in a musical, The Mikado. He had been chosen for the part of narrator. I don't know who took the following photo. My brother was standing on stage with his costumed servant. I think the curtains were closed behind him as he was introducing the play. His costume was quite something for an amateur production. He wore a long, dark-colored robe-if not made of actual silk, then some kind of a silky fabric. One of the more well-to-do mother's dressy bath robes, I suspect. It even had the long, wide sleeves affected by Chinese mandarins.

His enormous headdress was unique. It seemed to be about a foot high, wide and fan-shaped. It was of a light-colored material, probably cloth or covered cardboard. It was covered in sequins and someone had painstakingly glued some fuzzy material all along the edges. It was quite the fancy bit of head gear. I suspect my brother's ramrod posture and stern demeanor throughout the play had as much to do with balancing that thing on his head as 'being true to his character'!

He was the major character that tied the entire play together. Gary had a solo or two to sing and had been chosen for his unusually mature singing as well as speaking voice. Also, his ability to memorize and recite lines. His part was lengthy as I recall. (As I said, when he was in high school, we realized that he had a photographic memory.)

The important event was being held in the high school auditorium which had an adult-sized stage and 'official' ruby velvet draperies. The room was jam-packed with parents and other interested townspeople. My brother was exhorting loudly onstage probably to the tow-headed stooge who, in real life happened to be his best friend. The monkey-like little kid played the perfect foil for my ultra-serious 'mandarin' bro:

My brother as the Mikado at age eleven in 1960.

But, suddenly, a commotion erupted at the back of the room. A masculine voice boomed and huge feet made a startling racket as someone thundered up the aisle:

'Where's that little brother of mine? I heard he's hanging around in here somewhere. (I don't think that the strange personage had any idea of the solemnity of the occasion.) Where's that Jackie Ellesworth?

'Omigod, he's talking about my dad', I thought. All heads had turned. To our acute embarrassment, my old father stood up. He stepped into the aisle and almost collided with a tall, somewhat distinguished-looking old gentleman. The man appeared to be my father's age or a little older. He was a couple of inches taller than my dad's six feet and sported an enormous moustache. He was wearing a fairly formal but definitely-out-of-date suit (as was my dad).

My Dad spoke up:

'Wally, it's great to see ya. You haven't changed a bit!' (I later learned that they hadn't seen each other in over forty years!).

You can imagine the stern glare they got from my serious-actor brother as he was interrupted mid-sentence. Then, realizing where they were and who was listening, they decided to sit down. The big fella crammed in beside me and I realized who he was-my dad's oldest brother from Manitoba.

It seems that Uncle Wally had recently contacted my Dad from Manitoba after a long separation. They had had no contact since they had been young men in their twenties. My mother had told us there were rumors of a lifelong spat now, in old age, obviously forgotten. My Dad was by that time nearing seventy and his brother was several years older. He was close to being an octogenarian, but still stood straight and tall. His almost-handlebar moustache was still mostly dark and his face ruddy from years of working on the farm. His enormous hands were gnarled and work-hardened. He was not overly thin, but had not an ounce of fat on him. Like most farmers of his day, he had not 'run to fat' because he did not spend most of his day sitting on a tractor as they do today. And they mostly ate healthy foods off the farm. The term 'junk food' had not yet been coined when I was a kid!

So, our long-lost Uncle Wally joined us for the event which he said he thoroughly enjoyed. My mother must have told him we were there when he arrived at the house. We passed a memorable evening and, later, an interesting week with the old guy. To make it even more memorable, my brother, competing against kids from the senior high school, won Honorable Mention in the Festival for his performance. He was one of the youngest actors to ever win recognition.

A few days later, as Dad was bidding my uncle good-bye, he happened to query:

'Say, bro, what do you think of our little province of B.C. (It was the first time my uncle had been to the coast, and, sadly, proved to be his last).

My unc thought for a minute, then scratched his still-thick and unruly thatch of hair:

Well, I reckon there'd be some purty nice sights out here except for one thing'.

'Oh, what's that, Uncle Wally', we piped up.

Wally replied, (pointing a long finger in the general direction of Mt. Prevost):

'All these dang mountains. They get in the way of the view!'.

I remember with fondness most of my memories of Somenos School. The teachers were generally warm and encouraging, the students gutsy and fun. Even the support staff (only the janitor and bus driver? -I don't remember there being a secretary) were highly dedicated to the cause of elementary education. Many former students have done well in Academia, me included.

They Try to Close the School

Partial text of my letter to the School Board:

Ladysmith, B.C. 2004

It is with deep regret that I hear of your intention to close Somenos School. I attended that worthy institution from 1952-58. I found it to be an excellent school. The knowledge I gleaned there stood me in good stead through fifteen succeeding years of higher education, most at the University of Victoria. I achieved an advanced (Five-Year) Honors Degree in Education in 1980. I also qualified as a teacher-librarian specialist. In addition, I am still in touch with many loyal friends I made at Somenos- over fifty years later!

I think it would be a mistake to close this unique little 'country' school. The school has an ambiance and 'special feel' that cannot be duplicated in big city schools. The close-knit school community is a boon to the surrounding area. Many, if not most, of the students who attended there went on to graduate from Cowichan Senior Secondary and other high schools. The knowledge we gleaned there will stay with us forever. For that reason, I feel that closing this worthy little school would be a mistake at this time…...

Signed,

________ etc., etc.

Somenos School was finally closed in 2013. The former Education Minister, George Abbott, had fired the Cowichan School Board for failing to balance the budget. Six schools had to be closed, Somenos being one of them. Mike McKay, District Superintendent from Surrey was brought in to serve as 'official trustee.' However, I would hope that it was my comments and those of other former students that kept the little school open for the ensuing ten years.

Boy, scary to think that some of my former schools are closing because they're 'too old'. What does that say about me?? (Don't answer that!)

Reprinted by permission, Black Press

DUNCAN ELEMENTARY SCHOOL (1958-59)

Duncan Elementary was an architect-designed school built in 1913 by William T. Whiteway. He also built the World Tower on Pender Street in Vancouver, 1912. (Thank God for Google!) It has lasted all these years because it was built of brick. I later taught in one other brick school on the Island-Quadra Elementary in Victoria, (now Ecole Quadra) constructed in 1914. The old brick structure is still going strong! They had added a wooden addition in the mid-sixties just before I started teaching there. I'll bet the old brick school is outliving the addition!

One thing I liked about brick- it's relatively warm in Winter and somewhat cool in Summer. That came in handy because in those days, in the thirty-five-foot, high-ceilinged classrooms, it was a bit of a hassle to use the long 'window poles' to open the top half of the tall windows for ventilation. We usually delegated that task to a reliable kid and hoped he didn't mishandle the pole and break the window! I believe that Duncan El had similar high ceilings and similar poles.

Courtesy of an article I read in the Cowichan Valley Citizen* and, from which, I copied the above photo, I further learned the following:

Whiteway chose a Georgian Revival* Style the original of which was popular from 1714-1830 (the years that the four Georges reigned). It featured grey brick with red brick accents, an ornate, pillared portico* and hipped roof, unusual for a school, especially an elementary school, at the time. It replaced a small, two-bedroom school which had been built in 1891. It also featured a circular window in a gable with columnar support at the front. The hipped roof sported a decorative cupola*.

Remember, Somenos School was built in 1953 for approximately 25,000. Ironically, this school cost so much to build ($30,000- a fortune in 1913) that the Board could only afford to finish the main floor. The other school kids had to wait a year or two before the upper storey was finished!

So, in 1958, at the age of ten, off I went to Grade Six at the 'big' school in downtown Duncan. The school bus actually took us right to the school entrance this time. I remember being quite scared and felt strange for the first month or so. The much-bigger school (which had a separate Primary wing across the road) was quite daunting after attending such a small, country schoolhouse.

I also quickly learned that the academic competition was fierce. I believe there were two classes of Grade Six, so I had double the competition. I had grades that were good, but not as high as I had achieved at the little schools at Somenos. I don't remember much about my one year at Duncan El, but there were a couple of noteworthy incidents.

I had a tall, slender, middle-aged male teacher. I remember him as a kindly chap and a good overall academic. I don't really remember what we studied but assume it was the usual (then comprehensive) multi-subject curriculum. As an aside, when I started teaching in 1967, I was responsible for teaching up to fifteen subjects (see Appendix under 'Subjects'). In one class I had thirty-six students. No help, except for the occasional parent. How I did it, I'll never know!

An 'elderly' teacher across the hall at Quadra School, Victoria, had over forty students. Story has it that the fire marshall had to come in one day to measure her hips. That was to make sure that she could pass between the last desk and the doorway to lead the students down the fire escape!

Duncan El was the school that had the wonderful marble tourneys, some of which were even reported in the local paper, the Cowichan Leader. All I remember about my Grade Six year was my nice teacher and enjoying a study of the Ancient world- Britain, Greece, and Rome which I found fascinating. I believe we also studied Europe in general that year. That may have been the reason why, in 1971, I took a lengthy backpacking trip through Europe!

I also remember playing many great rounds of a game called 'tether ball'. It was a ball similar to a small basketball, tied to a tall pole by a thin rope. I think the idea was to hit the ball as hard as you could, trying to get it to wind itself around the pole. I think the winner was the one who could wind it completely around the pole with only one hit. (Or using the fewest number of hits). At least, that's the way we played it, anyway.

However, the fly in the ointment that year was that I broke my foot or lower leg. Had to wear a nasty old plaster cast for about six weeks! I had been outside skipping, stepped on a rock, mid-skip, and fell. Crack! I hobbled over to the duty teacher, but she wouldn't let me go inside. The leg ached abominably.

Mrs. R. didn't believe me. Again, because I was a 'chubby', she thought I was just wimping and told me to stay outside. She accused me of making an excuse to come in and not have to actively play outside. I was affronted as I did not tell lies and my leg really DID hurt. Ironically, I met her years later pumping iron at a local gym. By then, she herself had become quite rotund and I had slimmed considerably!

So, I suffered for about a week at home with a cast right up to my knee. I learned not to eat well-toasted bread when some of the crumbs fell into my cast. Talk about itch! (I think Dad rigged up a coat hanger I could put down the cast to scratch). In those days, broken limbs were just considered par for the course for kids-no big deal.... But, then, disaster befell:

Dad took us to the local pool on our usual Saturday so that my brother could swim. Being only a kid, I didn't realize that plaster dissolves in water! You can guess the result. When Pop came to get us late that afternoon, it was all but falling off my leg. That necessitated another trip to the doctor to get it remade!

View of Mt. Prevost, c. 2019

View taken from Mountain View Cemetery where my mother is buried.

Come on, Let's Cheer for Mt. Prevost'

(Sung to the tune of the 'Colonel Bogie March')

'Come on, let's cheer for Mount Prevost
Get up, and let's get on the go.
Winners, we're not beginners
Cuz we've been at it, and at it, before
　　　　(two-three-four)

Wake up, and let's get on the move
Right now, we're really in the groove
Show how, we've got the know-how
We're out to prove it, and score high today
　　　　HOORAY!!!!

I wrote the words. Can't remember if the school ever sang it or if the song was just buried somewhere. I sang it for my colleagues at my 2012 Cowichan District Teachers' Association Retirement evening. For the second round, I got them all to join in and sing it with me!

Almost directly under the majestic, twin-peaked mountain stood a large, low-lying wooden building. It was painted white. That was Mount Prevost School. I attended there for about two years in the early Sixties. For half of Grade Seven, we Duncan El students had to attend Cowichan High briefly while the new junior high school was being constructed.

Mainly I remember my lovely Scottish Grade Seven homeroom teacher, Mrs. Mac. Ironically, she was the wife of the second (and nice) male teacher I had had for Grade Five at Somenos. I believe she taught us English and was a pleasant, competent, if no-nonsense school marm. I believe it was that year that I began singing in choir.

Unfortunately, my memories of Mt. Prevost Junior High are also few. But I recall that times were different then. I like to say that–in those days, a teacher 'could be a teacher'. If a teacher felt that students were acting in a manner unbefitting the dignity of the school, he or she could take action. Witness our stalwart and no-nonsense principal, Mr G:

Crinolines and White Lipstick

In Grade Eight, to our horror, several girls were removed from class at Mount Prevost School. I happened to be one of them. We had come to school wearing crinolines* and garter belts. And even worse, some of the girls sported white lipstick and back-combed (substitute 'ratted') hair. Mr. G. marched us straight to the girls' washroom.

At first, he did not come inside, but just yelled at us to remove the undergarments and give them to him out the door. Then we were to remove the offending lipstick. Any girl who did not remove enough of it would have it removed for her with paper towel by the principal when she came out. We made sure we had it all removed. We were further ordered that, next day, we were to appear at school wearing proper ankle or knee socks and NO lipstick.

I don't think I had been wearing any white lipstick-honest! (I probably couldn't afford such a luxury!) But I had been wearing the offending garter belt and 'nylons' which came to mid-thigh. The dark band at the top was often not totally covered either, when one bent over, giving the boys a good look at the stark white garters as well. We were further told that if we wanted our property back, we were to appear at the principal's office after school to claim it. Any complaints and he would discuss the issue with our parents. We grudgingly complied.

Yep, them were the 'good ol' days' of teaching. Today there would probably be a huge protest march or at least a contingent of angry parents squawking about infringements of their children's 'human rights.' Or the students, themselves, would launch a protest. I cringe at the mini-tops and tight jeans with big leg holes sported by many of the high school students today. The girls currently are affecting REALLY LONG, straight hair, below shoulder length which is constantly hanging in their eyes. Many of them wear boyish workmen-style caps with the prominent brims to hold this hair back. I think that Mr. G would have confiscated those, too!

I don't remember too much else about junior high except the wonderful friends I made there and a few minor incidents. Mr. G., early recognizing my bent for writing, appointed me 'school reporter' to the local newspaper. It paid a few cents per line and he knew my family was poor. I thought it was going to be a piece of cake. However, I hadn't reckoned on the fact that I was a bus student. It was almost impossible for me to stay for any after school games or to keep track of the scores. Finally, the principal took pity on me and recorded the game stats himself.

I was also not much of a 'gossip columnist'. I didn't really click with a lot of the other girls and just had my own, close-knit circle of friends. It was difficult to discover any gossip to relate. Needless to say, being only thirteen, I didn't have a clue what a reporter really did. However, for whatever I did write, I was paid, the helpful sum of about eight cents per line. The money I made I added to my college fund.

My school chums were an exemplary lot. Nice girls all of them. No bullying or vicious gossiping that I can remember. Two or three were from my neck of the woods and we had attended elementary school together. However, most were town girls and had attended Duncan Elementary or other schools. They were all serious students and none were 'boy crazy'. I'm sure there were a few boy crazy girls at the school, but I didn't number them among my friends.

Because I had to catch the bus home right after school, I didn't join them at any malt shops or after school activities. But I do remember attending one excruciating school dance during Grade Nine. For the event, we had made these super-simple, but rather unattractive lined tops in Home Ec. Class. They were sleeveless and, to make the lining, we simply made the same simple top again and stitched it onto the underside.

As usual, I made a rather bad choice of fabric, a somewhat bulky denim-like cloth with green and white vertical stripes. I thought that the stripes would make me look slimmer. Not! The top sat on my chubby waist, giving me a boxy look. I also had the bad taste to pair it with a longish, white pleated skirt, all the rage that year. Good for the tall slim girls, but not for 'chunkies' like me. In the outfit, I looked across between a cardboard box and a circus clown. All I needed was the white ruff. And, as it proved, white was not a good choice of color for a school dance wherein messy food stuffs and dirty floors prevailed. I still have a black and white photo, though, of me standing outside the school with three or four of my girlfriends. We are all proudly sporting these awful school-made outfits. In retrospect, they all looked as crummy in them as I did.

Anyway, the dance in the sparsely decorated school gym commenced. I was wearing my boxy, unattractive, outfit. The boys of course, had ranged themselves along one wall, the girls the other. Somebody played a record and we were forced, by the teachers, to mingle. And how embarrassing, it was a 'piggy back' dance. The boys were to form pairs and go out to choose a girl to 'carry' across the floor. I kid you not- and I'd like to cold-cock the teacher whose idea it was! The boys were to put their arms out in front of them and link hands. Thus, they formed a sort of chair to carry the girl in.

I, being perhaps the heaviest girl in the room, was chosen last. To my utter mortification, there was only one boy left to transport me. And he was the runtiest. There was no way he could heft my bulk alone. So, a tallish male teacher came over to assist him. It was not fun to have them both thrust their arms under my bulging butt and haul me across the room. I was mortified. I seem to recall the dance went downhill from there, with most of the boys retreating to their side, and the girls to the opposite. But we braved it out and most had a good time by evening's end.

But it was events like those that, although embarrassing at the time, cemented my friendships with most of the girls and many of the boys for years to come. I have since attended my tenth and twenty-fifth high school reunions and am soon to attend my Fiftieth. I still remember most of those kids, both male and female, and they remember me.

I did have one 'close call' involving a school sports day. It was one of those where stations were set up and the students rotated from one to the other. They were standard and authentic sports events. No Egg and Spoon or Sack Racing for us now. We were expected to join in the more advanced sprints, long races, relays, high jump, broad jump, softball throw and the dreaded hurdles.

For a fat kid, I did O.K. with most, but was terrified when it came to hurdle-jumping. Ironically, the best hurdle jumper I've ever seen was a close friend and extremely short. She stood about four foot ten or eleven and told us that, had she been one inch shorter, she would have qualified as a 'midget'. However, she had the longest stride of any girl I've ever met. She must have had double-jointed hip sockets or something. At my suggestion she, years later, became a distance runner, partly to quit the smoking habit she had started. Years later, she won many amateur competitions running with the Cee Vacs in the Shawnigan area. Not so me.

When I went out on the track and saw those huge wooden hurdles, I nearly fainted. Those bulky monsters (designed something like my Dad's saw horses but without the angled legs) seemed to be about four feet high! I was only five foot one or so. My heart pounded just at the thought of trying to clear one of those things.

I tentatively tried to jump one and knocked it over, whacking my shin in the process. I was afraid that if I tried again, I'd break my leg. A sympathetic and also-chubby friend came over and we resolved to ask a teacher if we could 'opt out'. We knew we wouldn't have a chance if we talked to a 'Phys Ed' as he or she would just say 'go ahead and try, the exercise will be good for you'. (Broken leg, more like it).

So, we spied our tall, good-looking and kindly Social Studies teacher, Mr. M. We figured he'd have no vested interest in forcing us to perform. We were right. He merely said 'that's o.k. girls, just go on to the next event.' With a huge sigh of relief, we progressed to the softball throw.

Ironically, later on in high school, I had a young, Scottish P. E. teacher. We assumed that she was freshly arrived from the Old country as she had quite a burr. She had had excellent training and knew how to motivate young girls, whether they were athletic or not. The first time I tried to run a lap of the track non-stop I became dizzy, my lungs burned, and I had trouble breathing. When she saw that I could not run distance very well, she put me on a 'graduated' program.

I had had little difficulty with Phys Ed. in the elementary grades. About all that was required was softball and marbles prowess. Somenos School did not have a gym so we were not proficient at basketball or other 'running' sports and had no training in gymnastics.

When I got to grade seven (which, ironically for one year was at the high school), I encountered a starchy Brit Phys Ed. Teacher. I shall call her 'Miss P'. I panicked. She was teaching advanced gymnastics and I was constantly in trouble for my 'bad form'. Although I could do most of the basic level spring board, box and horse work, I did some of it with an unacceptable style. For instance, she kept me after school one day for 'coaching' because I would roll 'crooked' on the mat. She never did manage to get me to do straight rolls. It took Miss Mc, her successor, to figure out what was wrong. She was our wonderful young Grade Twelve teacher who obviously had up-to-date training and really liked teaching kids. She later figured out why I had such trouble with forward rolls and log rolls in gymnastics. More about that later.....

So, for most of Grade Seven I was a nervous wreck every time P.E. class came. My sympathetic M.D. gave me a note so that I could opt out of physical education for the rest of that year (even though he never guessed what was wrong with me.) I must have done O.K. with Grade 8 and 9 P.E. because I have no memories of it except for the rather disastrous track meet. I believe I had the same crusty P.E. teacher for Grades 10 and 11, but stuck with it.

I remember two further incidents about that class which have stuck in my memory. Miss P. was a fortyish, buxom, obviously, former field hockey star. I would be afraid to guess what she weighed (maybe 180?) She had what we would have called in those days- 'thunder thighs.' Because of that, I witnessed a highly embarrassing happenstance. (I was embarrassed; I doubt if she was.)

I had lost my gym shorts. Somehow, Miss P. got word that I came from a poor family and she offered to let me go through her extensive 'lost and found' to look for another pair. Her 'lost and found' was in a backroom off the gym. She had told me to come in after school and look for a pair.

Dutifully, that afternoon, I presented myself to the gym and was shocked at what I saw:

Miss P. had a habit of wearing a short field hockey skirt and 'bloomers'* rather than shorts for teaching. This, I think was an affectation from her playing days, possibly at a private school. I knew my friend, Flora, wore them at Queen Margaret's. T.G., Miss P. didn't make us wear them for her P.E. classes! To my chagrin, there stood Miss P. right in front of the very closet I had to enter. She had her one leg placed high up on the door frame, speaking to the principal! To this day, I have no idea why she had her bare leg in such an unladylike position. Cramp? Did he catch her mid-exercise doing a leg stretch? Seemingly unperturbed, she spoke with him at some length and never removed her bare (and somewhat hairy) leg from the wall. I was forced to wait, horribly embarrassed. It was patently obvious that the principal could see right up her skirt. However, I wasn't so intimidated by Miss P. in class after that!

In Grade 12, Miss Mc proved to be my salvation. She put all us 'chubbier' girls on a graduated walk-running track program. I not only lost some weight, I stuck with it. By the end of Grade Twelve, I was a pretty good runner and actually achieved a 'B' grade.

A few other flashes of memory reveal a tall, distinguished-looking male teacher standing, text book in hand, pounding Grade Eight and Nine English into our heads. Mr. M. was also the kindly staff member who had rescued me from the horrors of hurdle-jumping. But, it was the patient work of another tall, dark-haired male teacher who taught me probably the most valuable skill I ever learned in school-five finger typing. It was my efficient mastery of typing that allowed me to write these lengthy books, instead of just short snippets (such as emails and blogs?) The typing skills I learned those years at Mt. Prevost were well-used for the many college essays I had to write as well as letters and other documents during my teaching career.

I treasure my years at Mount Prevost Junior school, the experienced, close-knit teaching staff, the solid friends I made there and the benefits of a good, basic education from which I have profited to this day. Many of those same friends later joined my at Cowichan High which I tell you about next........

Drawing, Cowichan Sr. Secondary with School Crest

A stylized representation of Cowichan Senior Secondary School taken from the front of my Class of '65 Reunion Folder, 1990. On the upper left is our Thunderbird* motif in burgundy and grey/silver. I won three of those crests in 1965.

Cowichan High School Song 1965

'Cowichan high we salute you
Our hearts are bursting with praise.
For we know that we cannot measure
The worth of all that you gave'

'Hear us now singing your praises
For the battles won
And continue, Cowichan High School
Leading us bravely on, in days to come.'

Our school song- '64, I believe. Band played the tune and the whole school sang it during a school assembly. A bit schmaltzy, but what can I say. It was the Sixties. The Beatles were writing lyrics like 'She loves you, ya, ya, ya.' Anka's 'I'm so young and you're so old', proved him the King of Schmaltz. Yes, for the sCowichan High school song, I also wrote the words. Kind of interesting how that came about. That year, we had a Brit band teacher. Nice chap, but not very poetic. He told us he had an idea for a school song. I guess the staff had discussed it at a meeting and thought that a song to represent the school would be a good idea. They thought something should be written to go along with our rather tasteful school emblem. A native thunderbird on a shield in grey and burgundy.

Unfortunately, he picked a 'gawd-awful tune. Can't remember the name of the piece, but it had the most awkward phrasing to try to write lyrics to! He attempted it. We tried to be polite, but almost laughed him out of class the day he sang it for us. I remember it had one redundantly bland lyric-

'In Duncan, the Cowichan Valley….' (Well, Yeaaahhhh!)

The band kids were not impressed. I told him I thought that I could write better lyrics and he said 'Go ahead'. The above is what I came up with. I wish I could have done something about the tune, though.

From Grades Ten to Twelve I attended (what to me seemed to be) the immense high school on James St. (Compared to some today, it doesn't seem all that large now.) It was, at the time, named 'Cowichan Senior Secondary School', but we kids all referred to it as 'Cowichan High' or 'Cowie Hi'. Cowichan (Quwutsun') meant 'warmlands' in the local Coast Salish dialect. A bit of a misnomer in the Winters, however.

Cowichan High was kind of a neat place. Not the most picturesque of locations, with the school track fronting right on the highway, but what was really neat about it was the kids. We had everything from the science nerd to the 'latent cowboy'. Many of the kids were 'farm' kids, like I was. Then there were the 'town' kids. The Town Kids were usually polite and pretty friendly, but they did tend to shy away from us. Maple Bay was, and probably still is, the 'ritzy' area of town. Many of the families there lived on the waterfront and owned expensive boats. I considered myself privileged that one of my best 'school' friends, Maisie, lived in Maple Bay!

I can't believe our 50th is coming up soon. Fifty years since I graduated high school. I could say 'Where did the years go?' but I won't. I know exactly where they went and, most days, feel every one of them. Three husbands, one of them mentally ill and violent, one mentally ill kid, (He's featured in a partial biography I wrote entitled 'Episode' which I hope to publish next), a whole host of dud boyfriends, two or three careers and now, in my 'dotage' two more careers. One of them writing; one of them 'reparenting' for over ten years from the age of sixty! And it all goes downhill from there. Am I depressed? Definitely not. Just pragmatic. Have always held to the theory (as did my dear ol' prairie dad) that 'life is the pits, and then ya croak!) Occasionally the odd glimmer of sunshine in between the snowstorms. But, enough philosophizing and back to my story.

'The Boys of the Band' and Other Personalities

In High School, the 'boys of the band' were often hilarious. Especially when we had a quite elderly (sixties?) band master with classical training. The two worst culprits were the trombonist and trumpet player. When they weren't busy torturing the girls, they tortured the teacher. And for two years, I blush to confess, I played in the brass section as well. Euphonium. But I gave it up in grade 12 as being an instrument that was not ladylike. There was one awful photo taken of me, a side-shot and I felt the instrument emphasized my double chin too much! The clarinet was much more delicate (also sucky, no gusto). I later regretted making the change except for the fact that I learned valuable 'woodwind fingering'. That skill was valuable in later years when I taught recorder to elementary students -same notes!

I always preferred the rich sound, and perhaps still do, of the brass section. Today I play African drum at many of the local open mikes and coffee houses. Unfortunately, one cannot play a wind or brass instrument and sing at the same time!

However, our French horn player was also a girl. Quite straight-laced and serious although attractive and always dressed in the latest fashion. She helped me keep the boys in line-or tried to. Unfortunately, we'd just be finishing a classical piece, perhaps by Tchaikovsky. The two rapscallions (who stood behind me) would add their own–and totally inappropriate-jazz ending. Or, right in the middle of a serious piece, a fart sound. Aaaaaarrrggghhh! Then I'd feel the poke-right in the back of the head. Snider the Slider (I should have called him the Sidewinder!) hitting me with his trombone slide. One day, a hank of my longish hair got caught in his slide; he was a sorry kid. Oh well, with those two, band class was definitely never boring!

And then there were the kids that couldn't play. Percussion instruments 'marching to their own drummer'. The squeak'/squawk' of out-of-tune clarinets. The cacophony of noise was enough to cause permanent deafness. Maybe that's why I never opted to be a band teacher. But, incredibly, those elderly maestros whipped us into some semblance of musical competence. In fact, in Grade Twelve we won the Cowichan Music Festival. Quite an accomplishment since we had to beat out two prestigious private schools in the area. As we had done with out junior girls choir in Grade Seven. Yahoo! Again the public schools and the poor kids triumphed!

I think that, in the bad ol' days we 'poor' kids were loaned our instruments for free. I don't think we had to pay a rental. Because of that free service to impoverished band students, I learned quite a lot of basic music skills. I was subsequently able to teach everything from essential music theory to the basics of playing a woodwind instrument. Later, in Victoria, I taught recorder playing to my large intermediate classes for many years. (In those days 30-35 students was average.) To the principal's obvious chagrin. He'd often walk up the stairs from his office and ask me in a subdued voice: 'You're not going to teach recorders again this afternoon, are you?'

(If I were, he would discreetly manage to be 'away from his desk' for that time.)

Band class was definitely my most fun class after the boredom of Home Economics and the stress of the ever-enigmatic mathematics. But I also loved, Science, especially Grade 12 biology class. Not only was our youngish and dark-haired male teacher attractive, but I enjoyed both the subject matter and the competition. In my two English classes, I mostly competed with Geoff, a handsome blonde boy who, like me, had a flair for debate. It was more like 'intelligent arguing'- as much as the teacher would allow us to argue, that is. In Biology class, my chief competitor was a girl. Actually a relative of the very district principal who had facilitated my starting school.

Then there was the 'Science nerd' possessed an even nerdier name, which I have long forgotten- Gawaine, Galen, or something like that. He was relatively small in stature, definitely ugly, and seemed to have a knack for 'rubbing everybody the wrong way'. He was probably a nice kid, just socially inept. Probably had mild autism or ADHD. He had a penchant for such activities as 'going up the down staircase'. I kid you not, we actually had up and down staircases in our two-storey school. Even at that age, I felt sympathy for our elderly science teacher. This kid would speak out, argue, and had incredibly outrageous behavior for a kid of teenage. He was probably super-bright and definitely 'creative'. In Grade 10, he did such things as break microscopes and was always goofing up his science experiments. In Science class, it got so that no serious student would want to be paired up with him.

Especially after he almost blew up the classroom. Seems the rest of us were working on the properties of acids or some such. The kid got bored and decided to mix acids with a whole bunch of other chemicals (which he had filched from the teacher's back room one day after class). Yep-big, loud noise, right in the middle of class. Smoke everywhere. One nerdy kid with badly singed eyebrows, but otherwise unscathed. One trip to the office for 'nerdy' kid. Did it make any difference to his future behavior? Probably not.

There were at least three other very bright students in those classes, also boys. The six or so of us very bright students leap-frogged back and forth for grades for three years. In English 91, for example, I'd score a ninety on a test. Geoff might score a 92. Then, next term, I'd have an 87 and he an 84. Ditto English 12, Biology, Geography, and French. Math, however, was another story. It was my weakest subject. Most of the time I struggled just to get a decent pass (C+) and didn't try to compete with anybody!

It may have been the year that we were at Cowie High for Grade Seven because the junior school was not yet completed. Not only did we have the science nerd; we also had the class clown. And this guy was a kid you would never suspect of clowning. Not tall, but slimmish-muscular, he was actually the backbone (pun?) of the boys weightlifting club. He was definitely handsome and one you would never suspect of being a 'shit-disturber'. He was a good student and very intelligent. However, he was most noted for his off-beat, at times embarrassing, sense of humor. I remember one day in English class, our unsuspecting and somewhat straight-laced Scottish school marm had asked him to read a section of the text. The performance he put on-nonchalantly sauntering his way to the front of the class, would have tried anyone's patience.

After about five minutes of practiced sauntering and an equal time of slicking back his well-greased, blondish hair, he began to read. Suddenly, we heard a loud 'ahem' from nearby. He looked up. Another loud clearing of throat. A sudden pause in the reading and an exaggerated, puzzled look. He peered down the aisle, raising his arm, sailor-style with the perfect inquisitive look. (I hope that kid became an actor because the performance he subsequently put on was 'classic'.)

He eyeballed the 'cuing' kid. Next he held up his index finger and thumb, mimicking a measuring device. As he put his hand to his crotch, most of us caught on-his zipper was down. With the kid in the audience cuing him and him excruciatingly slowly, responding to the cues, he raised the zipper. For each eighth inch he showed on his fingers, that was exactly how much he raised the zipper. Then he'd look back at his accomplice to see how much more he had to raise the zipper. And with such an air of annoying nonchalance. By the time he finally got that zipper up, (grinning hugely all the time), I was ready to wring his neck. I'm sure the teacher was ready to do more than that!

Aggression!

I thought of putting this in a separate section entitled 'Bullying' but I thought: kind of depressing to read all at once. Not that I was a victim of bullying very often. I can count on one hand the number of times I was majorly bullied, generalized name-calling not included. I decided to include this episode in the tale of my years at 'Cowie High' (as we kids called it) because that is where the incident occurred. The other and only major 'negative' incident I can remember at Cowichan High was regarding a threat with a school projector and

I include it further on.

So-I'm walking along, carrying my (rather large) baritone horn after band practice. Minding my own business, all dressed up, as I recall. It was a 'dress' rehearsal for the annual Music Festival in which the band was performing on the weekend. I'm walking towards my brother's jalopy for a ride home. I start to pass three big boys also headed home on the sidewalk. Suddenly-boom! Big shot to the left ribs. I'm down and crying. Didn't see it coming. Flattened right out, partly on the sidewalk, partly on the grass. Both musical instrument and skirts flying. One of the boys, as they passed by had given me a hard elbow to the ribs and chest. I had no idea why.

Soon after, my brother finds me slowly making my way up out of the grass. I'm lamenting the grass stains on my new dress even more than the blow to my side. My brother turns and spies the culprits just disappearing around the side of the school. He's madder than a hornet, but it's late and I'm anxious to get home. I ask him to 'leave them alone and just get me home'.

"I'll deal with them later," says he. I didn't think to try to argue with him.

I get home and survey the damage. The dress is cleanable, but to my chagrin, I have a huge bruise on my left side partially covering my left breast. I don't remember the breast bothering me much at the time, but the scar tissue did in future years. Took me a lot of years to figure out that that blow to the side was probably the cause.

However, I told my brother in more detail what had happened. He asked me if I could identify the offending kid. I told him I could and he said 'he'd take care of it'. I assumed that meant he'd warn the boy not to touch me again. Not! I pointed the big kid out to him at school the next day. Soon I heard a rumor that that particular boy had been found, injured in the school hallway. In fact, rumor had it, he'd been jammed into his metal (and, I assume, open) locker. The boy was sandwiched in it so tight that the principal had to get the janitor to help him extricate the hysterical kid. One of the times it was helpful to have a 'big brother'. Unfortunately for him, he got expelled for three days!

My brother was exactly fifteen months younger than moi. But he had by the age of sixteen, nearly attained his full height. Over six foot one in shoes. Weight probably one-eighty. That WAS tall for boys in those days. His best friend stood a mere five-foot-three and they looked definitely Mutt and Jeffish. Today, six-foot-one is nothing. I'm sure I've seen at least three GIRLS in our small town who are six foot one (or close to it). An extremely tall girl attends our church and has a penchant for wearing high heels-high, high heels. I'm sure that, in them, she's at least six-seven. However, she often removes them and stands barefoot to sing at the front of the church. No stockings, entirely barefoot. The shoes probably bug her after she wears them for awhile.

How times have changed. Never, when I was a kid, would we have removed our shoes and stood barefoot in church. Especially not up at the front. I guess, however, if we're good and loyal followers of Jesus we wouldn't fault anyone who was barefoot. Jesus and many of his followers often were! And I guess we shouldn't gape at any girl who stands over six feet tall, either. Seemingly, the added growth hormones in the meat and milk are making monsters of our children. I have seen several young basketball players in one of our two high schools who seem to be about seven feet tall. One is a girl!

In 1971, I did my 'backpack through Europe' Summer with a girlfriend, also a beginning teacher. We were shocked at the many suits of armor we saw in the castles. Big, strong Invanhoe? Mighty Sir Gawaine? Yeah, right. Many of the suits of armor were shorter than I and the men had to be skinny to fit those tiny suits!

My brother stood six feet or so, one hundred eighty lbs. –not considered huge today, but pretty tall for those days. And another thing- I never saw a 'fat' boy around our neighborhood or in any of the schools I attended. In all my years growing up in Cowichan, there were few, if any, fat boys. At least not 'fat' by the standards of today. Most of the boys were slim and muscular from doing farm chores and eating healthy natural garden produce. Wild meat whenever we could get it. If there was any junk food to be had, most families couldn't afford it, anyway. I don't remember ever having potato chips until I went to college. Candy of any kind (especially chocolate) was a huge treat, reserved for movie shows, Halloween and Christmas. Ice cream was a monthly, not a daily, event.

So, anyway, that is how we dealt with bullies in the 'bad ol' days'. Send out the Dad with the shotgun or the 'big' brother, or both. Shotgun weddings were common on the old frontier, too. I suspect there was less rape per capita and less bullying in those days. The threat of having your head blown off with a shotgun was a pretty good deterrent! And it wasn't till just now as I'm writing this piece that I realized why the kid probably attacked me. I'll bet he had a grudge against my brother and took it out on me. In retrospect then, I'm kinda glad my brother flattened him!

The only other example of anything resembling bullying that I can remember from my high school years was actually perpetrated by a teacher. Grade Ten or so. It was a Friday afternoon, I think. Late. Art class, other than Math, my most hated. The teacher was a short, feisty little guy who had a habit of making 'after school pals' of some of the art students, especially the females. A practice I always avoided (and which is now frowned upon) when I was teaching. The teacher was preparing to show us an old reel-to-reel movie on some Art subject or other.

For some reason, he took us out of the regular classroom and into a small, crowded room upstairs. Maybe it was the room that held the projector; I don't know. I can only remember that it was hot and stuffy. We were asked to sit on low benches which were ranged in rows. I think we were actually asked to move the benches, too. I remember a number of students, particularly boys were complaining of the close quarters and having to move the benches.

The teacher was getting decidedly 'hot under the collar' and yelled out something like: 'You kids get busy and move those benches, N-- O-- W!

The boys beside me were muttering under their breath. I, most inadvisedly, got in the spirit and also muttered under my breath—'What'll ya do if we don't?' Unfortunately, the teacher heard me. He targeted me to tackle and screamed:

'You move right now or I'm going to throw this projector at you! Get moving…..down to the office, right now!' (I think he even threatened me with the strap or somehow, I feared that that was a real possibility).

I slunk off, mortified, and am sure I was bawling before I reached the office. In my ten or eleven years of schooling I had never so much as had a detention. Never accused of 'sassing back' a teacher. Never even had to write lines.

I sat in the office. The secretary announced my arrival to the principal and gave me sympathetic looks, and possibly a handkerchief, while I tried to pull myself together. No dice. As soon as the principal called me in, the waterworks started. I did not know the principal well as he did not teach any of my classes. I had never been hauled 'on the carpet' before. I also found his title to be somewhat daunting. A stiff-backed, tallish man of fifty or so, he had been a colonel in, I assume, WWII. Everyone addressed him as 'Colonel L…….' That, to me, made the whole idea of 'principal teacher' even more daunting.

However, he looked at me in a kindly way and spoke in a soft voice. Words to the effect: There, there young lady, what brings you to the office?' Being the honest kid that I was, I explained to him that I had drastically spoken out of turn and did not mean what I had said. The teacher had mistaken a bit of flippant speech (which other students were also engaging in) for out and out defiance. I mentioned, even more hysterically, about the 'projector flinging' threat. I think Captain L. had trouble keeping a straight face. He probably realized that such a pipsqueak as that teacher, could not easily throw an unwieldy object like those old reel-to-reels were. The thing probably weighed over eighty pounds. I think I even queried in a shaky voice between hiccups whether or not I was going to 'get the strap.'

I guess the principal knew well enough that I was a good student and had never caused any trouble before. He patted me on the back and assured me that this was not a 'strapping' offense. I could go to study hall instead of back to class. He even stated that he would speak to the teacher on my behalf after school. I felt so relieved. I don't remember whether I apologized to the teacher at the next class or not. I guess it was a Mexican standoff-he should also have apologized to me for his threat! Teachers definitely got away with more outrageous behavior in those days than they do now.

But, as I said I have mostly fond memories of Cowie High. The material taught was hard work but I was lucky in having a host of capable, dedicated teachers. They made the job as palatable as they could considering that technology in those days consisted of a blackboard, usually slate, a wall map, and a library full of (mostly hardcover) books. The only projectors I remember were the old reel-to-reel and maybe filmstrip. I don't think 'overheads' (overhead projectors with special marker pens) had even come in yet. If they had, they weren't yet widely used in our district. Few or no mimeographs, Gestetners, tape recorders, laminators and other (by today's standards) primitive devices that I used extensively in the Seventies. Computers were barely thought of and largely confined to filling an entire wall in the Pentagon!

Teachers and Colonel Bogie

As noted above, I had a few doozies. But, eccentric or not, we called them by surname-Mr. X or Mrs. Y. It was unheard of then to call a teacher by his or her first name. It would have been interpreted as a sign of gross disrespect. In fact, I never knew the first names of most of my teachers until I attended my first high school reunion ten years later!

I've already mentioned the little Art teacher from Hell. But we mostly had good solid dedicated professionals. They were humanistic and fair as well as demanding. I'll have to introduce you to the following teachers in more detail. From Grade Ten I recall our band teacher, actually an American on some kind of work permit, I believe, from California. However, he somehow dragged me through the horrendous Math curriculum which I detested and avoided whenever possible. Ironically, years later, when I studied the New Math in my college 'methods' course, it made more sense. I did better with it and achieved a 'B' average.

Our Grade Eleven band teacher was a different kettle of fish. Elderly and very English, he was also a competent and super-nice chap. Our French teacher, a male, was European- German, I believe. He taught us French and English with a trace of a German accent! All the girls had a crush on the gorgeous, thirtyish, biology teacher who was actually a Canadian. Our Grade twelve Math teacher was also a kind and elderly chap. Today he'd probably have been fired. I'll tell you why below.

We had, however, two teachers who were pretty tough. They both happened to be female. Our super-competent, but super-strict English teacher and our Home economics mistress. Come to think of it, the old chemistry teacher's classes were no walks in the park, either. So, to tell you more about my high school studies in the early Sixties, I'll start with the 'nicer' teachers first.

In Grade Ten, We had Mr. P. for both Math and Band. What a character! Marked American accent and often wore a white suit, reminiscent of the wealthy old Southern planters. Definitely not a Colonel Sanders type, though. Slim and Fortyish; very energetic. But-liked to tell stories in class. American stories. Places he had lived in the U. S. What he'd done. The boys, of course, would entice him into telling even more and longer tales in Math class than he would have otherwise.

By Christmas, my Math grades, and those of several of the other girls were floundering. (Girls, inherently had more trouble with Mathematics than boys in those days; I don't know whether that still holds true today). Mr. P. knew his stuff, but he digressed from the topic too much. He assumed that we had a whole bunch of Math skills that we didn't. I needed more in-class instruction. So-we ended up going to a different math teacher after school who was willing to tutor us. He was easier to understand than Mr. P.

Mr. C. was a chubby and pleasant chap and a Math whiz. We weren't. He had an incredible talent for translating numerical 'gobbledegook' into problems we girls could actually understand! However, I credit him with teaching us enough Mathematics in our Grade Ten year to get us through all of Grade eleven Math and most of Grade Twelve. Algebra was just 'hieroglyphics' as far as I was concerned. I saw no use for it at all. X-Y equations bore no relationship to my life either then or now. Today, I could probably sweat through a few of them for the 'intellectual exercise'. In those days, I just wanted to learn enough to get the C+ required for college entrance.

So we 'banded' with Mr. P and learned our Math from Mr. C. Then Mr. P introduced an innovation that thrilled all us kids-a marching unit. On sunny days, the entire band could be seen marching and drilling on the rather limited paved area behind the school. I don't think we sounded very good. We found it was hard enough to play some of our unwieldy instruments without having to high step in the complex formations Mr. P. encouraged us to do. However, it was fun, it gave us a break from the classroom and a better appreciation of marching bands.

I assume that Mr. P. only stayed at Cowichan one year. Ironically, later when I was teaching in Courtenay, I heard he had moved up there. Shockingly, his house had caught fire and he had perished in the blaze.

The following year's band master was a classical music aficionado. Short, chubby and elderly, he nevertheless was clever at keeping the unruly boys interested and engaged. So what if Leonard, the class clown, liked to poke me in the back of the head with his trombone slide? Or his buddy, the trumpet player, (who stood right behind us) would mimic my girlfriend's kissy-smoochy lip movements on her French horn. Ironically, both went on to develop better skills in music and later formed their own band. I think they in fact became semi-pro musicians. I'm sure it was due largely to the ministrations of those dedicated Band teachers.

She was the toughest English teacher I ever had-and the best. I had her for both English 100 (standard Grade 12 English) and English 98 (necessary to all us 'English majors' who hoped to enter college). English 100 was a dog's breakfast-an omelet of English grammar, a mixture of Canadian, British and American poetry and prose (often in excerpt form) and a smattering of Shakespeare's plays. English 98 on the other hand was totally 'heavy-duty', mostly historical literature. The Classics (from early Grecian to Chaucer), the Romantic poets (from Shelley to Browning), and a more in-depth study of Shakespeare. However, just as the Math tutoring from Mr. C. carried me through much of Grade Twelve, good old Mrs. P's head-pounding got me through the dreaded English 200 (which I sweated through with a better-than-average grade in my second year at the university.

At U.Vic my first year, I had a rather sloppy, eccentric and controversial young 'prof' who taught us to think, to reason and to argue points. He expected us to already be pretrained in the vagaries of English spelling and grammar or refer to the necessary texts. Thank God, Mrs. P. had taught us the basics. However, in Mrs. P's class there was no arguing. It was the way she wanted it or not at all. Case in point-our English notebooks.

Had to be duotang so that additional lined pages could be added as our notetaking progressed. Also, so that the pages could be removed if too messy. Had to be virtually spelling and 'letter' perfect. A tough requirement for a leftie who definitely had latent ink issues. Yes, I had a few pages removed from both notebooks and had to recopy them at home that year. Shades of the dreaded elementary school Compendium-writing! I suspect that, today, the kids don't even use notebooks, unless it's the computerized kind. I suspect notebooks have gone the way of the old basal readers. (which I thought were good, by the way). Encyclopedia sets, through which we waded 'ad nauseum' especially in Science and Social Studies classes, have probably gone the way of the dinosaurs!

I remember that, in my Grade Twelve year, I spent up to four hours per night on homework-and most of it was English. The teacher required that we write a complete precis on every piece of literature we studied. We were often required to give our opinion of a piece or compare and contrast two selections. I remember competing heavily with an attractive Gilbert Blythe type who, ironically, later went on to become a teacher. (Secondary level, I believe).

Same competitiveness as Science and Biology classes. He'd get an 86; I'd get an 84. Next time the reverse. I remember that he was not in my Bio class, however. Probably took Chemistry and the Physics that we girls were discouraged from taking. (I always wish I had taken Physics instead of Biology and political Economics instead of Home Economics.) However, in those days, we girls just did as we were told and didn't question the educational 'powers that be'. Except for one time at college when I wrangled my way into an overcrowded Zoology class by obstinately standing in the line-up and refusing to budge. Wish I'd done it to get out of the sucky, too-simple conversational French, too. However, those are two other stories for my next book.

Back to the strict and white-haired English teacher. Her professional Waterloo consisted of a number of huge and intractable (I won't be mean enough to say 'dense') boys who had probably flunked a grade or two. She took it as her personal mission in life to pound as much English grammar into those 'lunkheads' brains as they could possibly hold. I remember two of those big galoots in particular sassing her back and walking out of class on more than one occasion. However, she talked to the principal, probably talked to their parents. She convinced everyone of the necessity of having a good solid English education and being able to speak 'the King's English' (the 'Queen's', actually) in a literate manner. The boys returned to class.

We had a German French teacher who also taught English. (Try to figure that one out.) His name was Mr. S. and he was at least trilingual. Spoke English with only a trace of German accent. But-he taught me French. In stark contrast to Mrs. P.- Mr. S., on the other hand, was a softie. Although large and muscular, he was an excellent teacher and very non-threatening. I believe he taught me French for the full three years and, in Grade 12, I received a major award.

He used a multi-faceted approach which I later copied with my students.

For instance, we had one bright student in the class who intended to major in Music. She played several instruments and was expert in music notation. She'd write the lyrics, and sometimes the music, to popular songs on the blackboard en Francais for us. The entire class, including Mr. S., would sing, led by Miss A. Sometimes, we'd even be permitted to sing French songs along with the class radio. 'Dominque', an old Sixties hit by The Singing Nun, was a favorite. Also- Entre Les Etoile (Between the Stars):

Entre Les Etoile

Entre les etoile, Le Seigneur est ecrit ton nom
Entre les etoile tous la ronde dans sa maison
Entre les etoile Le Seigneur a pose ta vie
Ente les etoile, pres de Lui, en Paradis.

Between the stars, God has written your name.
Between the stars, all around his house
Between the stars, God has thought of your life
Between the stars, next to Him, in Paradise.

It had a lovely tune- the music for which I wish I could include here. Where is Miss A. when I need her? (She later became a professor of Music at the University of Toronto!)

In contrast, our decidedly elderly Chemistry teacher was a martinet. Well, into his sixties, he used rather outmoded, but effective, teaching methods. He and I got along fine, though, because I generally studied the textbook and had the answers to his pointed questions. His methods, though old-fashioned were relatively effective. His method was thus:

-Teacher perched on high behind a solid lectern above the class.
-We, below, ranged in rows, quaking with the dread of not knowing the answer. (Even well into the school year, he didn't seem to know our names. He called on us from a class list using surnames even for the girls. I empathize with him now.)
-He'd pose us a question, each in turn, and invariably make a scathing comment if we couldn't answer it.
-If the question was too tough, he'd go on to the next student and give him/her a go. After a few defeats, the question would be open to anyone to try.

I remember the extreme embarrassment one day of being asked the following question: (one of the few 'trick' questions I remember failing):
What is the world's most common solvent?

Ans: (of course)   Water

Boy, did I ever feel like a dunce when I missed that one! The only saving grace was that none of the other students had the answer either!

He had a large, metal mock-up of an engine which we girls dreaded. We'd break into a sweat every time he posed a question related to the workings of the gasoline engine. Most boys, of course, had had experience in changing oil and helping their dads with other repairs. They knew how an engine worked! We girls not only didn't know, we didn't wanna know! I finally just studied the diagram of the motor and memorized as much of the guts of the engine as I could (not having a clue how most of it worked or why). It was of no interest to me; I wasn't even driving yet! However, I now wish that I had learned more. Might have saved myself from major bucks on car repairs over the years.

Our Home Economics teacher was similarly 'older' but, red-haired. We suspected she colored it- a rarity in those days. I think she'd been teaching the same course, the same way for over twenty years. I remember acing most of the cooking, but sweating over 'bound button holes'.

Sewing Hell

'Curse, Swear! Boy, I wish I could throw this thing into the garbage. But then, I'd have to start all over again! I CAN`T DO THIS!

I'm supposed to stitch all around it and then cut through what I`ve stitched. It doesn`t even make sense! And the slippery fabric keeps sliding out from under the presser foot or creasing up, then I stitch in a wrinkle. Aaaaarrrrggghhhh!'

Before our elderly, experienced, but long-suffering Home Ec. teacher would allow us to attack a real garment, we had to produce 'samples'. She'd pronounce to us daily (from under her suspiciously reddish, impeccably-coiffed hair): `Now girls, practice makes perfect, you know.' (Well, why don't you go practice your own hemming, ya ol' bat!) I was a victim of bound buttonhole hell!

And samples. Samples, samples, samples! Then more samples! Ad nausem. Hand stitching samples. Machine stitching. Zipper sample. Hem stitches, both by hand and machine. Bound button holes. Aaaarggghhh! The impossible tasks seemed to go on forever.

To me, sewing class was nothing more than an exquisite form of torture. A few of the girls loved the class. Those were the ones whose mothers sewed well and who were able to teach their kids. My mother, on the contrary, had rammed the needle of the old Singer treadle through her finger numerous times. She'd scream- and either my poor, tortured Pater or I would have to run and pull her finger off. One day I heard the bone crunch. That was it; Dad finally banned her from use of the machine. She shook too badly with her Parkinson's.

In Grade Eight we had made a hand-stitched blouse and apron. The teacher thought that 'set-in' sleeves would be too much of a challenge for us novice seamstresses. Therefore, she gave us a pattern wherein the neckline of the blouse was simply shaped outward like a short sleeve. However, (at least on my rather pathetic effort) it produced a blouse with a decided bulge under both arm holes. I wore it once or twice and then, one day, when doing something active, I heard a nasty ripping sound. I had torn a hole in it the size of a grapefruit! That white cotton blouse made a good cleaning rag. The hand-sewn white cotton bib apron had more lastability. There wasn't too much you could tear on it except, perhaps, the long ties at the back. It lasted me through three or four successful years of cooking classes.

In Grade Eleven, I'm sure our teacher quailed whenever two or three of us hopeless seamstresses showed up after school. She would attempt to help us. I remember that after several aborted attempts and much help, I was finally able to stitch in a mock-up of a zipper that actually opened and closed. However, the 'bound buttonhole disaster' remained (and to this day still remains) an impossible task for me. Yay for Velcro!

I did, however, have some successes at stitchery, mostly coached by my mother. I remember embroidering a tea towel with a yellow daisy which looked quite nice. But then there was the fateful sweater. I had just married my first husband and we were on a 'working' road trip to the Prairies. He worked. I got stuck in one boring motel after another. In enthusiastic anticipation of the impending Winter blasts, I decided to knit him a sweater. Ha! What a nightmare that was.

The project started out O.K. and I had a pattern to follow. I actually managed (after about three days and many rippings-out) to get the required number of stitches onto the enormous needles. However, it all went downhill after that. I worked on that son-of-a gun for several months-ripping and reknitting, ripping and reknitting. Parts of it ended up the required sixe 42, but, by mid-Winter the sleeves would have fit a Gorilla. The neck hole was so small he could hardly cram it over his head. Unfortunately, too, the thing had to be stitched together by hand.

After only one or two wearings, there were suspicious holes where my stitching had come apart. And then there was the painstakingly 'ribbed' edging which had a penchant for unraveling. Eventually, the sweater was such a disaster that my husband had to give up any attempts to actually wear it. After that, I made one or two fairly successful plain scarves and easy baby outfits. However, I never tackled a sweater project again.

Finally, Mrs. H. made one of the worst mistakes of her lengthy teaching career. She attempted to teach me how to make a lined Winter-weight skirt. First of all, since my mother was ill, I went to the general store myself. (No specialty fabric stores for us in those days-or if there were any, I didn't have access to one. I chose a totally inappropriate black fabric (thinking it would be slimming). It was made of wide-weave, burlap-like thick goods probably more suited to gunny sack-making. The stuff was so thick, I could barely fit it under the sewing machine needle. But, probably against advice, and too thrifty to waste a whole yard or two of goods, I persevered.

The pattern I chose was easy-peasy, or should have been – a simple A-line with only waistband, side zipper and hook closing. No bound buttonholes! Yay! Stitching the lining (made of a much thinner silky fabric and attaching it) went well. However, stitching it into the bulky skirt presented one of the first problems for which I had to enlist the aid of the teacher. We then struggled to make a waist band that was not too bulky to stitch in. The zipper proved almost impossible because the fabric was so bulky. Also, as you may recall, zipper-stitching was NOT my forte. But eventually, I think my teacher found one that would work. After me making several abortive attempts, she capitulated and sewed it in for me as I think she finally had to do with the waistband.)

So I now had a lumpy, crooked-zippered, uneven waist-banded creation which 'horror of horrors,' required a hem. In spite of all my efforts, and all my sewing partner's efforts, the hem just didn't look right. We tried measuring and stitching it every which way, but, no matter what we did, that skirt hung on me crooked. Later, it turned out to be our new young P.E. teacher who figured out what my problem was.

You guessed it-back to the after school tutoring session with the ever-patient Mrs. H. She looked at the tortured skirt, heard my sad tale and had me stand up on a large sewing table. With, it seemed like, half the girls in school watching, she measured that skirt from the tabletop up. She went around me in a circle inserting pins and admonishing me that I was to follow her markings EXACTLY. Wonder of wonders, the skirt was finally finished and acceptable in appearance. I looked forward to our annual Home Economics Class fashion show. I expected to look so svelte wearing the fashionable black long-sleeved sweater buttoned backwards with matching black skirt. The requisite fake pearl necklace would complete the outfit and give it a delightful flair. However, I realized to my chagrin, as soon as I put it on, that it added at least ten pounds to my already bulky frame!

Old Mrs. H would have a fit if she saw us 'modern' mothers and grandmothers frequently sashaying through thrift shops. Rebuying acceptable used items for as little as a dollar or so. Wearing them for a few months or weeks and then recycling or, in fact, throwing them out. I'm sure that many of the young mothers today don't know how to THREAD a sewing needle! But I do!

So, I sweated through the year of sewing class, but enjoyed the cooking. We worked in partners and shared a cook stove, oven and other kitchen paraphernalia. We wore white bib aprons which had been painstakingly hand-stitched by us in a previous year's Home Ec. Class. It was quite the social occasion and we often served 'tea' afterwards, sometimes to visiting faculty.

I aced the omelets, the baking powder biscuits, muffins and other 'easy' baking. At home, I routinely made roasts, complex stews, baked chickens and turkeys with home-made stuffing (from the beheading stage!). Other complex entrees, quick breads, and desserts were easy-peasy. I could also easily produce entire iced cakes with various decorated and colored icings, fruit cobblers, deep-fried doughnuts, homemade coconut marshmallows and other complex desserts. Because of that, I was often given a cooking partner who couldn't cook! I guess the teacher thought that because I was pretty expert at rolling pastry dough and actually understood the chemical properties of leaveners (baking powder, baking soda, etc.), I could teach the other kid.

So Cooking Class saved my bacon (an even better pun?). When it came to my final grade in Home Economics the teacher welded the two marks. So, although I only rated a C+ or B for the dreaded sewing, my solid A's and even A+'s in cooking allowed me to keep up my college-entrance average. Since I knew I was weak in Mathematics I was desperate to do well in all other subjects and keep up as close to an 'A average' as possible.

Bashed Knees and Bleeding Shins

Don't let the subtitle fool ya. Girls' Field Hockey (as well as Band and French class) were the highlights of my Grade Twelve year. Again, the feisty, but cheerful little Scottish schoolmarm. A terrific athlete herself, but knew how to 'bring the slower ones along' and encourage us. She convinced me that I should try girls' field hockey.

They were large teams. I may not remember all the positions, but there were three phalanxes of players. The 'forwards' with two 'wingers', one on each side. A line of halfbacks, the backs and the goalie. The forwards, especially the wing positions did the bulk of the sprinting. The halfbacks had to run, but not as consistently or as fast. The two backs played defense and rarely ran far. The goalie (a position I hated) just stood around, encased like a mummy and waited for action. Most times there wasn't any.

We were all supposed to wear some protective gear. But we had nothing like the 'body armor' worn by kids today. Ours mainly consisted of 'knee pads', the goalie's hip-high. Sometimes we didn't even bother to wear them and just took our chances. Many former players bear some vicious scars of their knees from neglecting to wear the pads.

The game commenced with the two center forwards teeing off in the middle of the field. Each would try to hit the hard leather (or wooden?) ball towards her own players. As soon as one side got control of the ball the game was on! The object of the game, of course, was to score goals by getting the ball through the opponent's goal.

Any kind of aggression or body contact was discouraged and the girls I played with mostly respected that. However, my close friend, Sherri, attended school up-island and played a lot of field hockey. She later coached it when she became a teacher. To this day, she limps on one knee from repeated injuries. (usually good whacks with those lethal wooden hockey sticks!)

I tried playing both goalie and fullback for a while but found the positions boring. My enthusiastic P.E. teacher suggested that I should try for a half back position. I spent as much time as I could every noon hour and for a brief time after school, running the track. Within a month or so, I was able to play Center Half and thoroughly enjoyed the sport of field hockey for the rest of the year. I achieved a 'B' average in P.E. in that Grade 12 year which was quite an accomplishment for me. I even placed third in the Discus Throw event at the District Sports Meet that year. I credit the encouragement of that excellent phys ed teacher for my success. In succeeding years, I remained active and even did some elementary school P.E. teaching and coaching myself.

That clever Scottish Phys Ed teacher also did me another favor. She illuminated the secret behind my 'crooked' forward rolls on the mat during gymnastics class. (And the crooked hem on my Home Ec skirt!)

It was towards the end of my Grade 12 year. It seems I had been doing a forward roll on the big box after having done a springboard jump to the top of it. I was, luckily, wearing a loose sweat shirt. I guess my shirt rolled up and the teacher noticed a prominent hump on the right side of my back. She told me she thought I might have a condition known as 'scoliosis' (sideward curvature of the spine) with an accompanying rib hump. Bingo! That also explained the teary bouts I had had in Gr. 7 P.E. when I was kept after school for 'rolling crooked on the mat'. I mentioned it to my father. My mother and I had always known it was there, but just assumed it was a lump of fat. However, we never thought to question why there was no corresponding lump on the other side!

About that time, my mother died in a care home in Victoria. With the funeral and grieving going on, my condition may have been ignored. My back was never x-rayed. I don't remember having an actual diagnosis of scoliosis until I was in my early twenties and teaching in Victoria. But at least I now knew that I had a 'back problem'. In Victoria, the chronic pain soon became unlivable. I tell more about that diagnosis, the resultant surgery, and ensuing years of partial disability from it in my other book 'Episode'. It is a fictionalized early biography of my severely mentally ill son. I will not repeat any details here.

Suffice it to say, that little Scottish teacher did me a couple of favors which have had favorable impacts on my health even today. That, I guess is one of the wonders of being a teacher. One never knows who will benefit (and sometimes benefit greatly) from a casual 'teaching moment'.

And, as I've mentioned, there were other teachers from whom I learned life lessons I still practice. For in those days, education was prized, even more than it is today. Since many did not attend college, a good high school education was a ticket to success, to enlightenment and, surely to a better status in life. Over the next few decades, a high school diploma became a 'must' for getting almost any kind of a job. In the Fifties, probably fewer than ten percent achieved a college diploma. Today, a good education is a given, often taken for granted. I don't think the students are willing to work as hard as we did in order to achieve it.

Surprises on Awards Day

'Tis a common proof, that lowliness is young ambition's ladder,
Whereunto the climber upward turns his face... *
Wm. Shakespeare   Julius Caesar

Awards Day was held every June in the large and intimidating school gym. It had collapsible bleachers which were normally stored against the wall. For the Awards Ceremony the benches were brought down along with many padded metal chairs for the dignitaries on stage. I think even some of the school board members attended. I don't think any June awards were given out to the lower grades. As I recall, the major awards, either metal cups or felt fabric school crests were only given to the graduates.

The crests were lovely, almost works of Art. They depicted our school symbol or mascot, a native thunderbird. The school colors were burgundy and silver. I had no clear idea of what these prizes represented.

So-one day in late June we were all trooped into the school gym. The appropriate area big wigs were situated on stage. The band played 'O Canada' and its usual numbers. Various teachers spoke and introduced the awards. The Valedictorian had her say, probably the District Superintendent, too.

And I, to my utter shock, was called up three times before this imposing assemblage. I won a school crest for Band, French Language, and shock of shocks, English Grammar. I didn't even know there was a separate award for English Grammar! It was announced that the Grammar exam had also included Spelling of which I was probably the school guru. I usually achieved 100% on every test. (I hope I haven't made any spelling errors in this manuscript to prove myself a fibber!) Even in later years, when I was teaching, my colleagues wouldn't bother looking anything up in the dictionary. They'd just come into the staff room on break times and ask me!

To my further shock, I was also awarded a number of minor scholarships and bursaries that Spring. That made me even more determined to 'get to the University at all costs'.

So, in 1965, I graduated from Cowichan Senior Secondary well-armed with knowledge and self-esteem. I headed off for the Big City (Victoria) bound for further enlightenment and glory.

DEPARTMENT OF EDUCATION

THE GOVERNMENT OF
THE PROVINCE OF BRITISH COLUMBIA

Secondary School Graduation Diploma

THIS IS TO CERTIFY THAT

a student of .... Cowichan Senior .... Secondary School, has reached a satisfactory standard of attainment and obtained at least one hundred and twenty credits in a four-year Secondary School Course. Accordingly this Secondary School Graduation Certificate is awarded.

June , 1965

Principal.

J F K English
Superintendent of Education.

NOTE.—The student can provide on request an official statement of his secondary school record.

I thought you might like to see a copy of my High School Grad Diploma from 1965.

POSTSCRIPT

I graduated as one of the top students from Somenos in 1958. I went on to complete my high school graduation from Cowichan Senior Secondary in 1965. Ironically, I did not attend my high school graduation. I had learned that the fancy dress and other paraphernalia I needed to present a ladylike appearance and compete with the belles of the town would cost me sixty-five dollars. I reckoned that I could buy second-hand nearly all the books I required for my first year college courses with that money. It never occurred to me to ask for charity.

In addition, a close girlfriend told me her mother was desperate to find a reliable babysitter for her little brother that evening so her whole family could attend the ceremony. She assured me her parents would pay 'extra' because of the event. So, while my well-heeled fellow school chums were receiving accolades on stage and dancing till dawn, I babysat. I have always regretted the decision. However, I've partially made up for it by attending all our high school reunions.

I enrolled at the University of Victoria at the age of seventeen in 1965 and received my teaching certification (two-year temporary) in 1967. I taught my first year, a grade six class, of twenty-eight students, in Nanaimo in 1967 at the age of nineteen. With that small class number, I thought I had died and gone to Heaven!

I taught in several different school districts over the next fifteen years and picked away at my advanced (five-year) degree. I finally graduated in 1980 with a Library Education specialty. I graduated 'With Distinction' achieving solid A's in my last two years. I then worked in other school districts up-island, finally returning to Cowichan in the late Eighties to complete my teaching career. I am now retired.

I believe it is a positive testament to small schools that I did well and had no trouble with my university studies. The excellent basic education I gleaned from our small Cowichan school system at the time stood me in good stead with the professors at college. Of course, the fact that I had elderly, highly literate parents who prized education above all things, helped too.

My success and that of many of my fellow students stands as a solid testament to the excellence of 'old style' teachers and the small, but knowledge-embracing country schools.

The Demise of Stratfords Crossing

I drove by our old homestead on Somenos Road a number of years ago. To my chagrin, I noticed that the big old red Crossing House had totally disappeared. Nothing remains except a large patch of tough grass. There is still rough signage where the road crosses the tracks, but all else is gone. I wish they had designated the old House as a heritage building and restored it to its former glory:

Old Stratfords Crossing House site

FIN

Glossary

ADHD pgs. 39, 153, 185, 213 - Attention Deficit Hyperactivity Disorder-a learning disability and lifestyle-altering condition of the frontal lobe of the brain. Many of my relatives, particularly the males, suffer from this condition. It can be somewhat described with the acronym HID (Hyperactivity, Impulsivity, Distractibility).

Often manifests with extremely hyperactive behavior, lack of focus, poor decision making and other high risk behaviors. It is largely an inherited condition common now, in up to 6% of the general population. CADDAC (Canadian ADHD support group) is trying to get it taken out of the realm of 'mental illnesses' and removed from the DSM V (Diagnostic and Statistical Manual of Psychiatric Illness) which psychiatrists use. They prefer it to be labelled as an inherited neurological disorder similar to autism.

agnostic- p. 46 someone who neither believes nor disbelieves in God.

alary ball - p. 180, 91, 92 a smallish, hard rubber ball used for bouncing on cement or pavement. I guess 'alarey' was the name of the game.
* I have consulted various references and cannot find a spelling for alaire/alarey ball. If you know the correct spelling, let me know.

bloomers - p. 210 rather baggy panties made of some heavy fabric and tied or elasticized at the waist. They were gathered around the upper thigh and 'bloomed' around your posterior sort of like the old pantaloons worn years ago, except they were a lot shorter.

Cairn - p. 109 a cone-shaped, tall memorial atop Mt. Prevost dedicated to veterans of both World Wars. The area is now called Mount Prevost Memorial Park, but was just The Cairn when I grew up.

The Cloverleaf - p. 9, 61, 70, 170 the shamrock-shaped pattern made where Somenos Road crossed the Island Highway

Cowichan Leader- p. 161/5, 190,204   for 110 years Duncan's main newspaper until it ceased publication in 2015. Its initial subscription rate was $2 per annum for a weekly paper.

Cowichan Valley Citizen - p. 130, 165, 203/39 March 26, 2014 edition: Article entitled: Architect designed Duncan Elementary at Peak of his Career by Carolyn Prellwitz, Secretary, Cowichan Valley Schools Heritage Society crinolines- p. 21, 206 those fluffy, stiffened,multi-layered) petticoats worn to make a full skirt stand out. If the skirt a girl was wearing was short and the girl bent over or was actively engaged in play, the boys got quite a view!

cupola – p. 204- a small dome on top of a roof of ceiling often used to admit light and air

'discretion is the better part of valor'- p. 143 a quote by Onate y Salamar, a New Mexican leader. He didn't have the three hundred Spanish soldiers he needed to confront his enemies. He retreated to New Mexico.
dyslexia- p. 36 a perceptual difficulty in which letter reversals and other distortions occur, making reading and language activities difficult

Eaton's Store, Duncan, B.C.- p. 126 -According to Wikepedia, at one time the Eaton's department Store chain was the largest in Canada. It was started in 1869 by Timothy Eaton, an Ulster Scot. Its catalogue department was well-used for many years. In Duncan, the Cowichan Merchants Building housed the store from 1912-1995. In 1995, the Duncan store was closed and other offices and shops were opened in the old building. In the early 2000's, Eaton's was bought out by Sears which also eventually closed its doors largely due to the online shopping craze.

4H Club- p. 117 a youth program whose goal was to develop citizenship, leadership, responsibility, and life skills. This was done via experiential programs and a positive approach. In rural communities like ours, the care and showing of animals was an important component.

Georgian Revival Style – p. 203 Georgian Style was named after the first four British Monarchs from the House of Hanover-all Georges. It was revived in the U.S. in the early 1900's as Colonial Revival style. The Georgian styles vary, but are based on three principles of Greek architecture-regularity, stonework, and symmetry. Because of this, most Georgian buildings are immediately recognizable.

gizzard- p. 86 a small organ at the top of the digestive tract which helped grind up the chicken's food. Small stones were often ingested for that purpose.

Katzenjammer Kids- p. 5, 6, 49 (according to Wikipedia) an American comic strip created by R. Dirks in 1897, later drawn by H. Knerr for 35 years. First published in the Humorist, Sunday supplement of New York Journal. The characters used the first speech balloons and strip became a stage play, was animated and included in U.S. Comic Strip Classics postage stamps.

'like a deep-toned grief….' p. 151 From poem, The Largest Life, Archibald Lampman 1899 looseleaf – p. 185 a leather or fake leather binder usually containing rings. It was used to hold 'loose leaves' of punched paper or thin notebooks.

Mark Twain- p. 96 (1835-1910) the penname for Samuel Langhorne Clements famous author of Tom Sawyer; inspiration for our Steamboat Stump games. He was probably my all-time favourite childrens' author.

matrimonial cake- p. 132 an oat cake or squares made with a sweet date mixture inside

Mikado- p. 6, 65, 198, 200 Emperor of Japan

Nestor (Nelson) - p.5, 26, 122, 141/3/4,   any wise old man

Pax Canadiana p. 6, 30, 234 by M. A. Webster

Pax Canadiana

Come, if you dare, to our Northmen's lair
The tramp of your armies shall not shake us,
Come, if you will, we are free men still
Words cannot break us.

For we have the brain and the brawn and the blood
Of the Saxon and the Celt and the Gaul
And we'll fight with all our might
When we know we're in the right
And we'll march at our country's call.

We are the men of the fair, far North,
The land of the maple spreads around us.
Here we will live, not an inch we will give
None can confound us.

For we have the brain and the brawn and the blood
Of the Saxon and the Celt and the Gaul
And we'll fight with all our might,
When we know we're in the right
And we'll march at our country's call.

Canada, dear Canada, men of the North are we
For thee we will live and for thee we will die,
But, aye, though shalt be free!
Canada, dear Canada, men of the North are we,
For thee we will live, and for thee we will die
But, evermore thou shalt be free!

-This has a rousing tune which I would put in this manuscript if I knew how to write music. However, I could sing it for you-anytime!

'Poems for Boys and Girls Book 3' – p. 198 by G. Morgan and C.R. Routley Copp Clark Pub. Vancouver/Toronto It comprised over 308 pages, but I could not find a publication date anywhere within it.

PTA- p. 166, 197 *PTA-Parent-Teacher Association, now called PACS (Parent Action Committees) I remember that the PTA ensured that goodies were always served after the Christmas and other concerts

Portico- p. 204 a roofed structure on columns usually attached as a large porch to a building

Russell Farm Market- p. 5, 115 as of this publication date, still exists on the highway a few miles North of Duncan. Although I have mostly used pseudonyms throughout, I used real names for the segment describing the Stewarts.

saran-   p. 154 a tough, flexible thermoplastic resin. Doll hair was made out of it in those days. It and other types of doll hair such as monofibre is now sold on EBay.

scoliosis p. 227- sideward curvature of the spine often accompanied by other postural defects such as lordosis ('swayback') and khyphosis (neck hump). If the main curve is in the thoracic region-as mine is-one often has a hump on one side of the back. I have all three. The condition can be crippling or life-threatening if it progresses, as mine did.

Somenos – p. 5, 7, and others- a local Coast Salish native place name denoting a village near the Cowichan River. It means 'resting place' in the Hul'qumi'num language.

stoneboat- p. 4, 15, 72, 87 a flat sledge used for transporting heavy articles. It was usually horse drawn or pulled by hand.

Subjects (1960's)- p. 204, 225 Arithmetic, Art, Composition (now called: Creative Writing), Drama/Fine Arts, French, Grammar, Health, Music, P.E. (Physical Education), Poetry, Reading/Literature, Science, Social Studies, Spelling, Writing

Sybil- p. 26 a shocking movie from the Seventies in which a distraught young female seems to have multiple personalities as the result of family abuse

'throw the hooley ann- p. 13 an old bulldogging expression. It involved dropping from the back of the horse and wrestling the steer to the ground.

thunderbird – p. 211, 212, 227 in Coast Salish culture, a mythical bird that causes thunder

'Tis a common proof.... p. 227 Julius Caesar, Act II by Shakespeare quoted in Woman of Substance Part Three by Barbara T. Bradford

Webster, Frederick – p. 21 my maternal grandfather. Supposedly 'assassinated' in the Winnipeg General Strike of 1919. Family said he was a wealthy boiler making company owner. Census lists him only as Fred Webster, 'boilermaker.' If any historian out there has better info on Fred and the Strike, please let me know.

Women's Lib- p. 7 Women's Liberation Movement-comprised about twenty years starting in the Seventies (?) I attended women's consciousness raising groups and was a B.C. Teachers' Federation rep for about twenty years. We had a Status of Women Committee. The main thrust was to stop violence/disrespect against women both in the workplace and the home. To some degree, I believe we succeeded.

Another positive outcome that is often forgotten is that, with the liberation of women, also came the liberation of children. In the Fifties, for instance, the strap was liberally used- both in school and at home. Many boys, particularly, were recipients of the 'woodshed treatment'. Thank God, my dad did not believe in corporal punishment.

End of Glossary

Acknowledgements:

Bev (last name withheld) from Tim Horton's, Ladysmith, for pic and info about the Punkinhead doll; Bill Vandersluys, computer skills teacher; Brandi Sheldon, my granddaughter- artist, 'computer glitch doctor' and copy editing assistant; Karl Maxwell, my ex-husband, who, even then, gave me the freedom to write; Ken at Uforik Computer, Ladysmith; Nick Campbell, now deceased, dear friend and computer guru; Rick Collins, fellow writer and helpful critic; Sharon Cox-Gustavson, owner of a rustic cottage on Cameron Lake, where many years ago I did the original writing for this manuscript-longhand!; Suzanne Anderson, author and fellow B.C. Writers' Federation member, who wrote the incredibly helpful 'Self-Publishing in Canada'; Vivian Johnson, substantive text editor who suggested I split a very long Chapter Two into two chapters; and, finally, all the 'kids from Stratfords Crossing' (remet over the years at reunions and even on the street), who gave me ideas for the manuscript (especially if my memories at the time did not coincide with theirs!)

1950's Skipping Songs and Rhymes

'Betty Botter'*

Betty Botter bought some butter
"But," she said, "this butter's bitter!
It will make my batter bitter,"
So, she bought some better butter
For a better, bitter batter.

This was also what we called a 'tongue twister' in those days and could be used strictly as such.

Lulu Had A Baby

Lulu had a baby-
His name was Sonny Jim.
She put him in the bathtub
To teach him how to swim.

He drank all the water,
He ate all the soap.
Lulu called the doctor
To see if there was hope!
How many days did Sonny Jim live.......?
Pip, Pap, Pepper!

'Pip, Pap, Pepper' was what we yelled out as we turned the rope faster and faster to try to put the skipper 'out'. And I guess poor Sonny didn't make it!

The oldest version of this rhyme (taken from Wikepedia) is as follows:

Miss Susie had a baby

His name was Tiny Tim

She put him in the bathtub

To see if he could swim.

He drank up all the water.

He ate up all the soap.

He tried to eat the bathtub

But it wouldn't go down his throat.

It is thought that the 'Miss Susie' version goes back as far as the late 1800's possibly in Britain. A 1970's version began: 'The Johnson's had a baby.' The American version was thought to begin: 'Miss Lucy had a baby'......These regional variations in skipping songs and school yard rhymes were the norm. So, any variation we kids came up with was valid to our particular time.

As you can see, many of our rhymes contained a delightful component of gore. If you think of it-many of the old nursery rhymes were pretty violent and gorey, too. Witness poor Humpty Dumpty who smashed his head open, ditto Jack who fell down the hill and 'broke his crown'; I guess he died, too. Then there was Peter, the pumpkin eater, locking up his poor wife in a pumpkin shell which wasn't exactly a nice thing to do. The Old Lady who lived in a Shoe was a child beater, I guess:

> She had so many children she didn't know what to do.
> She gave them all soup without any bread
> Then smacked them all soundly and sent them to bed.

We talk about the Natives' oral language history. We Whites had ours, too. For the 'Betty Botter' rhyme, for instance, I have no idea how to spell 'Botter' (Boughter? Bought her?) as I had only ever heard it spoken. I never saw any of our rhymes in written form. That is one of the reasons I am putting them in print now. Sometimes the skipping or ball bouncing songs were interchangeable. Example: another old skipping or ball-bouncing song of my mother's circa 1920's or so: (I'm guessing at the spelling)

Eerie, iry, ory, iry, ickery-Ann,
Filsey, falsey, Nicholas John.
Creever, craver, English knaver
Stickle-'em, staggle 'em, buck,
And OUT-GOES-YOU!

I'd guess back in merry ol' England, the rhyme had something to do with a naughty knave named Nicholas John. He probably met a bad end and was stabbed. But, again, I'm guessing.

2018/19 editions of the Cowichan Valley Citizen can be viewed online under Cowichan Valley Citizen-E editions or some of my writings under my name on B.C. Federation of Writers' website.

www.ingramcontent.com/pod-product-compliance
Lightning Source LLC
Chambersburg PA
CBHW080900160726
48000CB00009B/2794